Women Like Meat

Women Like Meat

The folklore and foraging ideology
of the Kalahari Ju/'hoan

Megan Biesele

UUP

Witwatersrand University Press

INDIANA UNIVERSITY PRESS
Bloomington and Indianapolis

Women Like Meat was first published in 1993 in the Republic of South Africa by Witwatersrand University Press, University of the Witwatersrand, Johannesburg, 2050 Wits, South Africa.

ISBN 1 86814 212 4

Published in the United States of America in 1993 by Indiana University Press, 601 N. Morton Street, Bloomington, Indiana 47404, United States of America.

ISBN 0 253 31565 4 (Cloth)
ISBN 0 253 31566 2 (Paper)

Royalties from this book are to be shared by the following organisations:

The Kalahari Peoples Fund (Botswana)
3100 Ninth St. NW
Albuquerque, New Mexico, USA

and

The Nyae Nyae Development Foundation of Namibia
PO Box 9026 Windhoek, Namibia

Library of Congress Cataloging-in-Publication Data

Biesele, Megan
    Women like meat: the folklore and foraging ideology of
    the Kalahari Ju/'hoan/Megan Biesele
        p.   cm.
    Includes bibliographical references
    ISBN 0-253-31565-4 — ISBN 0-253-31566-2 (pbk.)
    1. Ju/'hoan (African people) — Folklore. 2. Women. $\frac{1}{m}$
    Ju/'hoan Folklore. 3. Tales — Namibia. 4. Tales —
    Botswana. I. Title.
GR358.82.J83B53   1993
398.2'096881 — dc20   93 - - 12414

1 2 3 4 5   97 96 95 94 93

Cover design by Diaset
Typesetting by ORBiT, Pretoria
Printed and bound by Creda Press, Johannesburg and Cape Town

For Patrick

Jùa n≠àngn≠àng kxà,
N//àú //'à ì g/áé bạmm̀//óé
Khòè n/úí wàqnke ye ì n≠áú

Author's Note

The state of debate about 'San' or 'Bushman' as possible appelations for the general group can be illustrated by the case of two Ju/'hoan brothers, both active in local and national politics in Namibia. At a large community meeting in 1991, each of them argued differently about the word 'Bushman'. One said he never wanted to hear the term used again in post-apartheid Namibia. The other argued that the term could be ennobled by the way in which they themselves now chose to use it. As for 'San', many people at the meeting had heard of it, but knew it has a pejorative connotation in Nama, the language from which it comes. No one advocated its use, or knew of any other over-arching term. However, as 'pan-San' or 'pan-Bushman' political conciousness grows in Southern Africa, we must assume that a general term will emerge. Until then, I choose in this book to use 'Bushman' when possible, in accordance with the suggestion that the term may gradually be 'ennobled'. I suggest that this book should be seen as a transitional document.

– Megan Biesele

Table of Contents

Acknowledgements

My main acknowledgement of thanks must go to my good friend !Xoma of Dobe, Botswana. !Xoma not only acted as my Ju/'hoan language teacher and as interpreter for the Tswana and Herero languages, but was an unfailing source of comfort and understanding throughout my stay in the field. This book would have been completely impossible without his patience and wisdom.

Next, though I cannot list them all, I want to thank the other Ju/'hoan people of Botswana and Namibia who so generously shared with me the meanings and the great fun of their oral tradition.

My thanks go too to the Government of Botswana for allowing me to carry out my research, in particular to the Hon. M.T.M. Kgopo, at that time the Permanent Secretary of the Ministry of Health, Labour, and Home Affairs. I am also grateful to Chief Letsholathebe II of the Batawana tribe for permission to work in the Northwest District. I also thank Jackson Matenge, then District Commissioner at Maun, and the late Isak Utuhile, then Headman at !Xangwa, for their permission and constant aid.

The research was made possible by a grant (MH 13611-04) from the United States National Institute of Mental Health and by the support of the Danforth Foundation of St. Louis, Mo.

The interest and encouragement of other members of the Kalahari Research Group at Harvard has been of great help. In particular I want to thank Irven DeVore and Richard Lee for allowing me to join the project and for their continuing interest in my work; Pat Draper and Henry Harpending for giving me an excellent introduction to the Ju/'hoan language, and for training my two valuable field assistants; Marjorie Shostak and Mel Konner for the time and care they took in introducing me to life at Dobe; and Richard Katz for years of productive collaboration in the study of the Ju/'hoan trance dance.

While in Southern Africa I profited greatly from discussions and other help from Bernhard and Renate Clauss, Dr Trefor Jenkins of the South African Institute for Medical Research, Mr Alec Campbell of the Botswana National Museum, Mary Kibel, Patrick van Rensburg, Fritz Metzger, Miss Jane Crook of the Botswana National Library, and Alcidio Reis Esteves (then Administrator of the Concelho do Lubango, Angola).

My understanding of Ju/'hoan life and of folklore in general has been greatly enriched by correspondence and discussion with the following scholars: Roger Abrahams, Paul Devitt, Alan Dundes, Maurice Godelier, Roger Hewitt, Dell Hymes, Albert Lord, Henry Murray, John Pfeiffer, Robin Ridington, Peter Skalnik, Jan Swearingen, Eric Ten Raa, Tony Traill, Rodney Vlasak, and Annette Weiner.

To David Lewis-Williams and Sigrid Schmidt I owe special thanks for lively scholarly correspondence and discussion which have gone on for nearly two decades.

People who have read parts of the manuscript and made helpful suggestions include James Fox, Stephanie Krebs, Susan Rain, Eric Ten Raa, Rodney Vlasak, Naomi Mitchison, and Alan Dundes. Melissa Heckler has been this book's most constant advocate.

Particular thanks goes to Dr T. Walter Herbert of Southwestern University, Georgetown, Texas, for reading the entire manuscript and making extensive comments. Discussions with Walt have been a source of great insight in both general and specific ways. For a long series of fruitful Wednesday afternoon conversations on oral and written traditions I thank Dr Stephenie Yearwood of Woodville, Texas. Without her help I might not have creditably approached the problem of presenting a complex oral process in written form. Stephenie, too, read the manuscript and made a comprehensive series of suggestions.

I thank Bruce Lane for the extended use of his sound equipment and Constance Coulopolous, Andromache Sheehey, Lorraine Brady, and Fax of Toronto for typing. I also thank Anne Winkler for volunteering to type certain sections and for discussion we had about them; Caroline Dowell for a year's loan of her electric typewriter; Betsy Traube for proof-reading; Dr Jim Jinnette of Woodville, Texas for the use of an air-conditioned dental operatory to write in for a summer;

Jean Stephens for permission to use her arrangements of the Marshalls' folktale collection; Richard Lee for permission to use 'The Haba-Utwe Oration' and the 'Sky and Earth Song'.

For the revised orthography used in the book I gratefully thank Patrick Dickens. Patrick has made not only future education projects possible for the Ju/'hoansi but also a lifetime project in Ju/'hoan texts possible for me.

Final and most important acknowledgements are to the Marshall family of Cambridge, Massachusetts: I am more grateful than I can say for their friendship, for hours and hours of shared ideas and reminiscences about the Ju/'hoan people, for the work that each of them has done, and for the unwavering encouragement that in writing this book I was doing something meaningful. In particular I want to thank John Marshall for having pointed out to me, early on, the enormous tolerance in Ju/'hoan belief for the individual's point of view. It is characteristic of John's, Elizabeth's, Laurence's, and Lorna's work that their straightforward ethnography has never obscured, but has quietly and firmly maintained in anthropology the will and presence of individuals.

The Author and the Witwatersrand University Press would like to thank Mrs Lorna Marshall for the photographs taken by Laurence Marshall which appear as the frontispiece and on p.xxii, and Claire Ritchie for the photograph on p.50. All the other pictures, including those on the front and back covers, are from the author and from Jean MacGregor, courtesy Anthro-Photo File, Cambridge, Mass., USA. The map on p.xviii was drawn by Thomas Dowson.

Note on Translation and Presentation

Because this book views oral forms from an evolutionary perspective, their translation into texts presents special challenges. My first concern has been to render as faithfully as possible the ease and fluency which, among the Ju/'hoansi, unite storytelling activities with ordinary discourse.

Storytelling, as the classicist Joseph Russo (1978:45) points out, is 'a verbal habit writ large', in that an individual's narrative abilities depend very much upon his general verbal resources. My point in emphasising the similarities between the language of tales and of speech in general is that the narrative option – whether to answer a question, to give an account of how a day was spent, or to construct an imaginative world – is regularly exercised among Ju/'hoansi, and there are important convergences among narrative styles used in these different ways. I raise the question, in fact, whether similarity in the narrative styles of ordinary and 'special' discourse may be widespread among hunter-gatherers for very good adaptive reasons.

Thus the texts are presented not as recently advocated by writers like Dell Hymes and Dennis Tedlock, to make a visual analogue of their verbal patterning in performance, but as prose narratives. Not only are Western readers more familiar with this form, but it is the one which most closely approximates for us the sequential experience fundamental to the tales' mnemonic function – and thus their adaptive importance – for Ju/'hoan listeners.

The reader will notice, moreover, an informality of word choice in the translations: I have tried to stay as close to the original as is practicable within the constraints of clear presentation, basing translations on as thorough an appreciation of the words' usages in everyday contexts as possible. Colloquialisms are allowed to stand (sometimes with annotation) and euphemisms have not been used except in cases where Ju/'hoan euphemisms were used in the original.

Though presentation and thus reworking have been major preoccupations, important elements like repetition and 'nonsensical' archaisms in the speech of certain characters have not been altered or edited out. It is understood that these are important mechanisms of reinforcement and recall.

Finally, serious attention has been given to the aspect of readability. As Harold Scheub (1971:28-36) writes,

the translation of a single narrative-performance involves profound transformations which defy equivalence. Indeed, the major problem centres on the translation from the oral form to the written word ... One of the greatest injuries that can be done to the original work is simply to 'retell' it without making any effort to give it a dynamic and artistic context.

Clearly, word-for-word translations misrepresent the verbal reality of the performance by chopping it up into alien linguistic categories. The flow of meaning in the original is made to seem discontinuous, and the effect in general is stilted and quaint, putting further distance between the story as read and the story as it was told. This effect is illustrated to some degree by the Bleek-Lloyd translation of a hundred years ago which appears near the start of the book and which mirrors the philological emphasis of its times. In contrast, a modern view takes the position that understanding the dramatic content of the communication is hindered by making speakers of the other language sound like bad or laboured English-users.

My goal, then, has been to put the stories into lively and correct contemporary English. The challenge was to stay as close as possible to the original words and word-order yet faithfully to transmit the sense and flavour of the message using the new medium. We are lucky to have the tape recorder: playing tapes even years later can help recapture the mood of a story. The gain in richness of documented atmosphere over the older written transcriptions is immeasurable. Tape recordings are always there to help a translator toward authenticity.

If the translator has been present at performances, if she has, beyond that, participated in many other daily contexts touched upon by the story, if she has seen to the construction of a reasonably unobstructed path for communication between herself and her informants, far more has passed into her knowledge than the mere words of a given story. Translation should draw on all this understanding.

A Note on Orthography

The orthography used in this book is the Practical Ju/'hoan Orthography developed by Patrick Dickens under the auspices of the Nyae Nyae Development Foundation of Namibia (NNDFN). An explication and justification of this orthography was published in the 1991 *South African Journal of African Languages*, Volume 11, No.3. It has been endorsed by the Nyae Nyae Farmers Co-operative, the educational and political organisation whose members represent the majority of the Ju/'hoan-speaking people of Namibia. The related educational programme of the NNDFN, which will use this orthography, has been made a recognised part of the Namibian Basic Educational Reform comprising child and adult literacy. A Ju/'hoan/English-English/Ju/'hoan dictionary with about 8 000 entries using this orthography has been completed by Patrick Dickens and should become available in print during 1992. Several Ju/'hoan people are fully literate in this orthography, and many more will become so as educational plans, including self-generated curriculum materials, mature.

In order to eliminate typing, typesetting and teaching/learning difficulties, the orthography keeps the use of diacritics to a minimum, and in some cases deviates from the conventions of the International Phonetic Alphabet (IPA). A brief and non-technical description of some of the sound-representations in this orthography (concentrating particularly on the above-mentioned deviations) follows.

CONSONANTS

The four clicks in Ju/'hoan are symbolised as follows (IPA equivalents in square brackets):

/ – dental (similar to the expression of irritation 'tsk tsk' in English)
= – alveolar (laminal) (no English equivalent)

! – alveo-palatal (something like the sound of a cork coming out of a bottle)

// – lateral (similar to the sound sometimes used to urge on a horse)

Each click may be released in one of twelve ways. This is shown below using as the example the alveopalatal click:

! – voiceless basic [!]
!h – voiceless with velar-audible aspiration [!k]
!'h – voiceless with velar-inaudible aspiration [!]
!k – voiceless with velar ejection [!k'] or [!kx']
!' – voiceless with glottal stop [!]
!x – voiceless with velar friction [!x]
g! – voiced basic [!g]
g!h – (pre)voiced with velar-audible aspiration [g!k]
g!k – (pre)voiced with velar ejection [g!k'] or [g!kx']
g!x – (pre)voiced with velar friction [g!x]
n! – nasal (voiced) [!]
n!h – nasal aspirated (prevoiced) [!]

The other consonants also more or less follow the conventions of the IPA, but there are the following exceptions:

c – voiceless alveopalatal fricative, [ ], as in English 'shoe'
j – voiced alveopalatal fricative, [ ], as in English 'measure'
' – glottal stop [?], as in Cockney English 'bottle'

The voiceless and prevoiced ejective affricates (which have no English equivalents) are written without the IPA apostrophe indicating ejection:

tz – voiceless alveolar [ts']
tj – voiceless alveopalatal [t ']
tk – voiceless alveovelar [tkx']
kx – voiceless velar [kx']
ds – prevoiced alveolar [dts']
dc – prevoiced alveopalatal [dt ']

Prevoiced aspirated stops and affricates (again, no English equivalents) are written as follows:

xv

bh – bilabial stop [bp]
dh – dental stop [dt]
gh – velar stop [gk]
dsh – alveolar affricate [dts]
dch – alveopalatal affricate [dt]

VOWELS

There are five basic vowel phonemes in Ju/'hoan.

i – high front [i], similar to English 'kick'
e – mid front [e], similar to English 'egg'
a – low or mid central [a] or [ ], similar to English 'but' and 'about'
respectively (the latter is used if a is followed by m, i or u)
o – mid back [o], similar to English 'saw'
u – high back [u], similar to English 'bull'

These may occur in combination with themselves (rearticulated) or
with other vowels (diphthongs), for example:

ii – [ii], similar to English 'seen'
ae – [ae], similar to English 'pie'
ai – [i], similar to English 'say'

In addition, vowels may be nasalised (indicated by an 'n' following
the vowel or vowel sequence), pressed (a harsh sound caused by
constricting and tensing the pharynx and indicated by a 'q' following
the pressed vowel) or both pressed and nasalised (indicated by a qn
following the vowel). It must be remembered in reading that q and
n represent modifications to the quality of the preceding vowel, and
should not be pronounced as consonants. Examples of these vowel
qualities (no English equivalents):

in – [i]
aq – [a]
an – [a], similar to French 'sans'
aqn – [a]

TONES

For most practical purposes, it is not necessary to indicate tone except when two or more items of the same grammatical category would otherwise be identical. A high tone is shown by an acute accent above the vowel and a mid-low tone by a grave accent, as in !u 'name' and !u 'tree sp.' respectively. Low-toned vowels have no diacritic symbol, but are generally followed by an h, which not only serves to indicate the low tone, but also shows the breathy modification (caused by a decrease in tension of the vocal folds) of a low-toned vowel, for example in !uh 'footprint'.

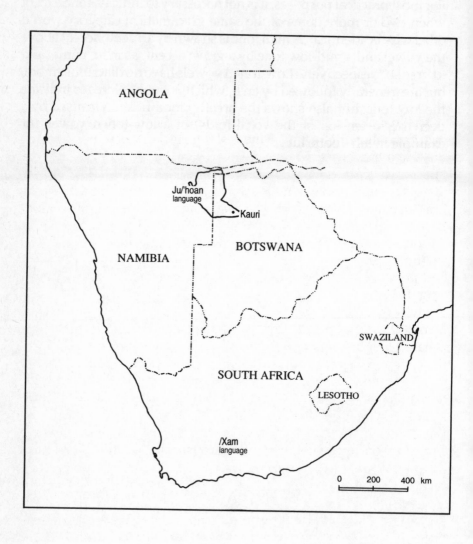

ANGOLA

Ju/'hoan
language

Kauri

BOTSWANA

NAMIBIA

SWAZILAND

SOUTH AFRICA

LESOTHO

/Xam
language

0   200   400 km

Preface

THE JU/'HOAN BUSHMAN PEOPLE

With their slight stature, yellow skin, and other distinctive physical features rather different from those of their black African neighbours, Bushmen hunter-gatherers have lived south of the Congo-Zambezi line for at least eleven thousand years (Clark 1970). The largest linguistic subdivision of the Bushmen, the Ju/'hoan,[1] inhabit northern Botswana, north-eastern Namibia, and south-western Angola. Recent excavations near Dobe, Botswana on the Namibia border by Alison Brooks and John Yellen point to continuous habitation of the Ju/'hoan area by hunter-gatherers for at least several thousand years and possibly as many as forty thousand (personal communication Aug. 1977).

Living for thousands of years in little groups widely scattered across a huge subcontinent, Bushman peoples developed many isolated languages and dialects. All the languages share, however, the common characteristic of having prominent click consonants. A detailed review of the linguistic literature on the different click languages is included in Lorna Marshall's book, *The !Kung of Nyae Nyae* (1976:24-28). While !Kung or Ju/'hoan with its three dialects is the Bushman language spoken by the largest number of living people, /Xam, once spoken in the western half of South Africa, is now extinct and known to us only from the written material preserved by linguists and folklorists.

Before the Dutch colonists arrived at the Cape of Good Hope, perhaps a hundred and fifty to three hundred thousand Bushmen covered all of Southern Africa from the Zambezi southward (Lee 1976:5). During the two hundred years after the first arrival of the Dutch in 1652, the Bushmen of South Africa were reduced to near extinction through bitter warfare with the settlers.

Towards the east Bushmen also experienced some conflict with pastoral Bantu groups. In this case, however, many groups were assimilated by intermarriage rather than killed off in fighting. In Botswana (once Bechuanaland), for instance, Bushmen were not systematically eliminated but were assimilated, exploited, or tolerated by the pastoralist Tswana tribes. Ju/'hoansi and other Bushmen form a small minority now within the Tswana-ruled republic, their populations concentrated in the most arid areas of the country.

THE SETTING OF THE JU/'HOAN FOLKLORE COLLECTION

This book presents a group of tales collected orally from Ju/'hoansi in western Botswana between 1970 and 1972. The tales are part of a collection made from several different groups of people showing varying degrees of influence from Tswana and Herero pastoralists from the west, as well as from white settlers. Most of the tales come from a group of Ju/'hoansi who were in substantial contact with economies other than hunting and gathering. This particular group lived a semi-sedentary life at a place called Kauri (see Map, p. xviii), twelve miles west of the Tswana settlement of Tsau, Northwest District.

Travellers' accounts from the earliest European contacts with Bushmen, and the excellent anthropological records of the last few decades, provide the background for the tales. Though regional variations in culture, and variations within the different linguistic groups, are colourful and striking, there are surprising similarities within the portrait of Bushman culture over the whole of Southern Africa.

ARCHAEOLOGY AND ETHNOGRAPHY OF THE BUSHMEN

What we can glean from first-contact reports by travellers, the early colonists, and missionaries, points to a way of life strikingly similar in its broad outlines to that reported by anthropologists for first-contact situations as late as the 1950s. The Peabody Museum Kalahari

Expeditions, and the Peabody-Harvard Smithsonian Kalahari Expeditions begun in 1950 by the Marshall family, encountered Ju/'hoan groups in Namibia (then South West Africa) who said that they had not yet seen Bantu, let alone whites. Though there is an academic debate over this issue, it is clear that for some long period of time these groups had lived as hunters and gatherers of the Kalahari without agriculture or domesticated animals of any kind. They did not even have dogs: their hunting pitted only human skill and an excellent arrow poison against huge and wily animals. Well over half their subsistence was provided by the vegetable foods gathered by women.

The Kalahari, though forbidding, is in some respects a very favourable environment for gathering. Peculiarly abundant in this semi-desert are plants possessing nutritious storage organs beneath the sand. These provide both food and water to those who know how to find them and dig them out.

During the course of eight expeditions between 1950 and 1961, the Marshall family and their co-workers studied the social structure of the most independent groups of Ju/'hoan and other Bushmen still living. Their studies centred around what Lorna Marshall has called the Nyae Nyae area of Namibia, and have resulted in a number of excellent articles and books on Ju/'hoan life. These documents are priceless, because they record the way life was for the Ju/'hoansi before change began to accelerate through greater and greater outside contact.

Published in the journal *Africa* between 1957 and 1969 (see Bibliography), the papers are titled '!Kung Bushman bands', 'Marriage among !Kung Bushmen', 'Sharing, talking and giving: Relief of social tension among !Kung Bushmen', 'N!ow', '!Kung Bushmen religious beliefs', and 'The medicine dance of the !Kung Bushmen'. Lorna Marshall has recently published two volumes (*The !Kung of Nyae Nyae*, Harvard Press, 1976 and *Nyae Nyae !Kung Beliefs and Rites*, Harvard Press, in press) to bring together all these articles and unite them with the rest of her work.

The title of *Women Like Meat* is taken from the work of Lorna Marshall.

Introduction

Women Like Meat

The title of this book is a statement made to Lorna Marshall by Ju/'hoan informants which she presents on p. 270 of *The !Kung of Nyae Nyae*. In its context, it is a succinct expression of basic expectations between Ju/'hoan men and women of that time concerning sex and sustenance:

> A boy who never killed any large meat animal would not be given a wife, informants said. This was why the strange old deviant /Gaishay [/Kaece] had remained a bachelor. For reasons no one understood he could not hunt; he gathered plant foods like a woman. Gossip had it that twice he had tried to drag a woman against her will into his shelter, but had not succeeded. Informants remarked, 'Women like meat'.

I chose the quote because of the particular balance it embodies for the two major divisions in hunting and gathering society, men and women, between physical needs and social responsibilities. It implies a world of integrated collaborations between the sexes involving work and foodstuffs, marriage and procreation – negotiations whose continuing success assures the ongoing viability of Ju/'hoan society itself. The stories which form the backbone of this book incessantly explore these very negotiations, turning them every which way to see them well and to reinforce their importance. The theme of the book,

1

in fact, is the man/woman cognitive opposition in Ju/'hoan culture
and its symbolic mediation in folklore.

That the quote iterates most clearly the female point of view while
at the same time implying male concerns is apt in connection with
this book. As a woman researcher I received communications from
my own Ju/'hoan informants, both male and female, which have
resulted in a collection of oral literature with a distinct feminine
emphasis. The stories I present concentrate on women's strengths in
Ju/'hoan society, on what women want and what they do to get it.
But they do so in constant relation to what the men are reciprocally
doing and desiring. Thus they paint a picture of the give and take by
which the entire society is maintained. A 'women's story' is never
just that; in distinguishing themselves from men, women must
describe in detail what they know of their men's world and how they
will relate to it. The present collection shows women's stories and
men's stories in inextricable connection with each other.

The double meaning in English of 'like' in the title is also appropriate for Ju/'hoan folklore. A metaphorical equation of women with
prey animals and men with their hunters, sometimes delicate and
sometimes overt, pervades Ju/'hoan expressive life. As we will see,
this simple intellectual transposition provides a fertile landscape of
figures and situations for the exploration of many aspects of social
relatedness. Women both 'like meat' and are likened to meat among
the Ju/'hoansi: in one version of her story, the heroine G!kon//'amdima, after being pursued by men as prey, being killed, cut up, eaten,
and finally reconstituted as a woman, becomes by an act of her own
will a steenbok, the first game animal, so that all people – women and
men – ever after should have meat.

To introduce the Ju/'hoansi and their folklore, we begin with a tale
collected from a related Bushman people nearly one hundred years
ago. Towards the end of the book a similar tale from the Ju/'hoansi
appears, a contemporary one, to illustrate both continuity and change
in oral tradition. Both of these feature a young married woman who
is the object of enmity between her family of birth and her new
in-laws. The first narration was made in 1879 by a South African
/Xam Bushman[1] man named /Han=kass'o and was written down

and translated by Lucy C. Lloyd, who worked with the linguist
W.H.I. Bleek. I tape-recorded the second nearly a hundred years later,
in 1972, from a Ju/'hoan Bushman[2] woman named !Unn/obe in
Botswana. Vital issues explored in both versions, such as marriage,
residence, resources, and the tensions of affinal kinships have persisted across formidable barriers. Linguistic divisions within the click
languages, a thousand miles of Africa and a century of time have not
changed the narrative framework of the story nor its basic concerns.

As they were told, both stories spoke eloquently to their Bushman
listeners of the business of living as hunters and gatherers on the
African continent. For us, however, the several hundred pages which
intervene between their presentation here are not too many in which
to try to understand the ramifications of their meanings. This fact
alone suggests the great efficiency and utility of the story as a form
of communication.

For us to gain an entry into these stories as communication, we
must not only develop a theoretical framework for relating stories to
culture, but must explore in detail the world of Ju/'hoan expressive
life. In Parts I and II of this book respectively, I try to fulfil these
requirements. Throughout, I emphasise the contribution of oral expressive forms to the formation, honing, and sharing of the tools of
sapience – and thus to long-term human survival.

Here is the Bleek-Lloyd fragment from 1879:

=KAGARA AND !HÃUNU, WHO FOUGHT EACH OTHER WITH
LIGHTNING

They formerly, =Kagara formerly went to fetch his younger
sister, he went to take her away; he went to take her away from
!Hãunu; and he took [her] back to her parents.

!Hãunu gave chase to his brother-in-law, he passed along
behind the hill.

The clouds came, clouds which were unequalled in beauty
[lit. clouds which not beautiful like them]; they vanished away.

=Kagara said: 'Thou must walk on.' His younger sister
walked, carrying a heavy burden of things, [her] husband's

things. He [=Kagara] said: Thou must walk on; for, home is not near at hand.

!Hãunu passed along behind [the hill].

The clouds came, the clouds vanished away.

=Kagara said: 'Thou must walk on, for, thou art the one who dost see.' And he, because the house became near, he exclaimed: 'Walk on. Walk on.' He waited for his younger sister; his younger sister came up to his side. He exclaimed: 'What things can these be, which thou dost heavily carry?' Then !Hãunu sneezed, on account of it; blood poured out of his nostrils; he stealthily lightened at his brother-in-law. His brother-in-law fended him quickly off, his brother-in-law also stealthily lightened at him. He quickly fended off his brother-in-law. His brother-in-law also lightened at him. He [=Kagara] said: 'Thou must come and walk close beside me; for, thou art the one who dost see that husband does not allow us time; for, he does not singly lighten.'

They [=Kagara and !Hãunu] went along angry with each other. !Haunu had intended that he should be the one lightening to whisk away =Kagara. =Kagara was the one who was strong [lit. 'was not light' or 'did not feel light'], he continued to fend off his younger sister's husband, !Hãunu. His younger sister's husband was also lightening at him; he was lightening at his brother-in-law. Then he stealthily lightened at his younger sister's husband with black lightning, he, lightening; whisked him up land carried him to a little distance.

His younger sister's husband, in this manner, lay dying; he, in this manner, he thundered, while =Kagara bound up his head with the net, he, returning arrived at home.

He went to lie down in the hut, while !hãunu lay thundering; he thundered there, while =Kagara went to lie down, when he had rubbed them [i.e. himself and his younger sister] with buchu, buchu, buchu, buchu,[3] he lay down.

Note by the Narrator

My grandmothers used to say, '=Kagara and his companion are those who fight in the East, he and !Hãunu.'
When the clouds were thick, and the clouds, when the clouds were thick, and the clouds were at this place, and the clouds resembled a mountain, then, the clouds were lightening, on account of it. And my grandmothers used to say: 'It is =Kagara, with !Hãunu.'

A version which incorporates a fragment much like this one into a longer, episodic account of the adventures of a heroine, her husband, and her natal family appears near the end of this volume. I present it towards the end so the same characters and themes may be met in modern Ju/'hoan guise after they have been fleshed out for us by ethnographic reference.

The question which the intervening analysis attempts to answer is this: why did the /Xam Bushmen of a hundred years ago tell this tale and why are the Ju/'hoansi still telling their versions of it? Of what use, in other words, are stories that they should be so tenaciously, yet so flexibly, preserved? In particular, what did stories like these mean and do for a recently hunting-gathering or foraging culture like the Ju/'hoan, which has been taken as a contemporary exemplar of the most ancient and long-lived form of human organisation? Does narrative have specific enabling functions for society? What is the significance of ideological time-lag preserved in narrative form? Suggesting answers to these questions is the aim of this book.

Part I, Sapience and Survival, introduces the Ju/'hoansi and their folklore. It places the contemporary people in anthropological perspective as at least part-time hunter-gatherers and their folklore as part of the specifically oral hunting and gathering adaptation. Part II, Ju/'hoan Expressive Life, explores Ju/'hoan folklore in detail, using a simple strategy of explicating selected texts by reference to ethnography. It proposes that the social usefulness of the expressive forms can be understood by considering the relationship of the metaphors used by a society to its technology.

Part I

Sapience
and
Survival

Among the biological characteristics of the human species is the specialization of some parts of the central nervous system for storing and transmitting information symbolically. The older views that mental and cultural life set man apart from nature or that they constituted a remission from evolutionary selection are challenged by recent anthropological work. Comparative studies of many different primates suggest parallels to the prehuman situation of our evolution and the steps by which social, intellectual, and even ethical traits came into existence in an ecological context, associated with the human animal's niche, and more particularly, his place in Paleolithic food webs.

These studies are slowly delivering a picture of the human mind as an adaptation to the physical environment, to band, clan, and tribal organisation, to the division of labor in hunting and gathering, to long life and delayed maturity – in short, to the environment and the way of life of the Pleistocene hunter.

Together with physical traits, these are perfections generated in a hunting-gathering milieu, shaped during 99% of human time. Natural selection has directly created the most subtle and delicate aspects of thought, passion, and art.

Paul Shepard, 1972

Chapter One

The Ju/'hoansi and their Folklore

The studies of Lorna Marshall portray a people whose culture is closely and visibly connected to the activities of subsistence and survival. The water supply and its location, the plant food supply and its location, the meat animals and their movements, are pressing absolutes around which cultural life is organised. The size of groups, co-operation within and between groups, and the strategies of subsistence, labour, and rest are intimately connected with these environmental constraints. Other cultural aspects give the Bushmen flexible mechanisms for defying the constraints imposed by their environment. Among these are many variations upon the theme of co-operation and harmonious social relations, enormously detailed knowledge of the environment and of techniques to exploit it, and strongly institutionalised patterns of sharing.

The traditional group structure is egalitarian, with an oldest man or woman who acts more as a focus for collective decision-making than as any kind of authority. Around the elder lives a small group of nuclear families linked to him or her and each other by kinship. Kinship ties and a fictive name-relationship link the individuals of one group with those of others, and sharing patterns (*xaro*) draw together members of different groups in reciprocal obligations. Women take an active part in decision-making. The respect given to women's opinions is linked to their importance in providing over

9

half the edible food by weight and their intimate knowledge of the whereabouts of plant food and resources.

Habitation and government are based on flexible, opportunistic exploitation of the best resources available at any given time. Because of the need for mobility in following the movements of game, and the water sources usable at different times of year, Bushmen traditionally have very little property. Since they must walk wherever they go and often have to carry babies and small children, they usually have no more possessions than they can comfortably carry. A woman has a few ostrich eggshell water carriers, her digging stick, a wooden pestle and mortar perhaps, and some ornaments and skin bags. A man has his bow and quiver, a spear, sometimes a hunting bag made from the whole skin of a small buck, and a carrying net made of twisted *sansevieria* fibres and not much else. Most of Bushman technology is carried in the mind as information and technique, in fact, rather than in the hands or on the back.

Since the Marshall expeditions major research efforts have been carried out among Botswana Bushmen groups by anthropologists and other scientists of the Harvard Kalahari Research Group, and more recently by the University of New Mexico Kalahari Project. Results of these multi-disciplinary efforts are presented in Lee and DeVore 1976 and the publications of the UNM Kalahari Project. Many of the more recent studies focus on the changes that have occurred in the last few decades to Bushmen peoples. Like many other traditional hunting and gathering societies, the Bushmen are now threatened by pastoral, agricultural, and industrial activities of neighbouring ethnic groups. These other groups are now able to move into the once remote, arid areas inhabited by the Bushmen because of improved borehole technology. In the case of Botswana, it is most often cattle-owning peoples who encroach on Bushman hunting and gathering grounds. The cattle compete with the game for forage and water, and with the people for the very plant foods on which their diet is based. Often cattle begin the process of range degradation in the fragile Kalahari environment. Bushman peoples tend to lose their land and economic autonomy to cattle interests, and their cultural independence to the more aggressive incoming society. Many seek cattle

work with the pastoralists, entering a subservient client-patron relationship. Others, who fail to find work, end up living as squatters
around agricultural and pastoral settlements. People once dependent
on the spontaneous produce of the land are finding every familiar
resource closed to them and an entirely foreign set of rules governing
land use and tenure. Today less than five per cent of the Bushmen
are in situations where hunting and gathering can provide their sole
subsistence.

THE 'ETHNOGRAPHIC PRESENT' OF THE TALES

If so few of today's Bushmen are now 'pure hunter-gatherers', to
what reality do their obviously hunting-gathering folktales refer?
The historical experience of Southern African Bushmen has all along
included varied environmental and social changes, though these
have accelerated greatly in the recent past. It is reasonable to assume
that there were prehistoric changes as well, which may have had
impact on Bushman belief and traditions. What do we know of these
prehistoric changes which may have affected Bushman systems of
procuring a livelihood, their social organisation, and possibly their
folklore?

Robert K. Hitchcock (1982:47-65) now at the University of Nebraska
outlines such changes on the basis of archaeological and geomorpho-
logical evidence from Southern Africa. During the late Stone Age,
which began twenty thousand years ago, he writes, the climate
gradually became drier. Mobility for foragers had to increase and
group size to decrease, so that they could maintain themselves in this
sparser environment. More species of plants and animals gradually
had to be used to provide a living. Significant technological advances
such as the bow and arrow and arrow poison compensated for the
reduced food supply under these more arid conditions. Camps
tended to be located in areas providing not only water points but a
mix of plant and animal resources.

In general, the move of hunter-gatherers in large numbers into the
Kalahari was a late phenomenon correlated with certain technological advances. These included increasing use of sip wells and other

alternative water sources like melons, digging sticks to get at nutritious plant storage organs deep in the sand, and of course effective arrow poison from insect and plant sources for use on increasingly scarce game. Perhaps most important in their adaptation to the semi-arid ecosystem, however, was the development of efficient means of communication and social links to ensure reciprocal access to resources. Marital and trading links and nexuses of co-operating bands observable today over large areas of the Kalahari were part of a pattern which may have arisen only over the last two thousand years in response to drier conditions and/or larger populations. (Hitchcock, personal communication, March 1983)

Sedentism as a relatively new Stone Age adaptation was eventually resorted to for several reasons. Population pressure, resource dealing and the depredations of livestock caused groups in some areas to reduce their mobility and shift subsistence strategies. But in recent years Bushman groups have been seen to move back and forth relatively rapidly between different subsistence options and between sedentary ways and mobile ones. The picture of human adaptation in the Kalahari is overall a flexible one, then, with hunter-gatherers making the most of the environmental opportunities available at any given time.

Having suggested the range of adaptations Bushman hunter-gatherers made in response to changing environmental conditions, let us turn back to the question of the ethnographic present of Bushman oral traditions. We must ask which reality grounds an oral tradition – the present, or a past going back thousands of years through great environmental and social fluctuations.

My answer in part parallels the argument of a recent, innovative book linking Paleolithic cave art with its environmental and social context. In *The Creative Explosion: An Inquiry into the Origins of Art and Religion*, John Pfeiffer (1982) writes of a proliferation of cave art which appeared in Europe at the same time as population and resource pressures tended to weaken the long-lived hunting-gathering lifestyle as an effective adaptation. Pfeiffer argues that the art was a response to a need for new communication networks and the assimilation and sharing of the ever greater amounts of information that came with social complexity.

Pfeiffer also suggests that the Cro-Magnons of the time were living 'at the dawn of the oral tradition' (1982:189) and that their mythology probably reflected contemporary survival pressures. Though speech does not fossilise, it is clear that oral tradition consistently preserves enough material to be recognisable over time as 'the same tradition' while processing and incorporating new material. Tales of today represent, in Pfeiffer's words, part of a 'vast untapped linguistic archaeology' (1982:217) reflecting no single point in time but an accumulation of realisations out of the past mingled with attempts to encompass new realities. Seen this way, contemporary Ju/'hoan tales can be understood as a combination of conservative elements from the deep hunting-gathering past with elements introduced by recent changes and pressures.

Both the Bleek-Lloyd tales collected in the last century from Bushman prisoners in South Africa and the ones I taped during the last decade show a hunting-gathering imaginative substrate. They deal with problem points in living which must always have characterised the hunting-gathering adaptation, such as uncontrollable weather, difficulty in procuring game, danger from carnivore attacks, and correct relations with in-laws. These sorts of concerns, expressed and explored in artistic verbal forms, have been part of hunter-gatherer living arrangements through many sorts of environmental change.

However, late technological advances which made possible the exploitation of the Kalahari Desert by hunter-gatherers, like sip wells and melons for water, digging sticks for root excavation, and the all-important bow and poisoned arrow, also appear prominently in the tales of this century and the last. The tradition is conservative but it has brought the innovations of the recent Late Stone Age with it into the imaginative present.

Tradition's adoption of new material is uneven, however, and this is a fact with which we must reckon. Other than passing mention of imported goods and domestic animals and a few borrowed Bantu and European tale elements, almost everything in the modern tales is in a traditional hunter-gatherer vein. Such recent innovations as the *xaro* trading network, status differences due to sedentism and population pressure, new attitudes to territory, and so forth, do not appear in any obvious way in the stories.

Why are some innovations chosen for inclusion in oral tradition and others not? Why do old fealties persist in art when it is clear that a new reality has superseded them in life?

The answer, of course, is that folklore is no simple sort of mirror for society. The choice of its elements clearly reflects other concerns – aesthetics or psychological stress, for instance – beyond the one-to-one representation of reality.

The elementary fact that many stories, rather than a single universal story purporting to explain all facets of society and environment, are told in cultures should alert us to the pervasive indirectness, the artistic 'licence' of oral tradition. Some innovations, even vital ones, may be ignored as 'goods to think with' while others may be used over and over again.

The insistent reiteration of the norms of the old order in the stories may in itself be a way of expressing that they are under fire. Pfeiffer suggests that artistic comments on egalitarian foodsharing, for instance, may reflect not its prevalence at a given time but that it was then 'for some reason, under stress, increasingly violated as a policy' (personal communication, March 1983). In any case, we can say that treatment in artistic genres demonstrates concern with an issue and/or the usefulness of an idea, whether that issue or that idea be a contemporary reality or not.

Hunting and gathering remains, then, as we see in the tales that follow, a major source for the content of the expressive forms of even semi-acculturated Bushmen. Pastoral and agricultural concerns had barely penetrated the tales of modern Ju/'hoansi in the 1970s, even those who lived on farms. Most of the oral expressiveness of the Ju/'hoansi is still centred on the concerns of a foraging economy and on the social attitudes necessary to keep it working. Even where new implements from a new way of life are mentioned, the power of the ancient form of social organisation still informs and structures Ju/'hoan stories.

But oral reworking is a flexible process, and new elements, new tools, culture contacts, and wider concerns may quickly appear in the tradition. Metal implements, for example, are prominent in the tales collected during the 1970s, supplanting the bone or stone tools that characterised stories collected a hundred years ago.

Storytellers, then, artfully select their elements to weave a seamless web that includes both past and present in a single coherence. The ethnographic present does not necessarily coincide literally with the imaginative present of tales, because recreating the past to explain how it merges with the present is one of the important metaphorical tasks the tales perform.

JU/'HOAN FOLKLORE: AN OVERVIEW

Specific hunting-gathering emphases and other characteristics strikingly differentiate Ju/'hoan tales from the tales of their agro-pastoral neighbours. Since these neighbours, chiefly Bantu peoples, are living in the same Kalahari environment, the contrast in folklore points up differences in world-view related to technology and economy.

Up to the time the Ju/'hoan collection in this book was made, the only substantial collection of Bushman oral texts was Bleek and Lloyd's *Specimens of Bushmen Folklore*. This valuable collection consists largely of fragments of ethnographic information, life histories and song texts, but also incorporates some twenty to thirty stories with original transcriptions, roughly divided into myths, fables, and legends. Another collection, published in English only, was made by Bleek and Lloyd in the 1870s. It appeared as *The Mantis and His Friends*, and also contains twenty or thirty stories. In the same decade, J.M. Orpen was hearing stories among the Maluti Bushmen of Basutoland (now Lesotho). He published an article in the *Cape Monthly Magazine* containing eight of them. In the early 1920s Dr Bleek's daughter Dorothea collected and translated a number of Naron Bushman tales at Sandfontein on the border between what were then South West Africa and the Bechuanaland Protectorate. Seven of these appear in *The Naron: A Bushmen Tribe of the Central Kalahari*. A few more non-Ju/'hoan Bushman narratives appear in scattered sources (see the Bibliography).

Since the 1920s a few collections have been made among widely spread groups of Ju/'hoan and other Bushmen. A book of tales adapted from the Ju/'hoan tradition by Fritz Metzger and set down in German under the title *Und Seither Lacht die Hyäne* was published in Namibia in 1952. In the 1950s Manuel Viegas Guerreiro collected the material for his *Bochimanes !Khu de Angola*, which includes several Portuguese translations of Ju/'hoan stories from the region between Pereira d'Eca and Serpa Pinto. Also in the fifties, stories were collected in South West Africa and in the Central Kalahari Reserve of Bechuanaland by Elizabeth Marshall Thomas and Lorna Marshall. A few of their G/ui Bushman stories appeared in Elizabeth Thomas's well-known book, *The Harmless People*, and roughly eleven G/ui and fifteen Ju/'hoan stories, some in many versions, are among the materials still being worked on by Lorna Marshall. Four Ju/'hoan stories and references to several more are included in her '!Kung Bushman religious beliefs' (1962). George Silberbauer includes one G/ui story in his 1965 *Bushman Survey Report*. J.M. Swanepoel made a small collection of Ju/'hoan tales at Tjum!kui in Namibia several years ago, but to my knowledge he has not published it. Other members of the Harvard Kalahari Research Group, notably Richard Lee and Melvin Konner, have collected tales from Ju/'hoansi but have not published them. Patrick Dickens collected Ju/'huan tales, for desktop publication as curriculum materials. Thus the Ju/'hoan collections in print present only a small number of tales taken from several different parts of an extensive area. The most extensive new collection of Bushman tales printed appears as part of Mathias Guenther's *Bushman Folktales* (1989) which presents Naron and /Xam stories.

In attempting a comprehensive collection of the stories still being told in one part of Botswana, I have tried to expand our knowledge of Ju/'hoan oral traditions. The collection is full enough to allow some generalisations to be made regarding both the 'ethnography of speaking Ju/'hoan tales' and the content of the Ju/'hoan repertoire.

It should be emphasised, however, that this overview of Ju/'hoan folklore does not constitute, except in the area of artistic techniques, an introduction to the folklore of the Bushmen in general. Comparing the Ju/'hoan material with Naron and !Xoo Bushman material I have collected, and with material from Bushman culture in other parts of Botswana, from Angola, Namibia and South Africa, one finds an extremely variegated content in Bushman oral literature. Just as anthropologists cannot answer the question 'What do Bushman gatherer-hunters eat?' without reference to very localised and specific ecological conditions, neither can the student of folklore easily generalise about the content of their oral traditions. The Ju/'hoan stories about Kaoxa the trickster-god are very different from those of the G/ui god Pisiboro, even though the latter is also a trickster. The mantis god of the long-ago /Xam people of the Cape, though he bears some resemblance to Kaoxa, has a whole set of adventures of his own which, though they also involve trickery, are unlike any found among the Ju/'hoan stories. The Narons, in addition, have a genre of dramatic stories with the musical accompaniment of a single *damagari* bow played by up to five women at once. This whole genre is lacking among their close neighbours the Ju/'hoansi.

Yet there are fascinating connections to be found among some of the traditions. Especially interesting comparisons can be made with traditions of neighbouring cultures, notably the Nama Khoikoi. Though the Ju/'hoansi seem isolated to us their culture is a complex mosaic of influences, and of references to other times and places.

The Ju/'hoansi's cast of characters revolves about the roguish trickster-god Kaoxa (sometimes called Haqice, or G//aoan, or G!ara) and his heroic daughter-in-law, G!kon//'amdima. Their stories reveal concerns and relationships which may further illuminate what we already know about Ju/'hoan society. A partial list of story themes includes problems of marriage and sex, the food quest, sharing, family relationships, the division of labour, birth and death, murder, blood vengeance, and the creation of the present world order.

Though Bushman oral literature contains a number of other forms, folktales are the most frequently performed. The Ju/'hoansi call these *n=oahnsi o n!àusimasi*, 'stories of the old people'. They are all set in a long-ago time when the trickster walked upon the earth, when animals 'were people', and when many bizarre things occurred which do not occur in the world today. There are also hunting stories and historical stories, but these are just *n=oahnsi*, or stories. Synonyms for 'stories of the old people' include *n=oahnsi o n//aahnmasi* (stories of ˙ long ago) and *n=oahnsi o kxaicemasi* (stories of the beginning). To *n=oahn n!àu* is to 'tell the old people's stories'. Among the =Kao/'ae Bushmen of Ghanzi it is to *n=oahn Hoesi* or *n//ae Hoesi*, to 'tell the doings of Hoe [trickster] and all the people who were with him in the ancient time'.

When I first went to Botswana I expected to find only a limited number of competent storytellers among the Bushmen. I imagined I would find a special class of raconteurs, and that other people's narrative abilities would be decidedly inferior. I assumed that it would be the individual's way with words, more than detailed knowledge of the lore, which would determine the worth of a storyteller. I was proved wrong in all this.

Not only is the number of Bushmen who tell stories competently quite large, but virtually every old person (among Ju/'hoansi this is every man or woman who carries the appellation *n!a'an*, or old, after his or her name – perhaps forty-five and older) is able and usually willing to tell stories. Of the many old people whom I heard performing there were very few who could not tell the stories of the old time with confidence and vigour.

On the other hand, younger storytellers are much rarer. Younger Ju/'hoan people, when asked for stories, most often protest that they 'have not grown old enough to have learned the things that old people know'. This observation seems to hold both among semi-acculturated groups and groups still gathering and hunting in the ancient way. Thus professed lack of knowledge is not to be equated simply with changing times. It seems, indeed, that there are definite social constraints reserving storytelling to older people. It may be part of a general practical stratification of knowledge in Bushman society. The old people seemed to take great interest in hearing the stories told by others, too. One does not see only grandmothers sitting by the fire telling tales to small children. As Lorna Marshall has commented, Ju/'hoansi seem to have little interest in actively teaching the lore of their forefathers to the children. The storytelling groups I observed consisted most often of a small group of old people getting together for some genuinely grown-up entertainment. The telling of stories among Ju/'hoansi is no watered-down nursery pastime but a substantial adult pleasure – old cronies over a bawdy or horrific or ridiculous tale. A woman might elaborate the gruesome details of her story as much for the grown-up women in her audience as for the children. But however horrific the tales, children are not barred from listening to them: toddlers and adolescents wander in and out of a group of storytelling adults freely, as they do at a trance dance. Often they stay to listen with considerable interest for a while, then go on to another activity.

Younger adults too are often present at storytelling sessions, and listen attentively. Sometimes they also tell stories, and tell them well. But there is usually a slight flavour of restraint in their participation: they seem to indicate by a respectful passivity that they are disclaiming primary knowledge of the things of ancient times. If no old people happen to be present, younger people are more likely to tell stories forthrightly. Some of them do so with good command of detail, but in general their narrative abilities are less well formed, and they do not hide the fact. The general respect accorded to age, and to the fluency and knowledge that come with it, is a salient characteristic of storytelling.

Further, those with the strongest and most unabashed interest in hearing and learning the details of past doings are not the children but the old people. Most old people appear to feel reasonably qualified to tell the stories, though as a rule mediocre storytellers defer to the really good ones if they are present. Thus, though there is no distinct group entrusted with the stories in Bushman culture, the old people do in effect have something of a monopoly. It is not a jealous guardianship, however; younger people who tell stories do exist and are welcomed by their elders. But there is an unspoken sense in which 'stories of the old people' refers not only to the ancients of long ago but also to the ancients of today. The most important factor linking this age-group with the tales is 'factual' knowledge of the items of folklore. Ju/'hoansi of all ages are more or less able to tell a good 'story' if it concerns events through which they themselves have lived. But it is the combination of the general verbal ability perfected over a long life with the details of the early times usually known only to the old which produces a successful Ju/'hoan storyteller.

It is knowledge, not secret knowledge, but a large collection of items which are public but take a long time to accumulate, which makes for good storytelling. It is generally the case that by the time a person is a *ju n!a'an* (old person) he or she will have accumulated a good deal of this knowledge. An old woman I asked about the telling of stories said,

> *Ju n!a'an n/ui /oa n//ae, kom, koara. Ju !ae!ae'm ko ku n//ae/'an e ko Hoesi oosi, te ha n/ai /oa //kae toan te koara ka. Te ha n/ai ku //kae o kxae ka.*

The old person who does not tell stories just does not exist. Our forefathers related for us the doings of the people of long ago and anyone who doesn't know them doesn't have his head on straight. And anyone whose head is on straight, knows them.

Of course there are a few really excellent storytellers who stand out from this crowd of good talkers. In some cases they excel in verbal or dramatic abilities, in others by a gift for remembering and synthesising fragmentary episodes into chains of connected stories surrounding central figures. Some are masters of dialogue, some of special sound effects. The techniques of several fine storytellers are discussed later in this chapter. At present, however, I want mainly to emphasise the high degree of interest and participation in storytelling among most all elderly Ju/'hoansi. It is looked upon not as 'something to do when you are old', but rather 'something that you get to do when you are old'. Though there is keen enthusiasm over the performance of folktales, their contents themselves are looked upon with scorn. The stories are heard with anything but awed reverence. Instead, shouts of indignation greet the outrageous, bumbling adventures of the long-ago people. Ju/'hoansi have no explanation for why their ancestors related such absurdities to them. /Ai!ae N!a'an ended some of his stories this way: 'Hey! The doings of the ancient times were foul [/kau], I tell you!' To know of these doings is itself good: it is the wisdom of the old people. But the happenings themselves are rarely considered of great account.

The Ju/'hoansi make no distinction of genre between, say, trickster-creation stories and animal-aetiology stories. Nor do they distinguish between 'sacred' and 'profane' stories. No sort of folktale is considered to be 'more true' than another. I tried in vain to find verbal equivalents for 'stories which are considered true' and 'stories which are considered false' or for 'myths' versus 'folktales'. Even when I confronted Bushman people who also spoke SeTswana or OtjiHerero with such distinctions in these languages, the reply to them was that all of these things, in Bushman tradition, were *n=oahnsi o n!àusimasi*.

There is another reason, too, why the animal stories are not taken as a separate class of story from those of the trickster and his family. It is that for the Bushmen the animals were all people in the beginning. All stories dealing with animals, therefore, have them acting much like human beings, though they also already possess traits that will characterise them when they become animals. The story which deals with the day on which they are finally given their animal shape, is in a sense the termination of the magical time in which the other adventures have taken place. Many stories remark upon this termination, some of them expressing poignant sadness for a lost, innocent order. Since that time animals have been animals and people, people. The casting situation in the tales, however, is very fluid, with animals sometimes taking parts that in other versions are taken by humans and supernatural figures.

To begin to understand these 'stories of the old people', we can ourselves make an informal separation of i) the creation tales and those involving the trickster god, Kaoxa, and his relatives and animal associates, from ii) the animal tales which are never found connected into longer cycles and usually have aetiological endings.

Of the fifty distinct tales in my 1970-1972 collection, approximately two-thirds fall into the first category and one-third into the second. Primarily discussed in this book is the first. This group is unified by a central cast of characters which binds its many stories together. The second group is devoid of such a focus, concentrating instead upon specific and apparently unconnected characters and incidents. The first group, taken as a whole, imparts strongly the flavour of a mythical time when all these personages were present in the same world and vitally connected with one another. In different versions their adventures overlap, and it is hard to tell where one episode stops and another begins. The rest of this section introduces this first group of tales. The second group is only briefly noted.

In the Botswana Ju/'hoan stories centring around G//aoan, the great god, a trickster at the time he was still on earth, he is referred to most often as Kaoxa. This name is one of the god's less potent ones, and it may be used publicly and in a normal tone of voice (in fact, the word can also be used to refer to a human 'master' or rich person). At times this god is called 'Haqice' or 'G!ara' or 'Hoe' as well, however, and almost always 'Hoe' by the Naron Bushmen. It has been suggested that a good case can be made for translating his name in these tales as 'God', since Ju/'hoansi say he is the 'same' personage thought to have later ascended the sky and become divine. But there is little connection between the trickster in the world of the tales and the Ju/'hoan sky god conception: a similar distance prevailed in ancient Greek myth and religion. In consequence, I have kept to the actual Ju/'hoan name for the trickster.

Kaoxa's family includes his wives, whom he engages in endless reciprocal trickery, his adventuring sons Kha//'an and !Xoma, and his brother-in-law !O!otsig/a'asi, whose eyes are located on the insides of his ankles. Perhaps the most interesting and enigmatic personage in all the tales, however, is Kaoxa's daughter-in-law. G!kon//'am-dima, the name borne by this heroine, is an extremely obscure name which may mean 'beautiful antbear maiden'. But her antbear characteristics do not outweigh her human ones, nor do they prevent her from appearing at times as a female python. An exact meaning for this name is very difficult to arrive at, and there are some possible alternative translations. In some versions she is called !Xodi, 'elephant girl'. At times she is married to an elephant or hyena and at times to a human being who may be one of Kaoxa's sons, the older brother of Kha//'an and !Xoma. In some versions she is called merely !Au!aua or !Au!auadi; words whose reference was not discoverable.

One reliable informant even told me she was not a person or an animal at all, but an edible root called =oah !ama (Ceropegia sp.).

G!kon//'amdima stars in a fascinating series of tales touching on the themes of marriage and marriage-service, murder and blood-vengeance, the origin of meat animals, sex, birth, and the balance of power between men and women. Her story consists of a number of related episodes which are often told separately but fit together with beautiful logic when told by a very good storyteller.

The father-in-law of the mysterious G!kon//'amdima, the trickster-creator Haqice or Kaoxa, appears in a number of different stories. Most of the stories featuring Kaoxa relate the tricks he plays on his wives and has played on him in turn. These stories are bawdy and scatological, and cause great hilarity among the Ju/'hoansi. Because of the tit-for-tat nature of them, they are most effective when reeled off in rapid succession. The storyteller (or storytellers) become progressively more animated and the laughter more uproarious. Absurd as the contents of these tales may seem, it is nevertheless clear that they explore, like the G!kon//'amdima tales, some of the fundamental issues of social living.

There is another very important tale which concerns the kori bustard (a huge bird, Otis kori) as a kind of captain of the other animals. Considered to be Kaoxa's servant, he uses his strong wings to fan the fire of creation so that the animals may receive their distinctive markings by branding. The branding occurs on the day that marks the end of the magical time when animal and human identities were merged.

JU/'HOAN METAPHOR IN CONVERSATION AND FOLKLORE

Metaphor permeates Ju/'hoan expressive life, which in a few words can be characterised as highly oblique, indirect, and allusive. One of the many pleasant surprises I received was learning to what extent metaphorical play is part of everyday conversation among the Ju/'hoansi. For example, a number of 'respect words' are used in dangerous circumstances such as those involving lions or rain. I expected to learn a few, but it turns out there are hundreds of such respect words to be used when circumstances dictate. They can enhance the politeness, prudence, or delicacy of any utterance. Ordinary implements, parts of the face and body, items of clothing, huts, encampments, areas of land – all have respect words associated with them. These form what is almost a second language.

Working on these words one day with informants, I asked for the respect terms for various animals. We began with carnivores. The terms for these were given as I asked for them. When we got to the great meat animals, however, I no longer needed to ask. The respect words for these were reeled off in rapid succession, in a kind of litany form I had heard used previously for the meat animals' regular names.

Sometimes the respect words had significances which utterly escaped me. Some of them were unfamiliar words altogether, which could not be otherwise translated. But many of the words were readily translatable and their metaphorical significance apparent. For instance, one of the respect words for python is g!u-tzun-g/a'a, 'water-nose-eye'. Feet are called 'sand-pressers', faces 'what's-up-front', breasts 'chest meat'. A pestle and mortar are called 'speech' because of the sound they make. A territory is called 'tree-water' or 'sand surface' and a pot, 'fire medicine'. Water is 'soft throat'. Lion is 'night', 'moonless night', 'night medicine', 'cries in the night', 'calf muscles of nightfall', 'calf muscles', and 'jealousy'. The delicious flying termites are called kxani, which I translate in this context as 'luck'.

The process of making up new words to fit new situations is designated in Ju/'hoan by the term n!áukxui. This process produced words like 'iguana fingers' for fork, and 'European giraffe' or 'riding giraffe' when an experimental camel patrol went through the Ju/'hoan area. Puns and other linguistic jokes are known as //ore, and people enjoy them greatly.

One of the most interesting spontaneous metaphoric interchanges I heard took place over a teapot boiling on my fire. I had just shared a pot of tea with a group of old women. Now the tea was all gone, so we were boiling the leaves a second time. A man approached the fire and sat down. Politely not looking at the pot but staring off into space, he said, 'Are the com ['buzzings': respect word for bees] being chopped out of the trees?' (By speaking obliquely of bees he meant honey, which is used to refer to cane sugar, which in turn metaphorically implies tea with sugar.) 'The light-coloured honey up at the front of the hive has been chopped out already,' answered one of the women. 'Now the dark honey at the back is all that is left.' This metaphor, used in a simple social situation, operated not at one remove but at four.

The processes of abstraction used in ordinary conversation can help us comprehend what is going on in the metaphors of verbal art. As I have said before, Ju/'hoan narrative style grows organically from the style of everyday discourse. Both employ similar mechanisms for creating emphasis, such as repetition of verbal phrases to suggest sustained action (ha 'm – 'm – 'm – 'm – 'm – 'm 'he ate ate ate ate ate ate' or Ka ju g!ò'ó ku g!ò'ó' – 'when someone coughs and coughs'). Sometimes the words are doubled for certain effects (ha dshau n!a'an ko kxóni-kxóni n//hoo – 'the old woman fuss-fussed around') or the speaker may use onomatopoeia (tsxaetsxae – 'to chatter, as birds do'), or idiophones (tzap or tzop for a hail-cloud coming down or an axe chopping through a neck, or !khui! for a bang like a gun going off, mongongo nuts cracking open, or a closed pot full of meat exploding).

Also, both ordinary discourse and narrative contain many sentences ending on an upbeat created by varying the final repetition in a series: ha ko djxani te djxani te djxani te djxanin/ang – 'she danced and danced and danced-to-sit-down'). A beautiful upbeat series ending of this sort is found in one of the G!kon//'amdima narratives:

N!oma kehe'm cu. Te !u cu te n!oma kehe'm cu te !u cu. Te n!oma kehe'm cu te !u cu te n!oma ke tsi cu /auhn.

Here is one hill. Beyond is lies a valley of soft sand and then another hill and then another valley. Then there's another hill, another valley, and then comes a hill that lies green.

In imaginary narratives, mechanisms such as these are used to good advantage by expert Ju/'hoan storytellers. Though most adults are capable storytellers, a storyteller who is especially facile with such devices may become known as a *n=oahnsi kxao* or 'owner of stories'. This phrase refers, not to ownership of the stories themselves, but of the ability to tell any story well. Usually, having a large repertoire of stories goes along with the ability.

Individual raconteurs often have specific stylistic tricks and/or methods of advancing the plot which recur again and again in their performances. For instance, //Xukxa N!a'an was fond of using comical reduplication in her stories to emphasise instances of outrageousness. For her, arguers did not merely *n=uiankhoe*, contradict each other, but *n=uin-n=uiankhoe;* gnawings made by a rabbit on the moon's face were */'om/'omsi*, 'gnaw-gnawings'; dirty-minded speech was 'foul-foul' or */kau-/kau*; */'om-/'om* was to gnaw or gobble hard the way an animal eats; vultures could drop *//aba-//aba*, voraciously and scandalously, out of the sky on to corpses; people *n//a-n//aankhoe*, 'shout-shouted' at each other, and would 'kill-kill' someone, *!hun-!hun*. Where other storytellers merely say that a python falls out of a tree and ends up at the bottom of a well, //Xukxa N!a'an was careful to describe the scene graphically:

> *Ka ha ku //ae tama n/a o ka ha n/a ko '/hom!' ko '/hom!' Te n//a ka tuontuoni ku g/ai te n//a ka tuontuoni ku g/ai te n//a ka tuontuoni ku g/ai te ha //oa tia g/aea n//ao koa a kaqen ke. O =xa, ha //oa tia g/aea n//ao koa. Ee.*

When she missed her grip she certainly went '/hom!' [the sound of falling into water]. She went '/hom!' And she went down, down, down all the way to the bottom. To the mud, that's where she went. Yes.

!Unn/obe, on the other hand, was mistress of elaborate and funny dialogues between characters, which she used to great advantage to create a lifelike scene:

When the older brother came back he said to himself, '*Yau!* Where's my wife? Why is the child standing there all alone? What has happened – why has my brother made such a big fire and why is he cutting and eating fat?' He came up to his brother and said, 'What foul thing have you done? Where is my wife? Where does that meat come from?'

The younger brother said wearily, 'Oh, stop giving me this business about what kind of meat it is; just take a bit and taste it. Why do you look at a piece of meat and start calling it a woman?'

But his brother said, 'You big-penis ... you've ruined me. How do you think I can go on living? Do you just want to kill me? Did you pop out of my mother's stomach just to kill my wife for me?' The younger brother said, 'Oh, take some meat and shut up and just have a taste of it, will you? It's just eland meat obviously; not human meat. Just take a taste of it and leave me alone. Won't you just try it and talk later?

A JU/'HOAN STORY IN PERFORMANCE CONTEXT

The following story was told one day in 1971. People had eaten, and were sitting together on a little hummock-side near Kauri village. The sun was bright white and the sky very blue, but since it was winter the air was cool and exciting, so full of oxygen one wanted to breathe and breathe to the point of dizziness. Xoa//'an had her //oaci lute with her, and was adjusting its strings. Babies stood on their mothers' legs and bounced. /Kaece, an adolescent boy, sat near the edge of the little group and fired his slingshot at the trunks of small trees. People talked quietly, off and on, about some visitors from the west who were said to be on the way. Suddenly, from behind an anthill, popped the Ostrich Lady! She ran forward on skinny but elegant old legs, shouting Wanh, wanh, wanh!, and scattered the children. We were all startled.

'How did you creep up on us like that?' I asked accusingly, laughing to see the old woman point her lips like an ostrich's beak and scratch one toe in the sand as if it were a big claw.

'It's me, the old Ostrich Lady,' she announced in a comical voice, ignoring my question. She flapped her bent arms, pretending they were wings. Then she sat down and the children settled around her.

Who's been asking about G!kon//'amdima and the jackal over here? Here I am, come to tell you.

This is the story of G!kon//'amdima and the jackal. The jackal was the younger sister and G!kon//'amdima was her older sister. One day the jackal came to her sister and said, 'Let's go and pick *n=ah*. You can reach the branch with the berries and hand them down to me.' But G!kon//'amdima said, 'No. that branch lies out over the water, and I'm afraid of it.' The jackal insisted: 'Oh, come on, let's go and pick some. You can reach the *n=ah* branch and pull it down.' G!kon//'amdima replied, 'If I pull that branch down it's sure to flip me into the water. Now just stop talking about eating *n=ah*'. But the jackal said, 'If you start to fall in I'll catch you. If you lose your grip and start to slide in, if it looks like you're going into the water, I'll be there to jump and grab you. Come on, don't just sit there – let's go and eat *n=ah*.'

People were giggling in anticipation. We all knew what was coming. The old lady went on:

So they walked and walked until they came to the water. G!kon//'amdima jumped and grabbed the *n=ah* branch. All the while she was muttering to herself, 'What in the world am I doing here pulling down this dangerous branch? Why do I listen to this deceitful sister of mine?' Then suddenly she lost her grip and – *!Xom!* she fell into the water. She fell right into the water. It was a deep spring and a wide one, and it was full to the brim with water. When she fell, the jackal pretended to try and catch her, but let her fall between her arms.

Now, beside the spring was a pile of clothing and ornaments that G!kon//'amdima had taken off before she tried to reach the *n=ah*. She had stood beside the tree and peeled off her things, left them lying inside out. When her sister was out of the way, the jackal ran up to the pile in glee. She began putting on the clothes. But she put them on inside out. Finally she put her sister's hat on her head and marched off. She walked back to the camp. There she met her brother-in-law, her sister's husband. He said, 'What have you done with my wife? Where have you

left her?' and looked long and hard at his sister-in-law the
jackal. The jackal said, 'Well, um, it's like this. Um, we, well, we,
um, I took my sister and we went picking *n=ah* and she fell to
the bottom of the spring.' G!kon//'amdima's husband said,
'*Koo-oo-oo*. Are you standing there and telling me you took my
wife and the two of you went off and she fell into the well?' By
this time the sun was going down. At sunset the jackal sat
visiting with some other young girls who were there. They were
all telling stories. The jackal laughed harshly. '*//ka//ka, //ka!*' Then
she covered her mouth and said, '*Yau*! Why am I laughing like a
jackal today? What's happened to me that I should laugh like a
jackal?' Her brother-in-law, kori bustard, said, 'Oh, go screw
yourself, you are a jackal, you fool. It was my wife who was
beautiful G!kon//'amdi, and you are only a jackal.' But the jackal
kept up the pretence of being her married sister, and walked
proudly away from him. She tried to undulate gracefully like
G!kon//'amdi did. She wanted to glide away with regal steps
and sit down smoothly as her sister did. But all she could
manage was a bounce.

/Xoan N!a'an, the Ostrich Lady, bounced in place. '*Yau*! Why am I
walking like a jackal?' she exclaimed.

'Oh, screw yourself!' yelled the kori bustard. 'How come you've
always been a jackal and now suddenly stop being one?' And he
stomped off to bed early. He took all the jackal's sleeping skins
and spread them out, with his own, on the sand. Later the jackal
decided to go to sleep. Now the kori bustard had taken long
arrows, those bone arrows that the hunters poison, and stuck
them into the sand beneath her blankets. He stuck rows and
rows of them into the sand where she was going to sleep. The
jackal began to settle herself among the skins. '*Xai*!' an arrow
stuck her. '*Yau*!' she said. 'What kind of crummy places do you
choose to sleep in, anyway? It's all thorny here.' But the kori
bustard replied, '*Koo*, won't you just go to sleep quietly? What's
the matter with you? This is where I always spread out our
blankets. If you're really my wife, you ought to know that.' So

they slept. But the jackal wasn't sleeping because she was
already dead. The poison had killed her.

In the morning when dawn broke, the jackal's grandmother
sent her littlest granddaughter to see why the jackal did not get
up. 'Go and get her up. Wake up your sister. What's she doing
sleeping so late?' The little girl went to see what was the matter.
'Koo-oo-oo!' she cried.' [/Xoan N!a'an assumed the tiny,
high-pitched voice of a child.] 'As sure as all of us stand here,
n=ah seeds have dried last night in her arse-arse. She has died
and her shit has stuck in her anus. She died last night, and her
shit is stuck halfway out of her anus. That's what has
happened.' When the little girl said this, her grandmother said,
'Yau! what did you say? What's happened to the jackal?'
'Granny,' shouted the child a little louder, 'n=ah seeds have
dried in older sister's arse-arse. Didn't you hear me?' But the
grandmother couldn't understand her. Finally the little girl told
her to come and see for herself.

She came and saw that her granddaughter had died in the
night. 'Koo-oo,' she said. 'What happened to her, what has killed
her?' Then she broke off the shit that had dried in the jackal's
anus, and she ate it. Her other granddaughter said, 'Give me
some, granny, give me some too,' So they ate it all up. Then they
picked the jackal's body up and laid it out flat. They slit her
stomach open. Then they brought firewood and dug a trench to
put it in. The old woman walked to and fro bringing wood, and
as she worked, the fire burnt itself down to coals. The old
woman roasted the jackal; she roasted her own granddaughter.
The sun passed overhead and at last she went to take her out of
the fire. She knocked the ashes off her with a stick. Then she cut
the body open and separated the different parts. She and her
little granddaughter began to eat. They ate and ate until the
jackal was gone.

/Xoan N!a'an widened her eyes and stared solemnly at the little ones,
who stood it for a moment and then burst into giggles. The story had
been received with both knowing looks and a sense of suspense.

Everyone present knew the plot line, but we were all speechless with interest to see how the Ostrich Lady would tell it this time, especially since she radiated such energy and fun that day. We hadn't expected to hear a story that afternoon, but it turned out to be exactly what we wanted. /Xoan N!a'an had bounded into the group and taken its measure, and had added her own ebullience to what we already had. By the time she ran flouncing off to join some people going by, she had a gang of little ostriches pattering behind her.

I heard this story in 1971. How many times have the incidents in this particular story been retold, since somebody made it up somewhere long ago? Certainly it is not a story confined to the Ju/'hoan people: it belongs to Aarne-Thompson Type 403, The Black and the White Bride, Sub-type IVe, 'The True Bride is Pushed into a Well or Murdered' (Thompson and Roberts 1960). It has analogues in many other parts of Africa. But how does one put a story like this into cultural perspective, given the millions of changing stories which must have been told over Africa in the last few centuries by migrating, mingling, and merging peoples? Are stories like this one, or parts of it, borrowings from contact with other ethnic groups? What is the setting, in other words, of Bushman oral traditions in the context of Southern Africa?

In answering this question I will be referring to two main cultural divisions, the Bantu-speakers and the Khoikoi.[1]

BUSHMAN FOLKLORE AND BANTU FOLKLORE

There is a general and very obvious separation between Bushman oral literature and that of the Bantu-speakers. One is tempted to see in this gulf a simple division between opposing world-views, that of the hunting and gathering Bushmen versus that of the agricultural/pastoral Bantu-speakers. But we do not want to make this distinction too easily. As we have seen, archaeological evidence shows that some Southern African hunter-gatherers may have practised agriculture under favourable climatic conditions for the last several thousand years, abandoning it when conditions were unfavourable. In addition, among many Bantu-speaking agricultural

and pastoral groups, hunting and gathering has remained an important subsistence stratum in their adaptation, a kind of fail-safe.

The Lord of the Animals and the trickster themes – which seem to
link Bushman folklore closely to traditions of other hunter-gatherers,
such as some native American groups – are also to be found in
Bantu-speaking Africa.

Peoples of Africa have rarely been separated utterly from each
other. Contact has been intermittent but not completely broken. Some
of the motifs used by African storytellers today thus go back to the
very early times of mankind. New tales and motifs have been con-
tinuously taken over by neighbouring peoples. It is very difficult to
attribute tales exclusively to one or another culture by using historical
data. Very few historical-geographical studies of tale types have been
done for any African folklore.[2]

In general, however, we can group tales roughly as Bantu or
Bushman by making note of their relative frequency among the two
groups. If a story is to be found just once in Bushman collections (for
instance, Schmidt cites that of the All-Devourer and that of the girl
carried in the net in *The Mantis and His Friends* (Bleek *et al.* 1923) but
is very popular with neighbouring Bantu, it can be supposed to be of
Bantu origin. Stories of hunters going to the other world through a
hole in the earth may well be Bantu because the earth is the location
of the other world in Bantu religions. Though powerful Ju/'hoan
n/omkxaosi (medicine men, trancers) speak of travelling through the
earth to reach the other world, this place is ultimately located in the
sky. At some point in the journey they must re-emerge from the earth
and ascend the 'threads of the sky'.

I myself recorded a number of Bantu stories while making my
collections. In most cases these were easily identifiable. Often
enough, even though they were transformed in entering Bushman
tradition, the storytellers knew them to be borrowed. Once I got a
story about a man who was created from a woman's rib (*sic*).

'Where did you learn this story?' I asked.

'I used to live near the mission at D'Kar'.

Some characteristics of Bantu folklore identified by Paul Radin are shared by Bushman folklore, and some are not. For instance, both share an emphasis on the earthly nature of man (who is not thought of as having had divinity and lost it) and on the necessity for gods to 'lose their earthly constituent before becoming divine' (Radin 1952:4). The stark realism of Bantu folklore and its emphasis upon the contemporary scene, on the other hand, are not so often found in Bushman tradition. Nor is the overtly moralising tendency of Bantu tales identified by Boas (1915:333) shared by Bushman tales, which tend instead to be only indirectly didactic.

Storytellers were rarely as privileged a class in Africa as they were in Polynesia. However, Radin makes a useful distinction between two types of African storytellers: one was attached in some way to a ruler, the other was free. The former (found principally in West and Central Africa) had greater prestige. Their productions spread into societies with less stratified political organisation, for example the Bantu societies of Southern Africa. The stories told by these author-raconteurs tended to extol the status quo and the ruler who embodied it. Earlier cosmological myths were pushed into the background. Animal tales were redirected towards the historical world of human beings. Culture-hero tales were progressively lost. Radin (1952:14) feels that the existence of both of these types of tales in Bushman folklore indicates that they must have been much more widely spread in Africa than they are today. As a matter of fact, in unstratified Bantu groups with 'free' storytellers, the hare and other animals, such as the spider, appear as trickster/culture-heroes. The creative function of these figures has largely been lost, as Radin points out, among some native American groups.

I have observed some other characteristics which do not seem to be shared by Bantu tales. One of these is that the Bushmen have no stories of an historical 'Golden Age', but only of a time when the identities of animals and humans were merged.

In this mythical time, life was not thought to have been much easier. The Ju/'hoansi, further, have no story of a flood, though the Hai//'om Bushmen reportedly told one. There are no tales (except in recounting trance experiences) of imaginary journeys to the other world and thus no 'Orpheus' tradition.

In fact, a unidirectional journey motif stringing together adventures or progressing towards a climax is generally lacking among Bushmen. Instead, the *loci* of the tales are the camp and the bush. Journeys progress from camp to bush and back, or between camps. Also, cosmological figures are generally located in a separate realm from that of the stories (though the trickster Kaoxa lisps and quavers just like the cosmological *Kaqiankxaosi*, 'Masters of Torment' figures who are said to live in the west). Quite a few Bantu tales have as central characters children upon whom descends a frightening world of strange beasts, ogres, and authoritarian adults. The heroism of the children in escaping the clutches of these figures forms a large part of the story line.

Though there are some parallels in Bushman tradition, there is certainly not the emphasis on this situation that is found in Bantu folklore.

BUSHMAN FOLKLORE AND KHOIKOI FOLKLORE

Now we turn to the place of Bushmen within Khoisan tradition.[3] Bushman folklore itself is practically indistinguishable from Khoisan tradition as a whole: it is very hard to tell the difference between a Bushman story and a Khoikoi story. The two traditions overlap to a great extent, with a few interesting dissimilarities. The Bushman tricksters have a close equivalent in the 'Heiseb' of the Nama Khoikoi. The well-known Bushman story of Eyes-on-his-Feet is familiar, according to Sigrid Schmidt, to every adult Nama today (personal communication 1974).

The question of the nature of the connections and/or borrowings between Bushmen and Khoikoi involves all the unsolved problems about the relationships of the two peoples in prehistory.[4] The Central Bushman languages are closely linked to Nama Khoikoi. Serologically, Khoikoi resemble Bushmen in some ways and Bantu in others. They also possess blood-group peculiarities of their own.

Wherever they came from, the Khoikoi pastoralists continued to rely upon hunting and gathering as well as stock-raising. Much of their folklore is basically the same as that of the hunters and gatherers to whom they may be closely related. However, there are certain groups of Khoikoi tales not shared by the San (for example, the flying lion stories). The Nama also have only traces of the theme of the Early Race basic to both the Northern and Southern Bushmen. They have similar stories, but they do not place them in a long-ago mythical time. There are also Khoikoi tales featuring cows, which do not appear in Bushman folklore; these, however, may be tales borrowed from the Bantu.

There do exist some basic similarities, as we shall see, which tie Khoikoi and Bushman folklore tightly together. For example, here is an instance of how a fundamental idea operates in both traditions although its external manifestations are different: a common means of revivification in Bushman tales is putting part of the dead body into water; in Khoikoi tales the part is put into a calabash of milk. In neither Bushman nor Khoikoi tales does the smith, so important in the nearby Ovambo folklore, appear; this common lack links them as well.

The present differences between the folklore of Khoikoi and Bushmen are due to the addition of numerous European elements to Khoikoi tradition which has occurred in South Africa and Namibia. The folktales of the present descendants of the Cape Khoikoi are so Europeanised that they have been included in the Afrikaans tale-type index.[5] As I have indicated, a few stories that are obviously of European origin came to my attention while I was making my own collection among the Ju/'hoansi. In most cases it was possible to pinpoint the entrance of the European influence as contact with missionaries or a labour experience. In general, however, if European elements are discoverable in Bushman tales they have come through Khoikoi tradition on the way. Just as the Afrikaners acted as go-betweens in the spread of European tradition to the Khoikoi, so the Khoikoi in turn were go-betweens for the Bushmen. One difference between Khoikoi and Bushman traditions, which has emerged from comparison of my collection with published Khoikoi tales, is the relatively greater development of a series of heroine stories (which includes our tale of G!kon//'amdima and the jackal) among some groups of Bushmen. Schmidt reports a few Nama tales about a little wise girl like the one collected by Bleek (1864:85), but there is nothing like the development of the heroine figure found among the Ju/'hoansi and Naron. The Hai//'om Bushmen of northern Namibia have a little wise girl too, said to be the sister of the trickster-god Heiseb; she does not, however, have a set of adventures all to herself. Schmidt, who has likened the Ju/'hoan G!kon//'amdima to 'Snow White', 'Red Riding Hood', and 'Cinderella' all rolled into one, suggests that it may be a special local development.[6]

We will be in a better position to say whether this suggestion is valid when we have examined all the evidence relating to this figure. Great care must be taken with this heroine when discussing traits that are exclusive to Khoisan folklore. The story of the wise girl (or boy), for example, who saves the grown-ups from ogres is known all over Bantu Africa. The story of the 'false bride' is spread over many continents (Aarne-Thompson 408 and 533). This story, deeply rooted in widely diverse traditions, must be a very ancient one indeed. Bantu versions of it usually feature an evil supernatural being who substitutes for the bride. The Khoisan peoples, however, have a false personage substituting for the young married woman, who is herself killed, tricked, or enchanted. (In some Nama tales, a frog-woman is the substitute. In Bleek and Lloyd's *Specimens of Bushmen Folklore* (1968:84), it is a hyena. In *Reynard the Fox in South Africa* (Bleek 1864), number 24 is 'The Lion who Took a Woman's Shape'.) That the jackal is G!kon//'amdima's 'sister' should not blind us to the fact that this jackal is the typical Khoisan ogre. 'Typical ogre motifs are connected with it:' writes Schmidt, 'the child [who] has to wake up the ogre and does not understand that the ogre is dead; the old ogre grandmother [who] has to go and see for herself; the comical treatment of these scenes; finally, the ogres [who] eat a member of their own clan' (personal communication 1974). Ju/'hoan versions of this episode have much in common with the Khoikoi 'Aigamuchab' stories.

The question arises, of course, of the possible Bantu origin of these Khoisan ogres and cannibal figures. Certainly cannibals are frequently encountered in Bantu folklore. But frightening cannibal figures are very real to many Ju/'hoansi and Nama, and probably to other Khoisan peoples. However, Schmidt has told me that there is a rock painting of a cannibal scene in a Nama area of Namibia. It is one thousand years old and thus dates from a time when Bantu peoples – at least the present ones – had not yet arrived there. Other stories peculiar to Khoisan, as opposed to Bantu, folklore include the tricking away of one animal's shoes by another animal. Though versions of this story are found in both Khoikoi and Bushman traditions and are not easily discoverable elsewhere in Africa, the story crops up in Hungary with surprisingly similar details (Schmidt, personal communication 1974). In this case there can be no question of borrowing. But in the case of the stories about the division of the social world, popular with all Khoisan groups, the many variants spread throughout other parts of Africa seem to mitigate against an autochthonous Khoisan origin.

In general, though there are complex duplications and overlaps in tradition due both to borrowing and to shared life-style features, Bushman folklore may be differentiated with some ease from that of neighbouring peoples, particularly those furthest from dependence upon hunting and gathering. Next, we turn to discuss hunting-gathering societies and to explore the role that folklore may play in this form of adaptation.

Chapter Two

Folklore and Foraging

Until the end of the Paleolithic Era, about ten thousand years ago, hunting and gathering was the only form of economic organisation. The ancestors of all of us lived lives similar to those of the few hunting and gathering societies left today. Recognition of this fact should not blind us, however, to the historical experience of contemporary hunting and gathering cultures. These cultures have evolved, just as that of Europe has, and great care should be taken in generalising from present-day hunter-gatherers back to the European Stone Age.

We have, however, certain specific pieces of information about the ancient hunting cultures in archaeological evidence of their habitation, stature, and diet, and in the art and utensils which have survived until today. Comparing these with the material culture, body form, and economy of modern hunting groups sheds light on the functioning of ancient societies. Combined with archaeological evidence, modern Ju/'hoan ritual and belief may illuminate what we already know of the great Paleolithic religious traditions of Europe and the Middle East.

HUNTER-GATHERERS

Foraging – or hunting-gathering – peoples of today, though few in number, are widely diverse. They range from Alaskan and Canadian

Inuit using the sea and tundra to forest-dwelling Pygmies of Central Africa and Negritos of the Philippines. A series of international conferences has been held to bring together scholars studying these peoples, so that their adaptations to different environments can be compared and contrasted. These scholars have found that, despite differences in the economic resources on which they depend, there are great similarities in the social arrangements by which hunting-gathering peoples have contrived to exploit and share them.

The single unifying characteristic foragers share which differentiates them most from societies with more complex forms of organisation (agricultural, pastoral or industrial) is that they change their environments very little in order to live. Other forms of economic activity modify the land and expend energy converting one kind of commodity into others, including money, but hunter-gatherers generally consume the naturally occurring produce of their region virtually unchanged. They live in small groups in numbers well below the carrying capacity of their land, generally regulate internal relations by kinship, custom, and consensus rather than by inherited or acquired authority and bind themselves to share resources by clear rules of reciprocity. They maintain a flexible relationship to their land in most cases, aggregating when desirable to pool work and share localised resources, and fissioning and dispersing to resolve tensions generated by living with scarcity.

The patterns of subsistence and the social arrangements of hunter-gatherers of today are of interest to us partly because they provide some evidence of how ancient hunter-gatherers must have lived. With careful extrapolation, gaps in our understanding of our deep cultural past can be filled by observing how contemporary hunter-gatherers relate to each other, to their environments, and to an imaginary world beyond this one.

Human beings living in small groups with simple technology have much in common no matter where they live. As John Pfeiffer (1982:174) points out, such groups 'confront many of the same basic problems ... especially when they pursue a non-literate, hunting and gathering wilderness existence'. Basic to the adaptation which solved the problem of living successfully under these conditions are first, detailed knowledge and second, devices for remembering and transmitting it. Both are important parts of what has been referred to as hunting-gathering or foraging 'style'.

'FORAGING STYLE' AND EXPRESSIVE FORMS

Anthropologists have recently begun to explore similarities in 'foraging style' – including mental and psychological characteristics – among hunting-gathering groups.

Though much detailed comparison of the folklores and religions of hunting-gathering cultures has yet to be made, some general observations about them are possible. For instance, seasonal economic patterns are deeply etched in the folklore – summer aggregations and winter dispersal, or vice-versa, according to climate and food resources, with plant and animal species and activities characteristic of each season sufficing to signify it by brief reference. Marriage and residential arrangements are usually elaborate ideas in the imaginative world because alliances are the means for establishing reciprocal access to the resources of various areas. The division of labour and of social domains is almost always by sex and age only, with little hierarchical emphasis or specialised roles. Hunting as a male activity is typically valued and ritually elaborated over either gathering or fishing, despite the relative economic importance of the latter activities in specific instances.

Men's hunting is often symbolically opposed not to the complementary female activity of gathering but rather to women's reproductive capacity. In other words, production as an idea is symbolically parallel to reproduction: both are shown as necessary to the ongoing life of society. Life cycle ritual is connected to the economic 'readiness' for these activities of maturing youths of both sexes: thus there is often some sort of 'first kill' ceremony for boys balanced by the rites of menarche for girls.

Ideas regarding hunting involve sympathetic identification of hunters and prey and/or hunters' wives and prey. A sex/food equation is pervasive, and man/animal/deity relationships are ritually important and elaborate. The idea of propitiation for killing prey is prominent, and is often associated with a 'Lord of the Animals' figure. Food animals generally function as transformers, helpers, or in the apt phrase of David Lewis-Williams (1981), as *animaux de passage*, helping human beings from less desirable conditions to desired ones. Meat-sharing has both social categorising functions and religious ramifications. Some individuals in most hunter-gatherer societies undertake social projection into 'other realms' on behalf of the group as a whole, for example, as shamans, and shaman/artist/innovator roles are closely connected with altered states. Vision-questing for spirit guardians and for contact with a changeless world order – the Dreamtime, for example – is a widespread and important means of 'knowing'.

Though hunting-gathering societies of the world differ greatly, they are all alike in that unquestioning reciprocity along agreed-upon lines is essential to their continued operation. Thus sharing for most of these cultures has been a high virtue continually reinforced. Further, their subsistence technologies are information-intensive and demand both skill and co-operation. So expressive forms are important in codifying both attitudes like reciprocal sharing as well as a great volume of subsistence information.

John Pfeiffer has suggested that the rock art of the Upper Paleolithic hunters performed the function of imprinting such information in the absence of writing. I believe this view can be extended to the oral expressive forms of hunting societies as well. Folklore and other forms of narrative, for instance, provide a kind of scaffolding upon which explicit information about resources can be vividly and memorably hung. The cognitive ability to represent situations removed from the immediate sensory field is, as pointed out by Robin Ridington (1978:9) and others, basic to the social hunting and gathering adaptation. In particular, the capacity to recreate situations for others and to convey to them what has been found to be of interest and of value has been of great adaptive worth. Instead of seeing the symbol systems of hunter-gatherers as superfluous aesthetic activity, then, we ought to regard them as enabling features of their adaptation. Ridington suggests an analogy for symbolic expressions with the carrying net identified by Richard Lee as 'the basic invention that

made human evolution possible' (Ridington 1978:5). Like the inno-
vation of the net, human conceptual devices and expressive forms
have made possible the 'carrying' and thus the sharing of adaptively
significant information. Stories like the ones presented here thus have
an intimate connection with life as it must be lived with a particular
technology in a particular environment.

AN EVOLUTIONARY VIEW OF HUNTER-GATHERER
COMMUNICATION

What I am suggesting is that folklore, far from being a kind of cultural
froth, may actually represent an important phase in the systematics
of the knowledge of hunter-gatherers. Blurton Jones and Konner
(1976:326), writing about the role of expressive forms in the transmission of information among Ju/'hoan hunter-gatherers, make the
evolutionary point that successful habits of mind connected with
learning, storing, and communicating survival information will have
been strongly selected for. This selection pressure has left an imaginative legacy in the expressive forms, strongly imprinted with the
attitudes towards work, social life, and the supernatural which all
along have been adaptive in the foraging milieu. Folklore shares with
other Ju/'hoan information dissemination processes a characteristic
indirectness which may be fundamental to their success. Much verbal
sharing of information, about animal behaviour for instance, among
groups of Ju/'hoansi is indirectly rather than directly accomplished.
In fact, many sorts of knowledge are acquired (by young and old
Ju/'hoansi alike) through hearing the dramatised story of a day's
events rather than in a directly didactic learning context.

Ju/'hoan education involves no rote learning or teacher/learner
roles; instead, knowledge is acquired not when directly needed or
under social pressure but in relaxed times when the pressure is off.

Information is accumulated additively, and individuals benefit
from the contributions of many others rather than of a single teacher.
Free flow of information characterises the casual social contexts in
which learning takes place. This appears to be a system which makes
optimum use of what might be called 'group knowledge' by making

information-exchange both routine and enjoyable. It is also based upon respect for observed facts and for those who are in possession of them, a characteristic of human groups governed by what Robert Theobald (1972) has called 'sapiential authority'. This sort of authority, found in egalitarian societies, in contrast to 'structural authority' in hierarchical societies, promotes an open, highly social flow of opinion and information. In other words, selected habits of information processing exist in mutual reinforcement with the egalitarianism of the social structure. In fact, egalitarianism in Ju/'hoan information flow seems to be closely related to 'very basic features of their society and its ecology such as food-sharing' (Blurton Jones and Konner 1976:345). The mechanisms of information flow can be seen, thus, as having substantial depth in cultural time. The unstructured nature of the learning process may actually result, further, in a 'greater efficiency in the "filing" and retrieval of information stored in a system of the subject's own construction', say Blurton Jones and Konner (1976:344). These authors go on to suggest that old people among hunter-gatherers (most of whom, at least among Ju/'hoansi, are competent storytellers) should be regarded not as reference libraries for the young but rather as dramatised documentary television. They say that the elderly storytellers' art 'gives many pegs on which to hang the information' needed to be successful in life (1976:344-45). For listeners to stories, both attitude- and fact-learning are connected to the motivation involved in plot and conflict. It becomes possible to entertain the idea that communication for survival among hunter-gatherers may be an eminently rational and effective process but nevertheless one that is based on narrative or visual art, casual social contexts, and idiosyncratic modes of assimilation.

The evolutionary point of view is very useful here: intelligence itself, and how it is used socially in communication, can fruitfully be regarded as adaptations. For instance, it has been remarked that in hunting-gathering societies many people show adverse reactions to direct, rather than informal instruction: Blurton Jones and Konner link this tendency to these peoples' general devaluation of individuals who seem to set themselves above others (even the young) by telling them what to do.

Such a perspective calls into question certain limited notions we may have of information transmission in these societies (involving stereotypical didactic grannies around campfires telling stories with 'morals' to the awed young) and substitutes for them pictures of humane, permissive, but effective learning contexts for young and old, based on the enjoyment of narration.

The importance of storytelling in the communication systems of hunting-gathering peoples implies that a level of interest in acquiring information beyond that needed for immediate subsistence may be of adaptive value. Much subsidiary information about the behaviour of animals, the habitats of plants, and the customs of humans regarding them is tucked within the artistry of stories, and it appears to be utilised later as part of a general fund of knowledge. Discussing the growth of human intelligence in evolutionary history, Richard Lee (1973:94) points out that language, which is 'synonymous with human intelligence reduced to its essentials ... becomes elaborated far beyond the adaptive needs of the organism'. To me this elaboration appears to take place, or at the very least primarily to reveal itself, in expressive forms, whose latitude for multiple references, playful spending of cultural energies, and capacity for social communication seem to create a natural spawning ground for new meaning. Lee in fact goes on to ask, 'are we to conclude that the tremendous growth of human intelligence was largely for social and recreational purposes?' In answer I think we may say that though the growth of language and intelligence served social purposes, it probably took place largely in recreational contexts.

Now social and economic purposes may appear from our perspective to require rational means. And recreational contexts for the generation and spread of knowledge may appear to us on the contrary 'irrational'. However, it is becoming clear that in the oral transmission of information and values the 'irrational' can serve rational ends very well indeed. The very longevity of hunting-gathering societies attests to this usefulness. Since such societies have been successful for so long a time in human history, it seems reasonable that their apparently recondite systems of thought, with facts embedded in entertainment, may embody an essential practicality. Blurton Jones and Konner have shown, in fact, that Ju/'hoan knowledge, though it may be indirectly and dramatically communicated, is based upon principles of observation and inference no different from those of our own science. It has good predictive capacity for their subsistence situation, and it reflects a probabilistic view of the universe that has contributed to their long-term survival.

Much is known about the subsistence strategies contributing to hunter-gatherer success already, but this knowledge is mostly in terms of their external, measurable manifestations. Input-output studies (Lee 1969), optimal foraging studies (Winterhalder and Smith 1981), and risk-reduction studies (Wiessner 1982) have examined the economic and social patterns by which peoples with this mode of organisation have sustained life. But the internal workings of hunter-gatherer ecological systems, in terms of cognition and communication, have only recently been looked at very seriously (for example, Biesele 1978, Ridington 1978, Silberbauer 1978, Testart 1978, Yengogan 1979).

The study of symbolic activities within which survival knowledge is explored, reinforced, stored and shared is lately coming to be perceived in anthropology as central to understanding how a society maintains itself. The importance of non-written expressive forms, with their constant recreative character, is that they and only they systematically do these things for oral cultures. Thus oral literature is coming to be seen more and more as a source of real data about the vital communicative aspects of culture, rather than as an imaginative spin-off which bears no relationship to how it perpetuates itself. Stories and storytelling may be considered, then, along with other forms of communication, for the role they play in structuring a specific kind of human survival.

STORIES AND CULTURE

The case of a hunter-gatherer society and its folklore is very well suited to an exploration of the relationship between stories and culture. Among hunter-gatherers, simple physical technology, low material inventory, non-hierarchical social structure and a limited number of recognised social 'scenes' often combine with a sparse environment where a single species of animal or plant has a multiplicity of uses. From a heuristic point of view, the cognitive uses of folklore may be most visible to us in a tradition based on such constraints.

For one thing, there are many textual repeats – involving raw materials as well as instrumental techniques both physical and imaginary – to make the structure of agreement obvious. In addition, reading stories from a hunting-gathering people gives one a strong feeling for the sense-and-consensus-making value of narrated events. Stories tend to fix positive ambience around all aspects of the social enterprise of hunting wild game with handmade weapons, of gathering wild vegetable foods, and of sharing both in precise ways. Stories both state and call forth the attitudes towards these and other economic arrangements by which people have co-operated to make their resources sustain them. Stories thus play a part in engaging and motivating social energies in desirable ways: they can be looked on as part of the energetic basis of an adaptation.

Besides that, as we said, stories are makers of sense. Sense must be made, for human beings, of biological and social life, and consensus based on that sense must be reached concerning the rules by which social activity will gain its end, the perpetuation of society. What is more, social agreement or consensus must be reached not once and for ever but repeatedly in the lives of each group and generation in order for human life as such to continue. This is true whether the intervening time has been characterised by great change or has been relatively changeless. The process of incorporating new meaning into understanding is fundamentally the same as the process of reiterating old meaning: both are recreations, performances of already accepted and newly accepted imaginative realities which bear a relationship felt to be vital to the concrete realities of living.

So oral traditions make sense by maintaining both continuity and creativity. They are an ever-renewed source of cognitive and imaginative agreement. This agreement has the most intimate connection

with the details of procuring a livelihood and with the particular sort
of co-operation made necessary by a specific form of livelihood in a
given environment. The storyteller's art both 'makes sense' repeatedly and anew and provides a framework for remembering
survival information.

The classicist Eric Havelock (1963) has written extensively of a
similar mnemonic function performed by epic poetry in pre-
alphabetic Greece. Surrounded by a relaxed, celebratory atmosphere
as in Ju/'hoan tradition, performances of epic were important in
storing, and recalling for the public, the knowledge and values of the
society. Oral storage in what Havelock (1978b:30) calls 'enclaves of
contrived speech' such as epic was the preliterate analogue of the
permanent storage later cultures accomplished in print.

The Greeks of whom Havelock speaks, of course, had far from a
hunting-gathering form of society. Because their communication was
also exclusively oral, however, much that has been observed about
their expressive forms may be useful in understanding those of
hunter-gatherers.

Chapter Three

Oral Systems of Communication

All societies support and strengthen their identity by conserving their mores. A social consciousness, formed as a consensus, is as it were continually placed in storage for re-use. Literate societies do this by documentation; preliterate ones achieve the same result by the composition of poetic narratives which serve also as encyclopedias of conduct. These exist and are transmitted through memorization, and as continually recited constitute a report – a reaffirmation – of the communal ethos and also a recommendation to abide by it.
– Havelock (1978a)

ORAL VERSUS WRITTEN

Oral modes of communication are astonishingly different from printed modes, but it is only in the last few decades that Western scholars have begun to grasp the implications of that difference. With the work of Milman Parry and Albert Lord in Yugoslavia in the 1950s, Havelock's publications on the classical world from the 1960s on, and the ongoing contribution of the 'oralist' school of Ong (1967), McLuhan (1962), and Innis (1951), consciousness of ancient oral modes of knowing and of preserving knowledge has been brought

51

to the fields of folklore and comparative literature (see also Parry 1971, Lord 1978).

There has been a curious lag within social anthropology, however, in applying this new understanding of the preliterate world to the internal communications of societies. This lag has occurred because i) the concept of 'cultural storage', though articulated in anthropology, remained vague in that most anthropologists never gave it a genre locus in the expressive forms, and ii) profound differences between oral and alphabetic education systems have until recently been ignored by anthropology.

Both these reasons may be due to anthropology's deep-seated suspicion of artistic activity and of disciplines which deal with artistic forms. Take folklore, for instance, which has been considered a sort of 'stepchild' field within anthropology. Only mentioned, if at all, in the final chapters of traditional ethnographies, oral literature has been treated as a sort of cultural froth, an epiphenomenon of 'real' life. Anthropologists seem to pay it homage as a cultural achievement without allowing it to confuse the serious business of understanding cultures through kinship, economy and political organisation. At least until Lévi-Strauss made myth analysis seem scientific to some, folklore was seen as not only riddled with subjectivism but devoid of any theoretical or heuristic power.

Though schools of folklore have long been talking very clearly of the role of expressive forms in transmitting cultural traditions, the protean, changing, and often puzzlingly contradictory nature of oral media have tended to confuse anthropologists who were searching them (if at all) for mirrors and models for society. When these anthropologists found that the 'culture reflector' theory was largely to be abandoned, they generally turned away in relief from the whole topic.

In particular, the mnemonic functions of expressive forms in oral cultures, and their relationships to the reproduction of the conditions for society as such, have only recently been appreciated. Much of this recent realisation has come from anthropologists who study hunting-gathering societies. There is of course a large overlap between hunting-gathering societies and the category of oral societies in general. The point here is that hunter-gatherer societies have been, and in many cases have remained, oral societies because they have functioned successfully that way. Oral modes of communication, in other words, have sufficed well for the long-lived hunting-gathering adaptation. It seems important, then, to examine what characteristics of oral communication have contributed to a good fit between individual knowledge and effort and the world of co-operative endeavour necessary to sustain life for hunter-gatherers.

PERSONALITY AND CAUSALITY IN ORAL CULTURES

The work of the classicists and oralists mentioned above has created an awareness that printed communication fostered profoundly different personality structures from the ones which characterised the oral world. Havelock describes the moment, c. 700-650 BC, when the Homeric epics were committed to paper as 'a thunder-clap in human history'. It formed a kind of watershed dividing for ever the face-to-face, socially interdependent, participatory world of oral communication from the increasingly isolated, abstract experience of alphabetic cultures. Knowledge and custom as performed and created together orally gave way to individual and often silent contemplation of texts and rules.

In contrast with the personality structures of post-literate man, writes Havelock, there can be observed an 'ease of character and pragmatism of conduct diffused in preliterate societies'. The pragmatism of the early Greek character is continually brought home to us by reading the *Iliad* and the *Odyssey*: Havelock shows that we should see these books not only as entertainment but as 'encyclopedias' of fact and conduct. Milman Parry (1971) writes that the prescribed morality of a Homeric hero emerges not as a set of principles to which he adheres but rather as his practical response in specific situations to general rules of conduct imposed on him by his social situation. Havelock (1978b:36-37) relates this basic pragmatism directly to the way in which oral, as opposed to written, media regulate adherence to cultural norms: 'Without benefit of a documented speech which will arrange the terms of conduct according to fixed principles, oral wisdom is more free to express pragmatic attitudes which vary according to the necessities of various situations as they arise: it can index the contradictions of daily living... [Oral societies use] a rule of propriety embedded in action, recognizable not as principle but as procedure, working with varying effects to maintain an overall stability.'

Much of what Havelock observes about the 'pragmatism' and 'ease' of Greek character in the preliterate period foreshadows state- ments that have since been made about hunter-gatherer societies. Paul Shepard (1973) speaks of the 'generosity', 'leisure', 'humor', and 'joy' of hunter-gatherers, which he attributes to their practical affir- mation of the ecological relationships on which their life-style depends. Richard Lee remarks upon the Ju/'hoansi's successful adaptation to the realities of health and illness, life and death as connected to their constant focus upon the concrete manifestations of religion rather than with abstract theorising about it.

Among foragers a probabilistic philosophy encourages confidence in the predictability (within limits) of natural phenomena and optim- ism about the sufficiency of skills to tasks (see Ridington 1978:10).

This view of the universe is adaptive not only because it builds confidence but because it is based on respect for the multiplicity of specific pieces of information about the environmental relationships on which life depends. The need for knowledge of many species, and of specific cases of animal and plant behaviour rather than general rules, is met among hunter-gatherers by a healthy respect for detail. This respect for specifics, this unwillingness to generalise prema- turely, has clearly been a habit of mind favoured by selection pressure.

This habit is expressed unmistakably in oral forms such as folk- tales, where the interest is in characters' responses to specific, detailed environmental and social situations rather than in general rules which may be abstracted from them. Not one story is told, but many, and the 'truth' of what is believed lies somewhere in the dialogue among them all. More stories provide more pegs for adaptive infor- mation, too. As Jerome Bruner (1968:89) has remarked, 'a corpus of narratives may be what philosophy used to be'. I think we may also see the general absence of proverbs among hunter-gatherers as a reflection of this same tendency to regard useful information as situation-specific.

In the world of hunter-gatherers, the essence of 'technology' is detailed familiarity with the pattern of relationships that are adaptively significant. The things about animals and plants one knows from previous experience – one's own and that of others – allow the hunter to intersect advantageously with the prey, the gatherer to find and use nutritious plants rather than stale or poisonous ones. Most importantly, the range of successful social conduct – in areas like sharing and attitudes to kin – is explored in specific situations. No one final answer is given to the question of how to behave; rather, the consequences of good and bad choices are delineated in many contexts. They lead to the realisation that there is a lot to know about the business of living and that life is a process of accumulation of the necessary details.

ORAL MNEMONICS

Accumulation of details implies devices for remembering them effectively. In the absence of written documents, the characteristics of oral memory provide the basic structure of the expressive forms. Dry prescriptions for behaviour or lists of hierarchically-arranged information are simply not retained as well as dramatic stories about acts and events. Dramatic interactions involve the listener at an emotional level while providing him with a mnemonic device – the sequence of dramatic events – for recalling content. For memory's sake, narratives are agonistically toned, promoting empathy rather than distance in listeners. Emotional involvement reinforces retention.

Recent writings on the technology of communication have focused on the specifically oral mechanisms of reinforcement and recall. Ong (1982:37) has discussed the 'additive' rather than 'subordinate' patterns of intellectualising experience mnemonically which are evident in the 'and then ... and then' of oral narration. Much experience and opinion, as well as an outline of the bare facts of a situation, can be

condensed within the embroidered anecdote of past events. Information is assimilated in an aggregative rather than an analytic manner,
with redundancy and repetition highlighting the points most important for retention. Folk stories exhibit traditionalism in conserving
what is important: in a sense there are no 'new' stories in tradition
but rather inventive retellings which may incorporate new experience. They are homeostatic (a word used by both Ong and Goody) in
that they tend to slough away both old material and new develop-
ments which do not have relevance to the present. Learning and
thinking in oral cultures, being situational rather than abstract, show
little emphasis on either definitions (Luria 1976) or etymologies
(Goody and Watt 1963): words as spoken have direct semantic rati-
fication. Classifications of information may cross each other out
according to context and situational usefulness. Typically, ethno-
graphers discover that requests for information in these cultures are
interpreted interactively: an attempt to get a definition may elicit a
narrative. In other words, literate investigators may have difficulties
communicating with members of oral cultures because they are not
only speaking a different language but a different meta-language as
well.

EDUCATIONAL 'MEDIA' IN AN ORAL CULTURE

Retention of information and 'schooling' have recently been compared in hunter-gatherer oral societies and in literate societies.
Teaching procedures which have come to be conventional in literate
societies may not at all resemble the modes in use during much of
preliterate history, because the media – and thus the modes of memory used – are profoundly different. For one thing, teaching in oral
societies was most often accomplished by indirection, in 'hands-on'
and casual contexts. Havelock discusses the recital of epic poetry as
a vital channel of educational communication between adults and
children in early Greece, and this must have supplemented the
knowledge which youths acquired by helping older people with
necessary tasks. Formal schooling as we know it simply did not exist.
    Any anthropologist who has spent time with the Ju/'hoansi has

noticed that their use of the concept translated as 'teach' or 'learn' *(n!aroh)* does not correspond to ours. 'Teach me to do X', the anthropologist asks the Ju/'hoan person. The person, ordinarily friendly enough, goes right on *doing* X silently and allowing the anthropologist to be present while it happens, never giving him a verbal 'recipe' or set of articulated procedures to go along with the demonstration.

Previous notions of information transmission between adults and between adults and children thus come into question. It appears that, in contrast to his modern counterpart, a 'teacher' in hunting cultures may be less an active inculcator than a person who was salient as an example both socially and in terms of the information transmitted in the environment at the time a learning task was accomplished. Goody (1977:142) writes that 'oral learning tends to reduplicate the "initial situation", the process of socialization'. I believe that such informal learning contexts may participate in the general efficiency of the permissive child-rearing characteristic of hunting-gathering societies. Both have done the job – of creating informed and adaptive personalities – for many generations.

The numerous bits of environmental information – as well as adaptive attitudes – contained within the artistic framework of stories of hunter-gatherers lead us to ask whether tales do not perhaps perform educational functions similar to those Havelock claims for epic in Greece. The question we face in answering concerns the obviously metrical nature of epic poetry (as opposed to prose narrative), which Havelock sees as an indispensable part of its mnemonic capacity.

MEMORY AND RHYTHMICITY IN PROSE NARRATIVE

May the mnemonic capacity of the metric form of epic in fact be exhibited in other ways in prose narratives such as folktales? Let us take a closer look at the possibly veiled nature of the rhythms of such tales and also make an examination of the narrative form itself for its particular strengths.

Dell Hymes (1981), Dennis Tedlock (1977) and Harold Scheub (1977) have each in different ways called attention to rhythmic pat-

terns in 'prose' narrative. These are patterns which may be percep-
tible to us only in performance, only with considerable linguistic skill
in the original language, and only after repeated familiarity with
specific traditions. Hymes and Tedlock have been concerned with the
visual presentation of native American texts so that they make obvious the pauses, emphases, and other oral markers of significance
which play so great a role in their understanding by auditors. Scheub
has described the patterned non-verbal bodily emphases that give
rhythmicity and repetitive, imagistic design to Xhosa tale performances. Such patterns are in fact obvious in Ju/'hoan performances,
too, though their demonstration is beyond the scope of this book.

Narratives, then, may be 'a verbal habit writ large' (Russo 1978:45),
but in being writ large they take on a precise artistry of their own in
terms of phrasing and repetition. This artistry aids their being remembered for re-performance and for personal cognitive use. Hymes
feels that 'the art of verbal narratives and the shaping of lines is
universal', and that it is a very effective form of communication
'wherever it has the chance to work autonomously' (personal communication 1983).

THE ADAPTIVE VALUE OF THE NARRATIVE FORM

Though folktale narrative is 'special' discourse, it is also a verbal art
for which a lifetime of ordinary narrative experience may well prepare. Practice makes perfect, and experience in exercising the
narrative option in daily contexts seems to hone the storytelling
capacities as well.

This is clearly true among the Ju/'hoansi, where those who can
best answer a question with an illustrative story, tell the tale of a day's
events, or captivate an audience with a well-told folk narrative are
the same individuals. In fact, among Ju/'hoansi, as I have indicated,
most old people can do all these things creditably, whereas younger
people are generally less able.

It is clear that a lifetime of experience in using the narrative styles
of ordinary discourse among Ju/'hoansi contributes to expertise in
'special' discourse as well.

And the opposite – that practice in storytelling may contribute to fluency in general – may also be true. Taking the broadest view, since both narrative styles communicate, a facility developed in either of them by individuals may increase the communicative efficiency and cohesiveness of groups. For this reason the similarity in discourse styles may be viewed as a positive adaptation for certain oral cultures.

However, whether there is any necessary connection between hunting-gathering cultures and non-metrical prose forms is an open question. Dennis Tedlock does deny the presence of verse epic in what Ong calls 'primary oral cultures' and Havelock (1978b:364, n.13) concedes that 'the formalism of oral epic may become more sophisticated in sedentary societies than in nomadic ones'. In any case there was, at least for some time in human history, a set of conditions under which the 'prose' narrative form was useful enough to be selected for. More data from the oral traditions of both hunter-gatherers and other cultures would help us to locate and define these conditions.

Meanwhile, what else about the narrative forms of foraging cultures familiar to anthropologists may be adaptive for these cultures? Can we make evolutionary sense of the collections anthropologists normally obtain from such peoples, collections which often consist of a corpus of episodes gathered from a people at a point in time, sometimes articulated into longer sequences but just as often not, each story seemingly linked by the most tenuous references to the world of the rest of the stories? These paratactically linked fragments of tradition have an open-endedness about them, a seeming capacity for linkage in many different ways and for retelling in many different ways, that can be obscured by trying to make them fit the model of the epic cycle.

In fact this very open-endedness, this flexibility, this 'intratextuality', may be the key for understanding their adaptive strength. For one thing, the form provides a vehicle which is most receptive to the special contributions which may be made by different individuals. The repertoire of stories is an amendable, growing form to which individuals feel they may make genuine contributions without having to be in control of anything like an entire cycle. For another, its episodic nature, in which we may encounter a character acting in an approvable social manner in one episode and later find him doing something outrageous, may quite accurately reflect the situation-specific knowledge that hunter-gatherers are interested in inculcating.

But the most important mnemonic mechanism of these narratives, and therefore the basis of their adaptive value, is shared not only by epic but by other effective artistic forms. This mechanism is, of course, drama. Motivation to follow, to internalise, to remember the form and content of stories is compelled by the involvement with dramatic conflict. Detailing of environmental and social minutiae can be very full because it has a scaffolding in the unfolding of plot. Seen this way, stories can be understood as effective, ongoing mechanisms both for educating the young and for sharing information and creating consensus about attitudes which continue to be important throughout adult life in an oral culture.

NORMS AND TECHNOLOGY IN ORAL FORMS

Other mechanisms of oral remembering that Ju/'hoan narratives share with the Greek epics include an effective melding of norm-teaching with the teaching of instrumental techniques.

Havelock's (1963:79-81) statement about social values embodied in Homeric poems applies very well to Ju/'hoan stories: 'The realities of the familial situation are summed up and accepted. The formula "what is fitting" is characteristically both descriptive and yet prescriptive ... *nomos* and *techne* overlap ... In an oral culture the hoarded usages of society tend also to assume the guise of hoarded techniques.' Thus it is not far wrong to see oral literature as a bridging mechanism between information and attitudes. Havelock (1963:83) writes of 'a kind of relish' which enlivens the tallying of required procedures, such as navigational details, in the epics. A similar sense of enjoyment infuses the spelling out of environmental and procedural minutiae in the Ju/'hoan tales.

For instance, when Ju/'hoansi enumerate the animals, especially the large meat animals, whether in folktales or in ordinary conversation or in answer to questions, they do so in a highly stylised, almost rhapsodic fashion. They count graphically and visually, putting successive fingers up to their lips as each animal's name is called. There is a certain way of stressing the syllables that appears in no other context. '*N!hoansi* ... */aòsi*, ... *n!angsi*, ... *=oahsi*', and so on. The list becomes a singsong. Almost, the eyes glaze over. The first syllable goes way down in tone. The second, the pluralisation, goes up high and then comes down again, trailing off from near-singing into silence. People love to do it, and they count off the animals at every opportunity.

The effect it conveys is of a dream landscape dotted with an impossible plenty of 'kudus, ... buffaloes, ... eland, ... giraffes ...'. The order is variable, but the enunciation is extremely stereotyped. If a person thought you missed what he said the first time, he would start all over again at the beginning of the list. Storytellers definitely approach those junctures in their tales where this litany is appropriate with 'a kind of relish'.

Another device compelling attention through sheer interest that is shared by Ju/'hoan and Greek narratives is the use of gods and heroes as mnemonic devices for internalising information about cause and effect. The reason for the heroic paradigm is not romantic but technical: it allows men and women to stand not only for human actors in dramas but for phenomena other than persons. Natural phenomena are more dramatically memorable if they are personified as human beings with will and reactivity. 'The environment', writes Havelock (1963:168), 'becomes a great society and the phenomena are represented as members of this society who interact upon each other as they play their assigned roles.' Gods and heroes, such as the personifications of lightning and thunderclouds =*Kagara* and *!Hāunu* which appear in the Bleek-Lloyd fragment, are thus explicable in terms not of primitive confusion but of the psychology of oral memorisation. In particular, they are examples of the reinforcement of memory brought about by pleasurable participation in a sequence of dramatic events.

These characteristics of oral literature illustrate a secret basic to its effectiveness as a learning instrument: it combines instruction with pleasure at a level that is very gratifying, and thus very memorable.

Moreover, the narrative form itself, as we have said, embodies an essential pragmatism of outlook, and this in itself is adaptive. It seems that this kind of mnemonics – a mnemonics of imaginative practicality – has stood oral culture in good stead for long periods in human history.

ANTHROPOLOGY AND FOLKLORE

When the activity of 'cultural storage' is clearly located in oral expressive genres and it is understood that much of the instruction of young people proceeds by exposure to the same instruments, anthropology begins to see folklore in rather better terms. In fact, collected folklore can be recognised as irreplaceable documentation of past lifeways, since linguistic usage is the only direct evidence for mental phenomena.

Ironically, the very success of the oral adaptation in the past has robbed us of the evidence we need to understand it. Tape-recordings from pre-literate cultures which may still be made today are thus extremely precious, and they are doubly so when the performances they record still take place in clear relation to life as it is currently lived.

Seen in this light, the modern Ju/'hoan tales in this collection are relatively high on the scale of 'oral authenticity'. They were collected from a people who in 1972 had no contact whatsoever with literate schooling and only very infrequent contact (always through scribes and government personnel) with documents of any kind. Until the Ju/'hoan literary programme was begun in Namibia in 1989, their language was known in written form only to the handful of scholars who had devised the form as an approximation of their speech. The tales were recorded in spontaneous and naturalistic settings embedded in the minutiae of everyday life. Thus they provide a source for understanding oral storage processes which can enrich the more conventional sources of anthropology.

Part II

Ju/'hoan
Expressive Life

Chapter Four

Tradition and Creativity in Ju/'hoan Religion and Folklore

INDIVIDUAL CONTRIBUTIONS: PART OF THE CONSERVING PROCESS

Because the storytelling way of making social sense is by its nature continually creative and re-creative; it actually has its being only in its new performances. That is why variants in oral life are as uncountable as grains of sand. People who only encounter folktales in print should realise that any collection of living folktales is an accident – an accident of historical time, academic or belletristic fashion, personal characteristics of the collector, funding, politics and other factors. A collection may consist of a lifetime's worth of stories told in the collector's own community and in his own language, or just a year or two of tales communicated in an exotic place and in a language that the collector learned for the purpose.

Normally today all such collections are transmitted to a further audience in print. Normally they are transmitted as if the versions chosen for printing were the only ones, the main ones, the truest ones, the representative ones of the tradition. The countless other versions probably collected at the same time languish in notebooks and on tape and ultimately disappear, because they are not enshrined in the printed collection. Though they stem from diverse, equally accidental sources, the printed collections present a specious sameness to the reader; they are members of a genre whose canons are the physical and financial strictures of publishing as much as anything else. They fail to represent the single most important truth about a folktale tradition, which is its ongoing, creative life in the minds of its narrators and listeners.

This book presents part of such an 'accidental' collection of Ju/'hoan folklore. Its purpose is to show how new Ju/'hoan voices in the years 1970-1972 wove contemporary experience into a seamless web with attitudes and information out of the deep past.

Oral storage processes do 'conserve' the past, but a view of folk tradition as a highly 'conservative' mode of cultural storage is only partly useful. Too strict an interpretation of the faithfulness of folk tradition to long-accepted truth can obscure the role of individuals as active carriers of tradition. Because each new instance of traditional communication involves a unique combination of performance context, the performer's special concerns, and possible new cultural material within a flexible mnemonic framework, each new instance is a creative moment bearing the indelible stamp of the individual.

Different cultures, of course, allow different degrees of tolerance for individual contributions within specific genres.

It is difficult to emphasise enough the great latitude for individual artistry granted among the Ju/'hoansi, whether in the folktale form or in embellished narratives of everyday experience. Without presenting a full catalogue of the variant tellings of many tales contemporaneous with each other in Ju/'hoan tradition in the 1970s, I can hardly convey the richly individualistic nature of the tradition.

When I was first in the field I was perplexed by this richness and even apparent contradiction. I asked an old storyteller, !Unn/obe, about it. She answered, 'Yes, of course, some people tell stories one way, some another. Perhaps it is because people sometimes separate for a while and still go on telling stories. But in all these stories about the old times, people use different words and names for the same things. There are many different ways to talk. Different people just have different minds.'

This answer was accompanied by a shrug: the complexity was ordinary to !Unn/obe, and presented no problems. I think we must realise that where spoken communication is both the norm and the model for information exchange, two messages may be regarded as 'the same' though they are rarely verbatim equals.

This equivalence of message explains storytellers' insistence that they are faithfully 'repeating' an old story when what they are doing in actuality is telling it in their own words in a way that reflects the performance situation of the moment. Concentration on words *per se* is a phenomenon of alphabetic literacy which has long distorted our understanding of communication in oral societies.

Richard Lee feels that the Ju/'hoansi's high tolerance for individual contributions may also be related to the egalitarian nature of their society, whose norms are enforced not by dogma but by the creative participation of all members (personal communication 1983). I believe this tolerance applies not only to folktales but to the incorporation of individual religious experience into accepted oral tradition. As an instance of change in the traditional religious songs, we have the widespread acceptance of Beh's song and the 'giraffe' dance music during the last few decades.

BEH'S SONG

One story goes that a woman named Beh was alone one day in the bush. She saw a herd of giraffes running before an approaching thunderstorm. The rolling beat of their hooves grew louder and mingled in her head with the sound of sudden rain. Suddenly a song she had never heard before came to her, and she began to sing. G//aoan (the great god) told her it was a medicine song.

Beh went home and taught the song to her husband, /Ai!ae. They sang it and danced together. It was indeed a song for trancing, a medicine song. /Ai!ae taught it to others who also passed it on. Old men can name the people who learned the song in turn as it spread eastward from Namibia into Botswana. The giraffe medicine song tradition, stemming from a single inspired individual, has virtually replaced the earlier 'gemsbok'[1] singing and dancing over vast areas of the Kalahari. Old Beh, who 'received the first giraffe song from G//aoan' when she was a woman in middle life, was alive and well during my fieldwork in the 1970s, I was told.

Clearly, one otherwise ordinary person can have a remarkable effect on the Ju/'hoansi's local traditions. There was nothing very special about Beh. She was just a person, and G//aoan, the Ju/'hoansi said, just chose her as a way to send a song to people. Ju/'hoansi feel that a direct channel may open at any time between'them and this great god through inspirations, a happy event which may occur to anyone. As individual revelations are shared, they are added to and developed by others, until they form an integral part of the ongoing beliefs of the community.

Variant beliefs are often held in the same group of people. In the instance of the giraffe song, there is variation not only in belief but in beliefs about belief.

For the version recounted above is not the only account of the origin of the giraffe song. Some say it was Old /Ai!ae, Beh's husband, who received the song, and that he taught Beh and the other women to sing it for him so he could dance. He had been hunting, his namesake /Ai!ae of G!oce said, and the song was suggested by the thudding hooves of giraffe running, and by the sound of rain. He also received a rain song that same day. Someone else, a woman, said the first giraffe song was given by the great god to a boy named /Ui. /Ui taught his mother, whose name was Beh. Beh was the first Bushman woman ever to sing, she said, and Beh's husband was G//aoan himself. Lorna Marshall, interviewing these same people earlier, heard still another story: 'When Be of Samangeigei was given a Giraffe song, she did not see //Gaũwa. She only awakened in the morning with a song in her head. She sang it to her husband /Ti!kay who recognised it as a medicine song. Anyone with sense would know,' informants assured us.

There are other permutations of the story. In one version Beh was supposed to have seen a giraffe and run back to tell her husband about it. He hunted it, but it turned out to be a spirit instead. It gave them the song and they all tranced, even the children.

The most elaborate version of all, however, was heard by Richard Lee (field notes:1207-10). In this one, /Ai!ae, said to have had two wives, went hunting one day. He shot at an eland but it fled. The next day he went out and saw a giraffe. He shot at it but it fled. The next day he went out and saw nothing. He came home to his wives, wondering why he had killed nothing. He slept. As he slept, G//aoan came to him in the form of a person. G//aoan said, 'The first day you shot an eland but it fled, the second day you shot a giraffe but it fled. The third day you saw nothing. I will give you three things. I will give you an eland song. I will give you a giraffe song. I will give you a sky and earth song. These things I give you.'

/Ai!ae turned to his wives and said, 'Did you hear what G//aoan said?' The wives said, 'We didn't hear anything'. Then /Ai!ae said 'I will teach you three things. I will teach you an eland song. I will teach you a giraffe song. I will teach you a sky and earth song'.

Though by now they have begun to sound like mythological figures, Beh and /Ai!ae were actual people dwelling at a specific place in Namibia, near Tjum!kui, in Nyae Nyae. During my first four years of field work it was not possible for me to hear the story of the song from the old people themselves because permission to visit Tjum!kui was withheld by the South African government. In 1972 Ju/'hoansi who came across the border fence into Botswana reported that Old /Ai!ae had died. However, people continued to affirm that Beh was alive and well at a camp thirty miles west of the border. In 1991 I finally met her at N=aqmtjoha, Nyae Nyae and heard the story from her own lips.[2] Beh died in 1992 in an accidental hut fire, having outlived /Ui, her middle-aged son.

There seems no doubt that a case of inspiration did occur to a specific individual, and that once it occurred its benefits were quickly shared among the Ju/'hoansi. It seems even to have spread hundreds of miles south of the Ju/'hoan area to speakers of other click languages.[3] People have taken it up because it is beautiful and because it seems to work; it has efficacy as a trancing song.

The story of Beh's song introduces two topics which will be dis-

cussed in the rest of this chapter. They are i) the widespread occur-
rence of a sharing process in Ju/'hoan religious revelation, and ii) the
respect given to individual renderings of what is beyond men and to
individual ideas of how to communicate with it.

As we saw, even the story of the revelation itself may be varied by
further individuals as they recount it. What does not vary, however,
is the sense that Beh or /Ai!ae was experiencing some sort of altered
state of consciousness at the time of the inspiration for the song. These
states, whether dreams, trances, or day-time confrontation with the
spirits, are regarded as reliable channels for the transfer of new
meaning from the other world into this one.

TRANCERS AS CREATIVE CHANNELS

Though dreams may happen at any time, the central religious experiences of Ju/'hoan life are consciously and, as a matter of course,
approached through the avenue of trance. The trance dance involves
everyone in the society, those who enter trance and experience the
power of the other world directly, and those to whom the benefits of
the other world – healing and insight – are brought by the trancers.
Trancers are known as *n/omkxaosi*, meaning 'owners of medicine' or
'owners of supernatural power'. They mediate to the community not
only healing power but also information about how things are in the
other world and how people in this world would do best to relate to
them. Great attention is given to trancers' accounts of what they have
experienced, and no one's account of a genuinely altered state is
belittled.

An example of this seriousness of attitude follows in a vivid,
dramatic, and memorable story of a journey in trance to the gods'
village in the sky. Its narrator, Kxao Giraffe, and his listeners regarded it as an important piece of the truth and communicated such
great urgency that I also regard it that way.

Just yesterday, friend, the giraffe came and took me again.
Kaoxa [the god] came and took me and said, 'Why is it that
people are singing, yet you're not dancing?' When he spoke, he

took me with him and we left this place. We travelled until we came to a wide body of water. It was a river. He took me to the river. The two halves of the river lay to either side of us, one to the left and one to the right.

Kaoxa made the waters climb, and I lay my body in the direction they were flowing. My feet were behind, and my head was in front. That's how I lay. Then I entered the stream and began to move forward. I entered it and my body began to do like this [Kxao waved his hands dreamily to show how his body travelled forward, undulating in the water]. I travelled like this. My sides were pressed by pieces of metal. Metal things fastened my sides. And in this way I travelled forward, my friend. That's how I was stretched out in the water. And the spirits were singing.

The spirits were having a dance. I began to dance it, too, hopping around like this. I joined the dance and I danced with them, but Kaoxa said to me, 'Don't come here and start to dance like that; now you just lie down and watch. This is how you should dance,' he said, as he showed me how to dance. So the two of us danced that way. We danced and danced. We went to my protector and Kaoxa said to him, 'Here is your son.' To me he said: 'This man will carry you and put n/om into you.' The man took hold of my feet. He made me sit up straight. But I was under water! I was gasping for breath, I called out, 'Don't kill me! Why are you killing me?' My protector answered, 'If you cry out like that, I'm going to make you drink. Today I'm certainly going to make you drink water ...' The two of us struggled until we were tired. We danced and argued and I fought the water for a long, long time. We did it until the cocks began to crow.

[Kxao softly sang a medicine song.]

That's how my protector sang. He told me that was how I should sing. So, my friend, I sang that song and sang it and sang it until I had sung in the daybreak. Then, my friend, my protector spoke to me, saying that I would be able to cure. He said that I would stand up and trance. He told me that I would trance. And the trancing he

was talking about, my friend – I was already doing it. Then he
said he would give me something to drink. My friend, my little
drink was about this size ... He made me drink it and said that I
would dance the dance I had learned. And so, my friend, I have
just stuck with that dance and grown up with it.

Then my protector told me that I would enter the earth. That I
would travel far through the earth and then emerge at another
place. When we emerged, we began to climb the thread – it was
the thread of the sky!

Yes, my friend. Now up there in the sky, the people up there,
the spirits, the dead people up there, they sang for me so I can
dance.

The rendering of individual kerygmatic accounts (such as this one)
into culturally shared images is a highly important process in the
religious unity of Ju/'hoansi and other hunter-gatherers. It is an
interweaving of tradition and creativity which keeps the society itself
alive, so that individuals experience their own lives as contributions
to shared reality. But how does idiosyncratic experience enter tradition and stay there? Part of the answer lies in the fact that experience
itself is, from an early age, already culturally informed and mediated.
Initiates have certain experiences in trance because they expect to do
so, basing their expectations on other accounts they have heard. A
high degree of stereotyping is present in the verbal accounts of travels
beyond the self which are made after a night's trancing. Yet
Ju/'hoansi themselves treat these experiences as unique messages
from the beyond, accessible in no other way save through trance, and
they regard narratives of the experiences as documents valuable to
share. The narratives are thus 'preconstrained' by tradition but they
also add to it.

Assimilation of new material takes place simultaneously with
reinforcement of the old. Learning events as Bateson says, are communication events, and vice versa.

Robert Tonkinson (1978) has described a similar process among
the Mardudjara Aborigines, showing how individual dreams and
altered states are socially explored for the 'clues' they may provide

to the structure of the great Dreaming or other world. The process should be seen as a constant looping back of individuals' experiences (which are based to some extent – but not completely – upon those of their predecessors) into the tradition, where they become available to the individual again as part of a cultural repertoire he himself has helped to build. The fact of the individual's being a dynamic part of the looping process cements his allegiance to the tradition. The power of the religion itself may lie largely in its having provided an amendable, growing form to which individuals, working idiosyncratic experience into concerted social understanding, can add meaning.

Both the religious ideas and the folklore of the Ju/'hoansi, I believe, are characterised by this sort of sharing process. Both should be seen as evolving, ongoing systems of expression of meaning and experience. I think of them as a kind of language continually discoursing, through dramatic representation, upon valued ideas in the structure of man's relation to man and to the other world.

Both kerygmatic accounts and tales, far from codifying a single version of dogma, carry on a sort of dialogue among themselves about what is valued and what is believed. Belief is not enshrined somewhere beyond the tales but is rather within the tales themselves, in the intratextual repartee among them and even in apparent contradiction. In oral traditions the truth is in the repertoire rather than in the individual tales, and in the involvement of tellers and listeners with all the variants, much more than in immutable facts or principles.

As we have seen, in an oral culture there is simply a different attitude toward what literate peoples perceive as contradiction. It is only when, in cultural history, the absorption in a succession of dramatic narratives gives way to written texts which may be laid side by side for comparison that contradiction becomes salient and problematical.

DJXANI TCXAI: TO DANCE A SONG

To understand, in the context, the Ju/'hoan commitment to individual experiences in trance as having general truth, we turn to a discussion of what is both the central religious ritual and the most important artistic form in Ju/'hoan culture, the trance dance.

The Ju/'hoansi and other Bushman groups frequently gather together as communities to sing and dance. The dances may occur as often as once a week or more, when the spirit moves people, and ideally they go on all night. Their purpose is to heal people who may be sick and to ward away any ill fortune which may menace the group. However, far from being solemn, the dances are usually occasions for great fun, flirting and hilarity. Through the physical and artistic discipline of the highly structured dance, an altered state of consciousness is produced in some of the participants which has benefits for the entire community. Contact with the beyond is regularly made, and all who come to the dance experience an uplifting energy which they feel to be a necessary part of their lives.

Rock paintings made hundreds or even thousands of years ago in the mountainous areas of Southern Africa testify to the existence of a similar dance among the Bushmen of long ago. The Ju/'hoansi speak of it as an ancient part of their culture. When people *djxani tcxai*, medicine songs, named for 'strong' things like giraffes, gemsboks, honey, elands, or death, are sung to make rhythms for the dancing. Sometimes, as in the case of the giraffe song in recent decades, one song or group of songs is more popular than the others for a while. But always there are individuals who retain a special allegiance to some of the other songs, and they may call out for these, too, to be sung. The songs of the trance dance, in contrast to everyday songs of the Ju/'hoansi, are said to possess *n/om*, a special kind of energy or spiritual power. *N/om* is invisible, dwelling in the *n/om* songs and in the bodies of the trancers, where it was placed by the great god. There it lies latent until it is activated by the singing and dancing. Those who have learned to activate and control it (about half the adult men, and some of the adult women) are called *n/om kxaosi* or 'owners of *n/om*'. These are the ones who can alter their states of consciousness by going into trance (from here on I will call this 'trancing'). The *n/omkxaosi* are able, in trance, to pull out sickness from others through their hands.

There is a basic division of men's and women's roles in the dance, though individuals often cross into the other role without censure. The women provide the music for the dance, sitting on the sand in a circle around the fire, clapping and singing in intricate counterpoint. Behind the women, in an ever-deepening groove in the sand, the men make elegantly controlled stamping steps round and round in a circle, filling the night with percussive shakes from the rattles tied to their legs. Babies nod on their mothers' backs: people have absorbed from infancy the rhythm of the songs and they know how to make them fit together until the dancing and music become 'heavy' enough to cause trancing.

Early in the night, people stop and start the songs and fuss good-naturedly at each other about the quality of the singing; later they begin to praise themselves and all who are participating, as the music seems to 'come together' and people synchronise, growing finely attuned to one another. The power of the n/om begins to be activated. What has begun in play, in dancing for the sheer fun of it, has become a highly important religious occasion. Men who go into trance become able to contact the gods and the ancestors, who are suddenly visible to them beyond the circle of firelight. The trancers shoot at the spirits and hurl sticks, defying them to bring trouble. Trancers also go unerringly to those people within the human group who are sick or uneasy and cure them by laying on their hands, fluttering with n/om, to draw out pain. The Ju/'hoansi believe that sickness comes from the great god in the form of tiny, invisible arrows. The curer attempts to draw out these arrows from the bodies of the sick into his own body. Then he expels them through his upper back, called his n//au (a potent n/om spot) with a violent jerk, uttering at the same time a stereotyped curing shriek, 'kaohididi!' When they enter deeper trance, appearing unconscious, the curers are believed to have left their bodies in order to contend with the spirits of the dead. Some, like Kxao Giraffe, may travel to the village of the great god in the sky to ask that the souls of the ill and dying be returned to them. The trancers go through a fearful discipline, sometimes taking years, in learning to trance. They describe it as taking the courage a man needs to 'die and then come alive again'. It appears that the high degree of stereotyping in the accounts of what lies beyond the barrier of normal consciousness helps to relieve the great fear of initiates and prepare them to have similar visions. Trancers are respected for what they have gone through, and for the great service they are able to render to the group in terms of healing and comfort. But they in turn respect the singers' (women's) contribution in making the sounds which act as indispensable musical protection for the curers as they traverse dangerous realms.

The dance uplifts all who participate because all have participated – in a concentrated effort of the whole community to do away with sorrow and danger. Lorna Marshall has described this trance dance as the one occasion in Ju/'hoan life that draws all the people into a concerted activity. She comments that the psychological effect of this uniting for a common good may contribute to the group's survival. It reduces tensions: people become a unit acting together for mutual benefit, undivided by words. The dance thus embodies the values of egalitarianism and tolerance, and reinforces the idea of mutual effort against misfortune. In a generalised sense all these values and attitudes have aided the Ju/'hoansi to make, even with their relatively simple technology, a successful, long-lived adaptation to their environment.

TRANCERS, STORYTELLERS, AND THE RECREATION OF TRADITIONAL VALUES

As Richard Katz (1976:300) puts it, the experiential mystery of entering trance for Ju/'hoansi is counterbalanced by a great degree of 'conceptual clarity' in individual accounts which are socially shared. The hallucinations of actual n/omkxaosi become, by a process at once highly individual and highly social, conventionalised vehicles facilitating trance for the uninitiated.

Though individual accounts may be heeded with great attention, there is also a sense in which oral tradition 'swallows up' (in Jack Goody's words) the achievements of individuals into cultural anonymity. This observation is true of both trancers' accounts among the Ju/'hoansi and contributions to the folktale tradition. Both kinds of narration embody a kind of timeless, anonymous truth at the same time as they are being creatively renewed by individuals.

Because both individual accounts and folktale recounting deal with deep, long-term underlying assumptions, similar values and images occur in both. The rest of this chapter describes those facets of the dance which help elucidate the symbolism of Ju/'hoan folklore. Processes of social integration and reintegration evident in the dance are eloquently expressive of values prized in Ju/'hoan society and reflected in the folklore.

For instance, the egalitarianism and tolerance highly valued by the Ju/'hoansi are evident throughout the forms and procedures of the dance. Like other hunter-gatherers with small groups and unstratified social structures, these people place great worth on each individual and his idiosyncratic life path. Men and boys of all ages are to be seen dancing one after the other in a ring around the fire, each involved in a different stage of acquaintance with, and control of, his own *n/om*. For instance, G=kao =Oma from Dobe, a man in middle adulthood in the 1970s, was only then a serious beginner. He had not felt called to work hard at *n/om* before, but then it had become important to him. Others are serious about it from the time they are small boys. Stratified societies seem less tolerant of people at different ages being in different stages of learning something that is culturally important.

The Ju/'hoan dance has a way of including, of endlessly incorporating, human diversity. It brings the diverse individuals of a band into vital contact with each other in such a way that the uniqueness of each is felt as a contribution to group life rather than as a threat to it. Richard Katz has linked this feature of the dance with Ruth Benedict's concept of synergy: each individual, in the course of seeking for himself the joy and catharsis of dancing, contributes to the supply of *n/om* available to the whole group and to the creation of an art and curing form which no single person could create alone. The whole is greater than the sum of its parts, and what is good for one redounds to the good of all.

The very parade of men and boys of all sizes and shapes, joined from time to time by a woman who jumps up from the singing circle, itself an irregular little cluster of grown women and little girls, is a far cry from the age-segregated or hierarchically arranged dances of societies with age-grades or other stratifying institutions. Yet the circular frame unites all the different people, causing them to participate in the making of a single dynamic form. If there is bad feeling between two men, others will contrive to put them next to each other in the dance: participating in the form of brotherhood paves the way for brotherhood to re-establish itself. Sometimes, an unspoken tension in the community is voiced by the trancers and in this way its threat to harmonious relations is dispelled. Richard Lee recorded and transcribed a long, intermittent chant sung by a Ju/'hoan curer while in trance.[4] Some of the words of the chant have distinct reference to the specific social situation being aired and alleviated through the dance. The sick person is described to be sick as a result of tension in the group:

> ... Are you looking at each other?

> How is it that you are full adults yet you refuse to give each other an agreement? What makes you tremble at seeing each other? What do you see when you look at each other?

> You people here who are arguing and glaring. You people who are arguing and glaring. You people who are arguing and glaring.

> What makes you do that is your argument about your cattle. You are battling it out and you are killing each other.

> His blanket, help him put it over his shoulders; can't you see, he is trembling? Help him cover himself.

> He is exhausted; his arms are dry; his legs are dry. Help him take his blanket and cover him ...

> He lies there dying; while you sit above him wrangling and fighting, and arguing and glaring, arguing and glaring, arguing and glaring ...

Ancient as the dance form is, it can embody new realisations such as misunderstandings about recently introduced cattle through contemporary artistry. Dance is the one activity in Ju/'hoan life in which virtually all members of the group participate. Its greatest strength may lie in its inclusiveness, its ability to make a whole of whatever group is present but also to expand for a newcomer at any time.

While a dance is in progress, it essentially fills the social universe, taking precedence over all other activities. There is no formal pressure on individuals to take part, but nearly everyone does, most of the time. The delight in participating in a shared activity and the feeling of community that is brought about by interpersonal synchrony within an effort to banish trouble from the group are important elements in the meaning of the dance circle.

TRANCE DANCE SYMBOLISM: HOT AND COLD, MEN AND WOMEN

The fire at the centre of the dance-circle is invested with great power. It is considered to be one source of the heat required to heat up the n/om, or power, which has been placed by G//aoan in the curers' bellies so that it may be used for curing. Trancers seem to flirt with the dangerous heat of the fire, coming as close to it as they possibly can in the effort to make the n/om boil within them. Some pick up hot coals in their hands and rub them over their hair. Others actually walk through or roll in the fire. Often curers who are working over a sick person sitting near the fire will fling themselves down on the ground right next to the fire and proceed with the curing. The nearest women will stop their clapping briefly and push the sand into a protective little ridge between the prostrate curer's body and the fire. Men's 'hot' roles as curers complement women's 'cold' ones which protect against too much heat. Heating the n/om correctly is thought to cause it to boil up from the men's bellies into their spines and heads and out to the tips of their fingers where it may be used to draw sickness out of another person's body.

The metaphor of 'boiling' links the idea of activated n/om with

other ideas of readiness and efficacy in Ju/'hoan life. 'Boiling (n!óm
– "to boil")', writes Richard Lee (1968:434), 'refers not only to the
boiling of water on the fire but also to the ripening of plants. Water,
like medicine, is dormant when cold but powerful when hot. Similarly, plant foods are dormant when young and unripe, but become
nutritionally potent when ripe. Thus, there is a symbolic association
relating boiling water, cooked meat, ripened berries, and activated
medicine. Sometimes this metaphor is extended, in a joking manner,
to nubile maidens who have reached menarche. They are now considered "ripe" for intercourse and impregnation.' The n/omkxaosi
must become hot (kxui), their n/om must boil (n!om) so that they may
draw out pain (kxui also), letting the sick person become =a'u (cool,
well) again. The n/omkxaosi claim the sickness they draw out of others
'burns' them.

There are, of course, contextual differences in the attitude towards
fire: even during talk about its efficacy, it is acknowledged to be
dangerous. 'Fire is good if it cooks', said /Ukxa N!a'an, 'bad if it burns
you.'

The symbolism of heat and coolness and the operations that transform one into another appear over and over in individual, social and
supernatural contexts. Arrow poison that has become weak with age
is called =a'u, cold. If hunters eat certain food they should avoid, the
poison on an arrow in an animal would 'get cold' and fail to kill the
animal. A man's sexual potency is da'a, fire. The hot sun is considered
to be male, whereas 'night is female because it is cold', as //Xukxa
N!a'an said. The moon is also cold (=a'u) and female in most contexts.
The sun and moon married each other at some time in the past, some
informants say. Coolness is the desired state of well-being, being
neither hot nor cold. When a dance is going well and is thought to be
a good dance, it is described as khui, hot.

Those describing a dance this way take pleasure and joy in its
'heat'. But khui is also an instrumental sort of quality, an adjunct of
dangerous powers that have certain efficacies but may 'burn' their
users or others who come in contact with it.

Ku'u (to burn) is the same word, same tone, as ku'u, to cure.

Ideas of hot and cold and the processes for mediating between them are central to three Ju/'hoan folk concepts which are important in the folktales. !Aia, or trance, is a means for reaching physical and mental harmony by using dangerous heat for ultimately 'cool' purposes. N/om, the magical power or energy for healing said to reside in diverse animals, plants, and other objects as well as in the bodies of the n/omkxaosi or curers, is also associated in its activity with heat and boiling. We shall see, too, that n!ao, a complex of ideas relating atmospheric conditions, men's hunting, women's childbirth, and the great meat animals, is built on opposition between the desirable cool, rainy weather and that season of the year when great heat, dryness, and night-time cold conspire to make the Ju/'hoansi hungry and uncomfortable (L. Marshall 1957).

Two main aspects of the form of the trance dance, the circular dance path and the central fire, are basic to understanding two fundamental structures in the folklore. In the tales that follow, a central fire of creation, and the diverse animals clustered about a central spring of creation, appear to be symbolically linked to the form of the all-important curing dance. Two other rituals involving dance and celebrating 'production' and 'reproduction', the boys' hunting initiation and the Eland Dance for a girl at her first menstruation, have close connections to these main themes of the folklore and are also linked through them to the great curing dance. The main symbols in the dance and in the three related concepts, !aia, n/om and n!ao, are used as reference points in the analysis of Ju/'hoan folktales in Chapters 5 and 6.

Chapter Five

Understanding Ju/'hoan Tales

In the selected tales and analyses which appear in Chapter 6 following, basic polarities of Ju/'hoan thinking – many regarding men, women, and their work – emerge. Familiarity with these repeated polarities allows one to construct a comprehensible framework into which much story material can be fitted. I say 'can be fitted' to emphasise that what we are constructing here is an entry for ourselves into the tales, a heuristic framework which is one possible way of understanding a complex, multi-faceted tradition. We can use such a framework to explore the Ju/'hoan world-view and the dynamic processes of mediation working in the folklore to resolve cultural oppositions.

There are other themes, of course, beyond sex roles and the division of labour. But the tradition itself emphasises these and it has seemed worthwhile to follow its lead. In this section I outline briefly the main structural oppositions of the framework. These will then be scrutinised in greater detail in Chapter 6, in discussions of the specific tales. Throughout, clarifying the relationships these oppositions bear to the metaphor of the great curing dance is a continuing concern.

METAPHORS OF THE TRANCE DANCE

Concepts about heat and cold and their mediations (into coolness) play important parts in all contexts where the complementarity of

male and female roles is at issue. In the dance, men heat up their *n/om*
or spiritual energy so as to use it for curing. But if it heats up too fast,
it must be 'cooled off' or slowed down, and then heated more
gradually. Too rapid 'boiling' of the *n/om* annuls its healing power,
because the *n/om* owner goes into unconsciousness before he gains
control of the boiling. Men who feel trance coming on too quickly for
them will cease dancing and draw back from the fire and the concentration of forces propelling them toward trance. Women offer such
men water with which to cool off. Women also watch to prevent
insensate trancers from burning their bodies in the fire. Thus women
protect men from too much heat. Men use controlled heat to bring
about the health and well-being (=*a'u*, which also connotes coolness)
of members of the community. Men carry tortoise shells filled with
magical substances to produce hot medicine smoke for trancing. In
the tortoise shells carried by the women, however, is aromatic *san*
powder, never set alight, which is explicitly said to cool a person and
promote a sense of well-being.

These are some of the symbolic polarities of the dance situation. In
practice, however, role boundaries are sometimes crossed by both
sexes. Women's singing helps to heat up the dance and other things
they do help to cool it; men sometimes help each other to cool their
n/om down. The main point about the actions of men and women is
that they are complementary: the end-point of the men's and
women's collective activity is the re-establishment of a state of all
individuals involved which is neither hot nor cold – a state of physical
and social harmony for the entire group. That the trance dance
provides an expressive form by which this may be accomplished as
a matter of course has clear adaptive significance. The values of
egalitarianism and tolerant concern for individuals are also reinforced by this dynamic dance process. Men know they cannot do it
without each other; women know they cannot do it without each
other. Similarly, men cannot do it without women, and vice versa.
Women sing and clap for the dance and act as protectresses against
too much fire. They actually form a ring around the fire shielding the
men from it. Men are the ones who dare the devastating effects of

heat – mediated somewhat by women and by other men – to wrest benefit for the women and indeed for the whole community.

CULTURAL SYMBOLISM IN DANCE AND FOLKLORE

The complementary roles of men and women in the dance are paralleled by the social division of labour into hunting and gathering. Women gather plant foods, and their power and prestige are inextricably linked to their role as deciders about and providers of this food resource. Men are hunters and they make the decisions and do the things that are necessary to bring down animals. In the folktales their separate spheres are limned in great detail. Plant foods and meats are shared quite differently from each other among the Ju/'hoansi, and this social dimension is yet another important symbolic aspect of the male/female division of powers. While meat from large hunted animals is rigorously shared among all the members of a local group, plant foods belong to the woman who gathers them, to distribute as she sees fit among the members of her immediate family. The male/female opposition thus also contains in it an implied opposition between the idea of solidarity with the whole group and of solidarity within nuclear families. One story plays on the conflict which sometimes arises between the two allegiances. It shows the sexual confusion which can occur when a woman is gathering for her family on the same ground where a man has recently been hunting.

In fact, in many of the stories there is an indication of what both sexes are doing in terms of subsistence activities at any given time: only in their interaction, it seems, can a whole story be told. The stories are not just accounts of the adventures of a hero or heroine. They are organic pictures of the balance and interweaving of the powers of the two main categories in the society: men and women.

Next, just as the basic division of labour in Ju/'hoan society is that between hunting and gathering, the basic division of foodstuffs is between hunted foods – the province of men, and gathered foods – the province of women. The enumeration of both sets of foods is sometimes accompanied by identical drawings in the sand:

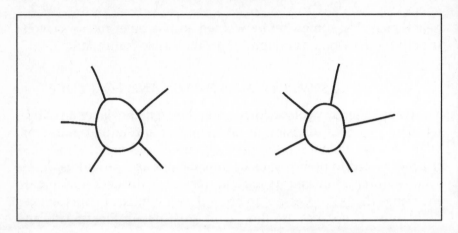

Gathered foods   Hunted foods

A rough descriptive division is made by Ju/'hoansi on the basis of
the mobility of these foods. Things that move are meat, *!ha*, and things
that stay put are *'msi*, which implies both 'plant food' and 'food in
general'.[1] The boundaries between these divisions are in many cases
crossed by both men and women, but there is overwhelming evidence in the expressive forms that the separation of the two categories
is symbolically important and closely connected to the sexual division.

Both hunted food and gathered food are cross-cut by a distinction
between wet and dry. Dry foods are 'eaten', and wet foods are
'drunk'. Some foods that we would associate with eating, like melons,
are 'drunk' by the Ju/'hoansi. Two very important foods transcend
the eating/drinking opposition, however; they are fat and honey.
Honey may be either 'drunk' or 'eaten', and so may fat. From the
folktales it appears that these two foods are conceptual mediators
between several other oppositions as well. Not only are they liquid
solids, unifying wet and dry, hot and cold, they are also symbolic of
the great mediation between men and women – sexual intercourse.
Euphemisms for intercourse, as a matter of fact, include 'drink fat',
'eat fat', 'drink honey', 'eat honey'. Another polarity which is symbolically mediated by the idea of intercourse is carnivore/herbivore[2]

– in Ju/'hoan, *!xoma/!ha*. There is much attention paid to the distinction between these two classes of animals by the Ju/'hoansi of Botswana. The mediation of this opposition – the killing and eating of the herbivore by the carnivore – is metaphorically accomplished in the folklore with the pursuit of women by men. Many clues, too, point to a delicate use of this same sexual metaphor to describe the collaborative processes of the trance dance. Men and women, and the objects and qualities in their respective spheres, are actors in the symbolic dramas of folktale and dance. Attributes associated with women (such as menstrual blood, breast milk, gathering utensils) are considered antithetical to those connected with men (like semen, arrows, arrow-poison). Though they are to be kept apart in daily life, these substances and objects often interact in the folktales, and in the dramas worked out among them lie mediation, resolution of dilemmas, and forward motion into new syntheses. An instance is the flowing of a woman's blood – female – into the fire – male – and the subsequent revelation of misdeeds that results, which occurs in a number of the stories. The forward motion of the tales into new solutions parallels the motions of the trance dance in that the desired state of social peace – the re-creation of the culturally important scene typified by the circle uniting diverse individuals – is established once more after an interlude of conflict.

A BASIC METAPHOR OF TRANSFORMATION: N!AO

A key role in the symbolic dramas of the folktales is played by the concept of *n!ao*. *N!ow*, as Lorna Marshall has spelled it (1957), is described as linking men's and women's great 'procreative' powers – childbirth and hunting – to the vitally important polarities of the weather. Weather and ideas about its control are of great concern to hunter-gatherers. Life and death, especially in a sparse environment like the Kalahari, are closely bound up with the vagaries of the weather.

The Ju/'hoansi have a set of beliefs which are both a way of commenting on the weather and the foundation for certain attempts to influence it. In the *n!ao* beliefs, men are thought to cause weather changes by their interactions with the great meat animals they kill. Similarly, women influence the weather by giving birth to one 'kind' of child or another – rain-bringing or sun-bringing. A child whose n!ao is good brings rain; one whose n!ao is bad brings sun and want. The desired weather is cool and rainy. Coolness in this climate is closely associated with water and the wet season of the year. Undesirable weather is hot and dry or cold and dry. Both of the latter conditions are associated with the hunger of the long Kalahari dry season. The wet season is life, the dry one death and privation.

As we shall see, the metaphors of the n!ao complex permeate to the core the folklore of the Ju/'hoansi. Several other key folk concepts are also of importance in relation to the folktales. These concepts are n/om (supernatural power) and !aia (trance) and the related concepts of n//ao (powers residing in the back of the neck) and !kui g!oq (danger from carnivores). These five folk concepts, highly 'visible' to us because we do not have exact equivalents for them, help us understand Ju/'hoan ritual attitudes toward the problem areas of sickness, initiation, hunting, childbirth, weather, and attack by carnivores.

THE POWER OF ANIMAL CONCEPTS

To understand the five concepts we must consider the power for the Ju/'hoansi of animals as metaphors. Every one of the folk concepts is based in some way upon the power of animals. Animals are used as metaphorical operators to mediate, within the bounds of these concepts, away from undesirable states and toward desired ones of coolness, maturity, individual and social well-being, safety, and hunting and gathering success. I have described the engaging 'litany' Ju/'hoansi use every time the great meat animals are to be listed, and the same rhapsodic recital which occurs with their 'respect' names. These recitals entertained me every time I heard the origin story of 'The Branding of the Animals', which was often. Sometimes the storyteller draws a diagram in the sand to show how each of the animals, when the world as Ju/'hoansi knew it began, left the branding fire and went off into the world with his new markings. The diagrams are shaped exactly like those used to show the categories of hunted and gathered foods. In everyday contexts as well, such as in telling the story of a hunting trip, Ju/'hoansi might use the same litany, savouring the name of each species as it rolls off their lips, to describe coming upon a plain full of animals.

The effect of this stylised repetition is to establish and reinforce the idea of these animals as a special kind of 'goods to think with'. Individually and separately, each animal has its beauty, its strength, its particular usefulness. Collectively, the animals work in concert around the central spring of origin and the central creation fire of the folktales. The way the animals work together in the tales is strongly reminiscent of the diversity and synchrony, the concerted co-operation of the human dance circle. Taken all together, the impression of multitudinous animal richness in these listings is very strong. With access to some of that power, one feels, a person could do anything. But what might a Ju/'hoan need animal power for, beyond protein nourishment? There are several realms of life in which Ju/'hoansi believe human beings cannot act all by themselves. Things like curing the sick by calling on supernatural sources of power, travelling to another world to plead for those dying, bringing game into range, changing the weather, fending off attacks by lions – all seem to the Ju/'hoansi to demand a source of power which is beyond ordinary human grasp. Accordingly, they seek ways of transcending human limitations, mediators between men and the forces of the atmosphere, metaphors with the strength to bridge worlds. Animals, because they are visible, visibly powerful, and near to hand, are a good choice for these purposes.

'MEN, ANIMALS, AND CREATOR DEITY'

A ritual relationship in hunting, linking man, animals, and creator deity, has been suggested for the Bushmen in general by Edmund Leach (1970:34). Patricia Vinnicombe (1972:195) examines this connection in her paper 'Myth, Motive, and Selection in Southern African Rock Art'. The three eland creation myths that have been preserved from the now-extinct Cape and Basutoland Bushmen suggest a widespread Southern Bushman complex of similar hunting beliefs in earlier times (see Lewis-Williams and Biesele 1978). This complex included ideas about absolution for killing and the creation of new game. At one time the /Xam, writes Vinnicombe (1972),

> also observed a complex set of rules when hunting eland, which is added confirmation of a ritual association. Shooting eland with a bow and arrow entailed a very close self-identification between hunter and prey while the poison was taking effect, and [for] killing the animal ... created with especial care by their deity /Kaggen, the hunter suffered temporary castigation.

The peculiarly intimate identification between hunter and prey in Bushman belief is traceable in part to the period of hunting during which a man can actively do no more, but must wait for the arrow poison to do its work. During this period the hunter's actions are no longer overtly instrumental; rather, they are ritual actions based upon sympathetic identification with the prey. Among Ju/'hoansi, for instance, the hunter must not eat certain foods which would cause the poison to stick to the arrowhead and not circulate well in the bloodstream, or certain juicy foods which might cause the animal to urinate out the poison, or fat, which would loosen and weaken the poison (L. Marshall, notes 23.7.55 and 18.7.52). His movements must be circumspect and his demeanour grave. The /Xam observed a hunting avoidance called !Nanna-sse which forbade a hunter's eating the flesh of the fleet springbok during the time an arrow was in another animal, lest the prey bound away like a springbok (Bleek and LLoyd 1968:271-75).

A similar ritual relationship prevailed among the Hai//'om Bushmen, as reflected in their concept of *soxa* (Fourie 1928). *Soxa* was a term applied to the meat of animals killed with bow and arrow. It was subject to certain dietary prohibitions and had to be rigorously shared.

Among different Bushman groups, different animal food avoidances and sharing requirements have been in force, but they all applied to 'herbivorous animals among which antelope predominate', writes Vinnicombe (1972:201). Certainly among the Ju/'hoansi it is true that formal meat-sharing applies only to the large game animals deliberately hunted by organised parties (L. Marshall 1961:236). Such hunting parties generally use bows and arrows. As with /Xam, there is identification between hunter and prey while the poison is doing its work. The hunter's actions while the poison is at work are believed to determine whether or not the animal dies (L. Marshall, notes 23.8.55). Further, the owner and distributor of the meat is not necessarily the hunter himself but *the owner of the arrow*, who might well not be present. Marshall (1961:237) suggests that the exchange of arrows among kin minimises the hunter's act and emphasises the sharing process. Apparently the /Xam exchanged arrows as well and similar rules of ownership may have applied (D. Bleek 1936:149).

These facts suggest that avoidances and sharing were part of a complex including the social nature of the organised hunting party, the hunters' relationships to the rest of the community and, as Vinnicombe (1972:202) suggests, 'the efficacy of a hunting technique rather than the prowess of an individual hunter'. A frequent Ju/'hoan expression for 'when an animal has been killed', or 'when I have killed an animal' is 'when an animal has died' (*ka !ha !ai*). This way of speaking further minimises the hunter's act and emphasises G//aoan's impersonal providence. It brings out, too, the high social value placed on sharing. This valuation is implicit in the organised hunting party and the meat of definite social significance – the co-operative rather than the individual nature of the pursuit and consumption of game.

In fact, the manner of meat consumption itself reinforces ritual relationships connected with the hunting techniques. John Marshall's film *The Hunters*[3] makes the point that the careful meat distribution which follows reasoned, deliberate hunting with bow and poisoned arrow is symbolic of social relationships within Ju/'hoan living groups. In *Bushmen of the Kalahari*,[4] a more recent film showing the effects of acculturation, Marshall points out that killing with guns from horseback seems to change the social nature of hunting. No longer is every scrap of the precious animal used, because it is too easy to get another. Division of the meat proceeds along lines of short-term material utility rather than as an affirmation of kinship ties.

HUNTING AND WOMEN

Ritual surrounding Ju/'hoan hunting also has ties to numerous other contexts which concern us. For instance, submission to certain observances with regard to hunting and menstruation are widespread among the Bushmen groups. The Ju/'hoansi tell of men killed by elephants for failing to observe menstrual taboos (L. Marshall, unpublished story, collected 10.1.53). Bleek and Lloyd (1968:77-79) recorded a /Xam story about a menstruating girl in which is it clear that she was thought to 'cool' the hot, effective bows, arrows and hands of young male hunters. The storyteller said further that menstruating girls should not look at springbok 'lest they become wild'. Nor was the moon, similarly, to be looked at by /Xam hunters when they had shot game and were waiting for the poison to work:

> For, if we look at him, when we have shot game, the beasts of prey will eat the game, when the game lies dying, if we look at the Moon. When the game does not die, the Moon's water is that which causes the game to live. For, our mothers used to tell us about it, that, the Moon's water yonder, [that] we see, which is on a bush, it resembles liquid honey. It is that which falls upon the game; the game arises, when it has fallen upon the game. It makes cool the poison with which we shot the game; and the game arises, it goes on, while it does not show signs of poison, even if it had appeared as if it would die ...

Much appears, thus, to connect the /Xam moon with menstruating women. Both cool into ineffectiveness the implements and poisons of hunting. That Ju/'hoansi make the same connection between women's cycles and the moon is evident in their expressions for menstruation, *ho n!ui* (to see the moon) and *u a n!ui khoea* (go to the moon). *N!ui ku guni mi* (the moon torments me) means 'I have menstrual cramps'. Further Ju/'hoan expressions for menstruation lead us into other ritual contexts. *Du n!om* and *ho n!om* (do *n!om*, see *n!ohm* or supernatural power) seem to indicate that the danger to hunters does not come from a condition of 'uncleanness' in the woman. Rather, she is in a state of extra-ordinary power; in fact, she is obviously at the height of her female procreative power. Ju/'hoansi believe that the blood of menstruation combines with the semen to form a baby (L. Marshall, personal communication 1974). The Ju/'hoansi say a man whose wife is menstruating should not go hunting for fear of carnivores and for fear the game will escape. A woman's menstrual blood had power, informants told Lorna Marshall: even if she touched a chopper, the point would bend when chopping a tree (notes 17.10.52). *Gao gaona* is the name of a bush whose roots provide a medicine to purify hunting equipment inadvertently touched by a menstruating woman (L. Marshall, notes 22.8.52). However, it is not merely female power as exhibited in menstruation which is antithetical to hunting, for the Ju/'hoansi. A hunter should also avoid contact with his wife's breast milk and her clothing if she is nursing (L. Marshall, personal communication 1974). All that is connected, then, with female procreative power is out of the men's realm and to be kept apart from their hunting.

HUNTING AND TRANCE: USING ANIMAL POWER

Trance, however, is a male context closely connected with animals and hunting beliefs. Medicine smoke from a tortoise shell is not used only in trance-curing but also to prepare a man for hunting. The *zam* (which means both the tortoise and the medicine box made from its shell) 'sends you to the animals'. This usage seems to be implied in one story, as we will see, when the trickster Kaoxa is led to the scene of an eland's kill by the tortoise. The *zam* sticks his head into successive campfires to track the progress of the hunt. He finally loses his shell to enable Kaoxa to trance (by sniffing aromatic herbs and eland fat lit by a coal in the shell).

The *zam* is not the only animal, however, whose special power is utilised to help men develop the *n/om* that is potential within them. A number of animals thought to be very strong are closely connected with the *n/om* of the trance dance. In the account given by the *n/omkxao* named Kxao Giraffe, for instance, the connection was quite explicit. Kxao (now dead) told me that his power as a trancer and as a curer partook of the giraffe's power. 'Just yesterday, friend, the giraffe came and took me again,' his account begins. Then he launches into the narrative describing his trance-journey to the sky using the *n/om* of the supernatural giraffe.

Elsewhere in his account, Kxao describes Kaoxa, the ultimate source of all *n/om* as a kind of Lord of the Animals as well. Leopards, zebras, locusts, lions, jackals, dogs, pythons, mambas, eland, giraffes, gemsbok, and kudus, he says, surround Kaoxa in his house in the sky. Many other trancers repeat a similar list of Kaoxa's animal possessions.

The attitudes toward animals' powers connected with trance seem a natural concomitant of general Ju/'hoan attitudes toward animals. As we have seen, the strength of the Ju/'hoan medicine songs is connected with the 'strong' animals or things for which they are named. The great buck like eland and gemsbok figure significantly in the symbolism of many different Bushman puberty ceremonies (see Vinnicombe 1972, citing Schoeman 1957; Silberbauer 1963; Schapera 1930:119; Heinz 1966). Animal materials used in ritual contexts are extremely numerous and include fat, marrow, certain bones, certain muscles, horns, tails, blood and urine. In most cases the particular species of animal providing the material is an important indicator of the substance's particular power.

THE GEMSBOK METAPHOR

Predominant among the species utilised for ritual materials and metaphors among the Bushmen are the great meat animals. Predominant among these, in turn, are the large antelopes kudu, gemsbok, eland, hartebeest, wildebeest, tsessebe, roan. The figurative powers of these animals help to transcend ordinary human boundaries.

Although the southern Bushmen emphasised the marvellously fleshy, imposing eland in their ritual and folklore, the more northern Bushman groups emphasised the gemsbok. 'In the desert regions of the Kalahari where eland are not so common,' writes Vinnicombe (1972:198), 'gemsbok (*oryx gazella*) appear to have replaced eland as a medium for ritual, both on the evidence of rock art in adjacent areas and ethnographic observation.' The gemsbok song, for instance, was the most popular dance song among the Ju/'hoansi before the recent giraffe music was composed. E.W. Thomas (1950:17-19) reports a gemsbok creation myth from the Hai//'om. It is similar in structure not only to the Ju/'hoan and G/ui stories which feature confusion between meat and women, but also to the eland creation myths of South Africa. In this story Heiseb (the trickster) secretly takes meat and honey day after day to his gemsbok wife. One day all this is discovered by Heiseb's wife and mother, who kill the gemsbok wife. His human wife says to Heiseb, 'Oh, foolish man. Why do you marry that which is meat and call it a wife?' Heiseb's mother says, 'Hereafter shall meat be meat, and men be men.' From that day, gemsbok have feared men and run from them. Heiseb's mother says, 'Hereafter those finding gemsbok in the plains shall hunt and slay them, for they are food to be eaten of men.'

In Namibia and Botswana, Ju/'hoansi believe that there was once an early race of people called the !Xoosi who had heads of gemsbok and the bodies of men. These gemsbok people are said to have lived towards the far south-west of the Ju/'hoan area and to be the originators of ostrich-eggshell beadwork.[5] Some of Bleek's informants called the figures in Basutoland cave paintings 'sorcerers wearing gemsbok horns and belonging to the ancient Bushman or to the race preceding the present Bushman' (Bleek, notes, following Orpen 1874:13). Maingard, writing of the prevalence of gemsbok in southern Kalahari Bushman puberty ceremonies, dances and other rituals, says,

The gemsbok pervades every aspect of their communal activity, and forms as it were, the focal point of their lives, the centre round which hinges all their philosophy, all their habits and customs. The Bushman's horizon, one might say, is bounded by the gemsbok.

It is this background of belief which we must bring together to understand the significance of those implements in Ju/'hoan tales which are made from parts of gemsboks' bodies. The connection with the deep past gives these implements a powerful aura. I was told, for instance, that magical gemsbok horns like the one given G!kon//'amdima by her grandmother in one version of the heroine story were also used in earlier times to warn of the approach of a vengeance party. Miniature quivers and arrows made from gemsbok horn may also have been used in magical vengeance contexts.

Other gemsbok implements in the stories include the gemsbok-skin hunting bag carried by Kaoxa when he and Eyes-on-his-Ankles go out to dig roots. (Ju/'hoan men today carry hunting bags made of the whole skins of small antelopes such as steenbok. A gemsbok bag, by implication, would be huge and somewhat special.) Then there is the gemsbok-skin pouch lovingly softened by the grandmother to receive the bit of blood which grows again into the heroine. Metaphors such as those connected with the gemsbok penetrate deeply into both folklore and ritual, linking them together in powerful and indefinable ways. The gemsbok metaphor, for instance, draws together ideas about hunting, women, and power – to name a few of the areas it connects. But it is subtle, indirect. Its very ambiguity gives it all the more evocative strength. When the mind must be active in drawing unstated, but implied, connections, when it ranges through all its experience for the details which build significance, it moves and expands and feels in itself new strength. Connection to a supernatural source of power has much to do with connection to the power of a metaphor.

The Ju/'hoansi's use of metaphoric animal power to influence environment gives us clues about how they regard their environment and their relationship to it. Certain areas of life for them – like the pursuit of animal protein in a sparse, semi-arid environment – are chancy, and men resort to supernatural power to supplement knowledge and skill. In folklore and other symbolic expressions, these special metaphorical muscles constantly ripple. Together they form a body of factual information about environment and attitudes toward the social and supernatural worlds which supplement this information and continue to mobilise action right into the present.

MEN AND WOMEN AND THEIR SYMBOLIC DOMAINS

Looking at its powerful metaphors reveals to us the significant structures of Ju/'hoan folklore. How do men and women in Ju/'hoan society align themselves symbolically in the folktales, how do they or their representatives interact? What symbols signify women, what situations, traits, and possessions are associated with them? Where do we see men in the tales, and what are they doing? We find that *women are connected in the stories with both the central spring of creation and with the origin of water*. One vision of world order emerges from a watery birthplace which has sequestered a fecund female python. Then, too, water becomes known to human beings because a woman forces her husband to share his discovery of it. In clear parallel to these associations, *men are associated with a central fire of creation and with the origin of fire*. A second vision of world order radiates out from this central branding fire which is itself closely related to male hunting power. Presiding over this fire is a male god/human or his representative, the kori bustard, who is also male. Also, fire becomes known to human beings in some tales because a man steals it from his wife.

The message is that without the other, neither fire nor water alone could keep human beings alive. The social message is clearly that both men and women are necessary to the continuation of society. The mutual interdependence of males and females is expressed in the tales, just as it is celebrated in the curing dance.

Once when I asked for one of these central stories, 'The Branding of the Animals', dealing with the central male fire, the storyteller gave me both this story and the one dealing with the central 'female' spring and drew an explicit connection between them. It became obvious that neither can be genuinely understood without the other. A listener new to Ju/'hoan tradition, in contrast, would assume either males or females were superordinate in the culture, according to which tale she or he happened to hear first.

Cool, gentle rain, the moon, the liquid light which drips from the moon – these things are female and therefore dangerous to men's pursuits. Men control lightning with their animal horns, use quivers and spears and bows, and their potency is connected with the hot, feared sun. The lists could be magnified considerably. The point is that where these items and attributes appear in the tales, they signify the social situation, in which the balance or pendulum-swing between male and female power is crucial. Men have trance-curing and hunting. Women have childbirth and plant food gathering. All are indispensable ingredients of traditional Bushman subsistence and social life. Their symbolisms interact to form the basis of the major themes of Bushman art and folklore.

Chapter Six

Selected Tales and Analyses

INTRODUCTION

The four major groups of Ju/'hoan tales discussed here are arranged to illustrate the basic theme of this book – the man/woman opposition in Ju/'hoan culture and its symbolic mediation in the folklore. The discussions following the texts deal with general metaphors of transformation commonly used in the tales; with male and female visions of creation and order expressed through tales of boys' and girls' initiations; with the strengths of women celebrated in the heroine tales; and with men's and women's symbolic power. Arranging the tales in this way rounds out the framework for symbolic analysis suggested in Chapter 5 so as to demonstrate the balancing of male and female symbolic strengths in Ju/'hoan expressive culture.

For each group of tales the text of a single performance is first presented, then discussed with reference to ethnography. The discussion in each case takes off from the tale it follows, but because many symbols and folk concepts are common to all the tales it also helps to explain those it precedes. In other words, the discussion in the four chapters is cumulative. It goes through symbolic associations in a variety of contexts, helping the reader to experience a simula-

crum of the Ju/'hoansi's own lifelong experience of their important
symbols. By the time the final tales are encountered, the reader
should feel somewhat familiar with Ju/'hoan mental territory.

Let me emphasise again that the stories presented here are by no
means all that the Ju/'hoansi are telling today. My own collection
contains fifty distinct stories, but in order to centre this book around
certain themes I have chosen to print only a few tales representing
some main story groups. Other important Ju/'hoan story groups
dealing with the origin of death, the division of the social world and
other adventures of the trickster will be presented elsewhere.

One reason for choosing the present four groups of tales, apart
from the fact that they illustrate the balance of Ju/'hoan gender
power advantageously, is that the central cast of characters in these
groups is linked together by close kinship. It is easy for us to keep
track of the relationships between characters, and we may also see
the same character acting under different circumstances in different
tales. In other words, I have chosen to arrange the tales so that they
are in a mnemonic form that is useful for us as readers. Without such
an arrangement, Ju/'hoan folklore is extremely perplexing in its
variability and obliqueness.

The four main groups represented in this selection of tales, then,
with the characters who appear in them, are as follows:

I   *The Trickster: Metaphors of Transformation*
     G!ara (Kaoxa) the trickster, and his sons Kha//'an and !Xoma.
II   *Origins and Initiations: Male and Female Visions of Order*
     Kaoxa's servant, the kori bustard, and a python heroine who in
     other versions is called G!kon//'amdima, Kaoxa's daughter-in-
     law.
III *The Heroine: Womanly Power*
     G!kon//'amdima as an elephant girl and her husband and
     younger brother-in-law, who are the sons of Kaoxa, also called
     Hoe.
IV   *Men and Women: The Balance of Sexual Power*
     The trickster Kaoxa, his wives and a son.

I

The Trickster

G!ara sired two sons, one named !Xoma, the other named Kha//'an.

Once the two boys were chasing an eland. G!ara followed their tracks but did not catch up with them. He had with him the tortoise, and the two of them were following Kha//'an and !Xoma.

G!ara and the tortoise came to the remains of a fire where the boys had slept along the way. G!ara told the tortoise to stick his head in the fire to see whether the centre was cold. The tortoise stuck in his head and left it there a while, then told G!ara that the fire was dead.

So they kept on tracking and tracking until they saw another old fire. Again G!ara told the tortoise to stick in his head and feel the heat. The tortoise left his head in the ashes a while but at last reported that this fire, too, was dead.

Again they tracked the boys. When night fell they came to the place where the eland had died. They came to the fire the boys had lit the day before, the fire they had lit when they killed the eland. This time the tortoise put his head into the fire and cried '*dzi dzi dzi dzi*!' G!ara said, 'My father's namesake, hooray for you!' They had come very close to where the boys were, so that the tortoise had burned his head in a living fire.

G!ara and the tortoise jumped up and ran, ran to where the
eland had been butchered. There they found that lions had been
making waterbags of the eland's stomach. They had taken out
the eland's stomach, and had made waterbags of it. With the
chyme from the stomach the lions had made a pile to bury
Kha//'an and !Xoma.

[Aside:] That's what lions do. Lions kill a thing to eat, and
they bury its chyme in the sand.

Yes, the lions had made eland waterbags for fetching water.
G!ara came up to the pile of chyme and saw his sons
imprisoned in it. '!Xoma and Kha//'an – is this you here?' They
said, 'Yes, here we are.' Then G!ara went to hang the bones from
the back of the eland's neck in a tree. He meant to make
lightning, this fire which comes down from the sky with the
sound 'huru'. G!ara hung the bones in a tree.

He hung them up, but they fell down and went '//oh!' in the
sand. 'No,' he said, 'these bones won't do.' So he went and hung
up the horns instead. The horns stood up straight and stayed
there. In this way G!ara was calling the lightning to come and
kill the lions.

When he had hung up the horns, G!ara moved off a little way
and gathered small birds together, gathered them so they could
speak to him. He tied the birds all around his head and they
cried, 'khoai, khoai, khoai.'

He untied them and said, 'Why do these things chatter so
much?' G!ara threw the birds away. Next he took the little bird
tcxoe and tied him on his head, and sat down to wait for the
lions.

After he had sat a while, G!ara made the night come. He
spoke to the night, saying, '/e/e!' Grow dark so the lions, who
have gone to fetch water, will have to return.' It grew dark, and
the lions returned. They came up to G!ara and offered him
water. They gave him the biggest waterbag, but he refused it.
'Give me that little waterbag over there, let me just sip a little, so
that the water will go around,' he said.

Then he took the biggest waterbag and gave it to the tortoise.
They all drank and drank and drank. Then G!ara said, 'Now
that you have finished, let's eat.'

So the lions cut the fat from the carcass and they all ate.

Next G!ara said, 'We're going to dance. Let's dance, so it will
rain.' G!ara led off and the tortoise came behind him.

The lions came behind the tortoise. G!ara said to the lions,
'Now you two dance together; don't separate. The tortoise and I
will also dance close to each other, so that there will be a space
between us and you lions.'

So they danced and danced and the dance began to be
'heavy'. 'Now descend!' bellowed G!ara. And the lightning
came down – 'hobo!' and struck the lions flat. G!ara called out,
'!Xoma, you and Kha//'an come out and help me beat these
pawed things!' The boys came out of the pile and ran to their
father's side to help him beat the lions.

Then G!ara stood back and said in surprise 'What will I do
now ... how will I powder myself with *san* so my brains won't
be spoiled by this killing I've done?' So he went and got the
eland's hoof. He put coals in it and took a big whiff of the smoke
– 'he-e-eh.' But it didn't work, he didn't go into a trance. So he
said, 'No good. What kind of dried up, tasteless thing is this?'
He walked back and forth thinking. Finally he killed the
tortoise, his nephew who had accompanied him. He grabbed the
tortoise so he shrieked '*ee!*' and snapped his neck in two. Then
G!ara scooped out the meat from the shell. He took eland fat
and poked it into the shell. He put in the fat and heaped coals on
top of it and sniffed the smoke, and this time he began to trance.

Told by /Ukxa N!a'an, Kauri, Botswana, 1971

DISCUSSION: METAPHORS OF TRANSFORMATION

G!ara the trickster, is often called 'Kaoxa' in Ju/'hoan tales. The name
Kaoxa is one of many which are applied by Botswana Ju/'hoansi to
their great god. Actually it is a term of respect, not strictly a 'name'
at all. Another term of respect for the great creator god is '//'aiha',
which may also be used for any rich or exalted person. This word
contains elements which can be translated as 'having many possessions and the power to dispose them'. The creator's names beyond
these, as reported by Lorna Marshall (1962:223) for the Nyae Nyae
Ju/'hoansi, include (in her spellings) =Gao!na, Hishe, Huwe, Kxo,
Gani ga, =Gaishe =gai, and //Gauwa. In Botswana I heard stories
which dealt with a figure who could variously be called Kaoxa,
//'aiha, Hice, Hoe, G!ara, and G//aoan.

This first tale is a central one in the collection of stories dealing with
the trickster god G!ara or Kaoxa.

G!ara's characteristics resemble those of tricksters in many cultures. Trickster tales are often closely associated with themes of
origin. The trickster is, however, not a conscious benefactor like a
culture hero, who would set out to seek boons for men. Instead he
discovers the necessities of life (fire, procreation and so on) in the
course of serving his own gargantuan desires (see Radin 1972; Boas
1915:329).

I have presented this tale first because it provides a good introduction to the use of a metaphor of transformation basic to all the tales,
the concept of n!ao. N!ao, as we have said, is a complex of ideas
relating i) men, the great meat animals they hunt, and the weather,
and ii) women, the children they bear, and the weather. The relations
among these elements involve two transitive verbs, $kxani$ and $//xui$.[1]
The actions of these verbs have, respectively, favourable and unfavourable results. For clarity I translate the two concepts into 'being
lucky' and 'being unlucky' in all subsequent discussion. This is a
rough approximation, but it will allow the main ideas to emerge.

The main result of luck in the n!ao complex is expressed in terms
of good or bad weather. 'Good' weather is the Kalahari summer, the
fruitful rainy season. To it is opposed the dry season, which unites

painful night-time cold at its beginning with the dryness and want which continue on into the scorching heat of springtime. Mothers and hunters cause either rain or drought when bearing children or hunting, because the *n!ao* they possess interacts with the *n!ao* of the newborn or the hunted animal. If a hunter is 'lucky' about an animal he kills, there will be cool, rainy weather. If he is 'unlucky', the sun will parch the land. As Elizabeth Marshall Thomas (1959:152) writes,

> when the blood of the antelope falls upon the ground as the antelope is killed, when the fluid of the womb falls upon the ground at the child's birth, the interaction of *n!ows* takes place, and brings a change in the weather. In this way, a mother may bring rain or drought when she bears a child, a hunter may bring rain or drought when he kills an antelope, no matter what kind of *n!ow* the mother or the hunter may have.

The words 'lucky' and 'unlucky' are used in a number of everyday contexts as well as in the *n!ao* complex. 'Luck' contains the meanings 'to suit' (as a hat 'suits' a person), 'to have a good relationship with', and 'to be good at'. One man said, 'Luck is if you have nothing and someone gives you something nice.' If a snake or an insect bites a person and no swelling or illness results, the snake or insect is 'lucky' for the person, 'goes with him'.

On the other hand, tattered clothes or ugly beads are said to be 'unlucky' for a person, to not 'suit' him. Also, what we might call an allergic reaction is 'unlucky', 'ill-suited'. Ostrich eggs, for example, are said to make some who eat them crazy. If ostrich eggs are 'bad luck' for a person, he will go crazy. If they 'suit' him, however, he will not. Further, if a person who is 'lucky' with ostrich eggs eats them, rain will fall. If a person who is 'unlucky' with them eats them, there will be no rain. These rules seem to apply not just to ostrich eggs, but to many foods. (I do not know, however, whether the concepts of good and bad 'luck' have closer connections with foods which, like ostrich eggs, are specifically avoided by some age-groups.)

It also appears that *n!ao* itself can be used as a transitive verb along with the other two. If a person (male or female) is 'lucky', he can *n!ao g!a*, 'bring rain with his *n!ao*'. If he is 'unlucky' he can take away rain and 'bring sun', *n!ao /am*. Means by which these transformations are accomplished include, according to Lorna Marshall, burning horns or hair, urinating in the fire, or cutting the throat of an animal with a predictable *n!ao* reaction and allowing the blood to flow on to the ground. Without going too far into it here, I provisionally suggest that what these acts have in common is the uniting of opposites to create a desired change in the weather. Ancient rain rituals of the Bushmen and Khoikoi share this characteristic. Generally they combine wet and dry, cold and hot, female and male elements to promote good weather and fertility.

Ju/'hoansi make an association between hair and clouds.

Clouds are called 'rain's hair'. In the *n!ao* beliefs, putting one's hair in the fire can change the weather: //Xukxa N!a'an told me that if she puts her hair in the fire the sun is so hot it kills people. Her husband, though, she said, 'is rain', *g!a*. 'If he puts his hair in the fire, it rains. It will also rain when he dies.' It all depends on the kind of *n!ao* the person has. Both men and women can be either rain or sun. Their type is determined at the moment of birth.

N!ao is active, therefore, at one's birth and death, and at occasions in between when one seeks to change the weather by using one's *n!ao*. It is also active when a woman gives birth to a child or when a man kills an animal.

Not all animals have *n!ao*, however. It is only the great meat animals like giraffe, eland, gemsbok, kudu, and hartebeest (the ones enumerated in the 'litany' form) which are *n!ao* animals and have an effect on the weather. The smaller *g=ah=xae* category of antelopes (steenbok and duiker) generally do not possess *n!ao* (which fact may be significant with reference to their low frequency in another Bushman symbol system, the South African rock paintings).

/Am and *g!a*, sun and rain, are the oppositions which informants connect with *n!ao*. If a hunter or a mother is 'unlucky' with an antelope or with a child, '*/am khui*', the sun will burn, they say. The opposite, 'good luck', brings *g!a*, rain, and *=a'u*, coolness. Because of the seasonal peculiarities of their area, the hot sun of spring is associated with the cold nights of winter: both fall within the dry,

hungry time of the year. To this pair of unpleasant atmospheric conditions is opposed the ideal of coolness, =a'u, associated with rain. One man told me that if a child is born and the day is one of searing heat, Ju/'hoansi might say, one man told me, 'What kind of child is this who gets born and the sun is so hot?' The answer implied is, 'a child with an unlucky n!ao'.

N!ao was associated by some Ju/'hoan informants with a certain part of the body, the skin of the upper back at the base of the neck. This area is called the n//ao or n//aosi pl.) and it is explicitly designated to be the spot at which sickness is expelled from the body of a working curer. Only the curers (n/omkxaosi), however, are able to see sickness leave this spot.

A person (curer or non-curer) with a foul or bad n//ao (n//ao /kau) will keep rain from falling. Furthermore, a lion may come to bite him. One informant stated that such a person would be bitten precisely on the n//ao spot by the lion. But a person whose n//ao was good, /'om ('fine' or 'beautiful'), the Ju/'hoan say, would not die 'even if he were cursed'. Special feelings are attributed to the n//ao spot: it 'tingles' if a person with whom one has an avoidance relationship sits behind one. If a young man is being given the power to trance and cure by an experienced curer who is sitting behind him, he might feel his n//ao tingle as well. In the story of Kaoxa and his sons, echoes of the beliefs about the sensitive n//ao spot and the n!ao complex regarding weather are prominent. An understanding of these two folk concepts points the way for comprehending yet a third which is involved in the trickster story – the relationship between men and carnivores called !kui g!oq. Finally we are brought back to further discussion of the concept of !aia (trance), since one of the things this story does is account for the origin of trancing.

In this tale, G!ara tries to resuscitate his sons after they have been killed by lions. He calls a dance for rain, then uses eland horns to summon lightning to strike the lions dead. To cleanse himself of the killing he makes a tortoise-shell medicine box, sniffs smoke from it and goes into a trance for the first time. The trickster and the tortoise, as in the traditions of many Bushman groups, are linked with rain;

the lions here, as often with other Bushmen too, are the anti-rain forces (Schmidt, personal communication).

Kaoxa wants rain so he can have lightning. Lightning, called *da'a o G//aoan hi* (G//aoan's fire), will do his bidding. To get rain and lightning, he hangs eland horns in a tree. (The eland's neck bones have not worked for this purpose.) In a similar story from the G/ui (L. Marshall, unpublished story, collected 22.7.55) involving eland hunting, the trickster throws his own hair into the sky to make rain. Hair and horns, as we saw, are two of the instruments for changing weather within the *n!ao* complex.[2]

Though the hair and horns are not burned in the stories, the way they are used as instruments of transformation is suggestive. Further, at least one storyteller connected the lightning thus invoked with the *n//ao* spot at the back of the neck, which as we have seen is connected with weather and *n!ao*. The lightning descends right into the *n//ao*s of the lions, this storyteller said.

If a person's *n//ao* is */kau* (foul), not only will he bring no rain but, as another informant told me, a lion may come to bite him. '*N//ao* is that you fear things [that is, dangerous animals] if you're walking alone,' said a young woman. 'Your *n//ao tsau* [hackles rise] when you are afraid.'

Still another informant expressly linked having a bad *n//ao* with danger from carnivores, or *!kui g!oq*. If a person throws a hat, it is said that a lion will come to bite him.

This induced bad luck is called *!kui g!oq*. The lion will bite the person on the back of his neck, on his *n//ao* spot. If he has a bad *n//ao*, he will die. If he has a lucky *n//ao*, on the other hand, he will live.

Other actions which can bring on *!kui g!oq* or attack by lions include gathering grass at night and throwing a stick at a crying child. Lorna Marshall (notes 3.3.53) also records other beliefs about throwing things and danger from lions. Certain plant foods must not be tossed in the air like a ball, or otherwise played with. Some twelve foods whose edible parts are underground and three whose edible parts are above ground will bring lions if they are tossed about by children or adults. Another plant must not be pulled up at all. A certain bird must not be played with when dead. Other objects which must not be tossed are wooden bowls, pots, ostrich eggshells, mortars, beads, knives, spears, axes, and digging sticks. Children are threatened with the bringing of lions if they play with any of these foods or objects. (Note that the specificity of these injunctions seems to reinforce the idea of attention to detail in the learning process.)

!kui g!oq is feared not from lions alone, but from other carnivores as well. Leopards and hyenas were specifically mentioned. The concept is even extended by Ju/'hoansi in Botswana to include aggression by people whom they call 'carnivores'. These include black people and 'angry' whites. Ju/'hoansi use the word !'homa or !'homh (pl.) to refer to this group of people as well as to carnivores in general, including the smaller ones, Another word they use for both carnivores and this group of people is jom or jomhi (pl.) which means 'pawed creatures'. The silent hand sign for a lion is clenched fists 'walking'.

To jom is for a person to become a lion and kill people.

The great n/omkxaosi of long ago used to do that, people said. When a person says 'lions are walking' he does not usually mean animal lions. Such an expression is used at an eerie or strange time. For instance, I heard it in 1971 when the Kalahari had a near-total eclipse of the moon.

Bantu living nearby still say that, if they wish, Bushmen can turn themselves into vengeful big cats and stalk human beings. Bushmen, in turn, express their fear of the more aggressive Bantu by visualising them as carnivores. Killing in the animal realm is thus metaphorically transposed into the human realm to express tension between groups.

Though it is clear that it involved magical danger from carnivores, the actual translation of !kui g!oq is difficult. Its elements may imply 'male (or strong) fear'. All we can say for sure is that it is an old compound word, part of whose meaning is lost, which refers to a set of beliefs about bad luck involving carnivores.

Lorna Marshall has speculated whether the word may not mean something like 'taboo'. As we have seen, she mentions that playing with certain plant foods was said to bring lions.

She has also recorded an instance of trance being used against real lions, which I will quote because of its relevance to our folktale:

A little group of two families was making a long journey. They were encamped in the night alone in the vast, flat space. A lion came and prowled around them. The moonlight was bright and the people could clearly see the lion circling. They were terrified. They took their screaming children in their arms and stood, shifting around to keep the fire between them and the lion, ready to throw burning brands at it. One of the men, Bo, cried out to the lion, 'You lazy beast. Why do you not go and kill an animal instead of coming after us? We are not equals.' The lion growled and did not go away. Toward morning, one supposes in response to the long-continued emotional stress, Bo fell into a trance. At sunrise the lion left, and the people said that Bo's spirit followed it and chased it far away, and they never saw it again. When Bo's spirit returned to his body and then came out of the trance, his nose bled severely. (L. Marshall 1969:374)

We do not know whether the verb *jom* was used to describe what Bo did. But in any case the tables were somehow turned on the lions, or the lions were persuaded away. The power which allowed Bo's spirit to go out to the lions was *n/om*. *N/om* boiled up in him and he went into a trance. To trance is to *!aia*, or *!aia n/om*. In *!aia* Bo had power against the lions.

In the folktales, Kaoxa uses dancing on a number of occasions to cure or cleanse himself. The most usual occasion for *!aia* is curing others in the trance dance – Bo's case was out of the ordinary. In fact, when Kaoxa in another story says he wants 'to dance so I can get my mouth back' he means, to all intents and purposes, 'to dance so I can trance and cure myself and get my mouth back'. In the lion story, G!ara or Kaoxa says, 'How will I powder myself with *san* so my brains won't be spoiled by this killing I've done?' He is again referring to dancing and trancing. This time the reference is through the medium of the ground-up magical roots (*san*) used in the dance context to remove a dangerous 'hot' condition or 'stigma'. *San* is said to cool. In the /Xam story at the beginning of the book, *buchu*, the /Xam equivalent of *san*, seems to be used as an antidote to hot lightning and the stigma of killing.

Usually *san* is thrown on the *n/omkxaosi* at a dance by women who wish to praise them. Women carry the powder in tortoise-shell boxes like those used by the trancers to produce medicine smoke. The aromatic *san* is the cooling counterpart of the hot magic smoke used in trancing and curing which the *n/omkxaosi* produce from powdered roots, fat, and a glowing coal.

!Aia (trance) is what G!ara uses to cleanse himself of the killing. The killing itself has required something else. Some very great power has had to be involved to reverse the man-carnivore relationship which would normally obtain between G!ara and the lions. To kill these formidable adversaries, G!ara has had to become the equivalent of *!kui g!oq* for them.

That he does so is evident in the lightning's deadly attack on the *n//ao* spots of the lions, those places at the back of the neck lions themselves would go for on men. In a version from Ghanzi the point is made even more graphically. The trickster is Kaoxa but he is also called 'The Big Frog'. He is revenged upon the lion for the loss of his daughter (whom the lion marries but then eats) by closing a forked branch around his neck. I have seen frogs brought home by hunters this same way. Here the hunter is the hunted.

How does G!ara manage this spectacular reversal of roles? This part of the story may involve some very ancient beliefs which have been lost. We have some very intriguing clues, however.

One storyteller told me that Kha//'an and !Xoma (G!ara's sons) 'are an animal's horn. They are an eland's horn. They taught Kaoxa to dance around under eland's horns in a tree.' In both versions of the story collected by Lorna Marshall (22.10.52 and 21.7.53), and in one I collected myself, this dance, which culminates in the lion's death, has a specific song to go with it. Kaoxa insists, in fact, on its being sung to the exclusion of others. The songs in the three versions are respectively (with the comments made on them by the storytellers):

> *//Nhon nhon chi /kay num.* 'These are not words. The song is the song of the eland horns.'
> *Now now jin ka gum, now now jin ka gum.* 'That music works with the eland horns.'
> *=xei ku /in /in.* 'I don't know what the words mean.'

The transcriptions are imprecise, but it can readily be seen that the first two songs, at least, are quite similar. Casting about for clues to the meaning of this song of eland horns for rain; we are reminded of a section from Lorna Marshall's 'N!ow' paper (1957:239): to change the weather a hunter

> would take a piece of the burning horn and point it to the sky saying *goichi goichi n!ow qui*. This we were told is speaking *n!ow*. The interpreters did not know and could not find out by questioning people what the words mean. We wonder if they are an archaic spell.

In 1991 I collected a story in Namibia from /Kunta Boo of /Aotcha which at last made the words clear:

> While they were dancing, G=kao N!a'an (the trickster) said, '*!aihn tzisi //xan //xan!*' (let there be light). And the lions said, '*G/u noqm noqmsi ku noqm!*' (let the dark of night fall!)

The actual words mean 'Let there be light between the tree trunks', and 'Let the dark darknesses of the night darken'. The opposition between men and lions as specialists in daytime versus night-time activities is clear.

Even more to the point than the words of the eland-horn songs, however, are the melodies. They are composed in a certain scale which Nicholas England (1968:401-402) calls the 'Rain-Eland Scale'. He surmises that this scale, one of several used in Bushman music, and an accompanying rhythmic pattern, 3 + 3 + 2, are very, very ancient in Bushman culture. They are found in both the Eland Bull Dance of the girls' menstrual ceremony and in the Rain Song, *G!a Tzi*. England remarks of the rain song that in Nyae Nyae it had a manner of performance unique among the *n/om tzisi* (medicine songs). He thinks it might be a musical vestige of a past rain-making ceremony which may have been shared with Central and Southern Bushman groups. These and other tantalising clues seem to link the trickster story presented above to rain rituals and the *n!ao* ideas.

The lightning brought down by the music and strange song, whatever its significance may be, is called in some stories 'G//aoan's servant'. Its respect word is /'hana. Another instance in Bushman tradition of the use of lightning as a weapon, of course, is to be found in our /Xam story of '=Kagara and !Haunu, Who Fought Each Other with Lightning' (Bleek and LLoyd 1968:112).

But this lightning, most often called by Ju/'hoansi 'god's fire', is far more than just an occasional weapon. One storyteller volunteered the comment that this 'fire' is the 'same as the fire used by the kori bustard to create the animals. He branded them with the fire and now they have gone off into the world.' Somewhat later she said that the kori bustard is Kaoxa himself, who 'calls any dance and was the one who made the fire of creation'. Next we will look at the story in which this fire of creation is used to brand the animals, marking them off into separate species. From the day on which the branding occurred, Ju/'hoansi say, the animals have 'ceased to be people' and have taken their places in the world as animals.

II

Origins and Initiations

THE BRANDING OF THE ANIMALS

Long ago, they were all sitting around talking together. They
talked and discussed things, and they said, 'Today we're going
to n=om ka n/om [create n/om]. Then we'll write the name of all
the animals on their hides. Today we'll n=om ka n/om, and we'll
use it to give a different design to each animal. From today
people will no longer be people but will have markings and be
animals.' So they created n/om. They gave names to all the
animals; they told each animal his name. 'Today we're going to
brand you all so that you will be animals from this day.'
  So they built a fire. Everyone crowded around to watch.
  The zebra came up to see what was going on, and so he was
the first to receive his markings. The zebra came up and they
drew stripes all over his body with the n/om. Then they stepped
back to look at the zebra's stripes.
  'This is a pretty pattern here,' they said. 'See how the n/om has
marked lovely stripes on the zebra. Let's make stripes on
ourselves to imitate him so we'll be beautiful too.'
  So they marked themselves with the n/om to look like the
graceful zebra.

116

Yes, long ago people imitated the stripes of the zebra on their own bodies.

They imitated the markings of the giraffe, too: they were busy making designs on the other animals when the giraffe came by to see what was going on. The giraffe stepped through the crowd and came rocking forward on his long legs.

'Sa-ay,' murmured the people. Isn't this one pretty?'

Then they drew giraffe designs on some of the people, and these were beautiful too. They drew and wrote upon the animals so they all had designs. Some of them walked away with lovely spotted hides. Some were one way and some were another. There was this one, and that one, and that one.

But one animal did not receive any designs. This was the hyena. 'I wonder what kind of animal I'll have to kill and bring to them so they will give me pretty designs too? What does a person kill?'

'You have to go and kill a steenbok, of course,' the people answered.

So the next morning, the hyena got up and went hunting. He laid his snare well, and he killed a steenbok. When he brought it home to his camp, his wife said, 'Now, I want you to cook that steenbok for our children. You are only a hyena and if you go over there where people are doing the markings you'll get into trouble. Those people are just naturally better than you. You're a hyena, a scavenger; hyena is your name and that's that. Even if you go to them they won't treat you like they've treated the other people.'

But the hyena replied, 'Don't be so crazy, dirty-face! I'm going to get my branding so I'll have designs like everyone else.'

His wife said, 'All right, it looks as if you're going in spite of anything I can say.'

So the hyena slung the steenbok over his shoulder and went to the branding place. Now his left leg was diseased and rotten. But he carried the steenbok over his shoulder and brought it to the people.

When he got there, the children of the camp called out, 'Hey! The hyena has snared a steenbok and brought it here.'

The people reprimanded the children, and said, 'Stop that talk; is that any way to behave when a visitor comes? Why do you insult our honoured guest by shouting out his name when he arrives?'

But all the while they were pinching each other and agreeing together on the sly about what they would do to the poor hyena.

When the hyena first heard his name called out by the children, he was frightened and stood stock still. 'Even the little children know that I'm a hyena.'

He stood there until some of the people said to the others, 'Bring him right up here to the fire: take his steenbok for him and lead him over here so we can give him his markings.'

So some of them brought him up to the fire, and others began to butcher his steenbok. Of course, they had already made their plans together. They told him that they were going to brand him with beautiful designs.

Then they took out a long iron and heated it in the fire.

Then they said, 'Now cover your face and lie down. Put your leg up like this. All right – just lie still now ...'

So the hyena lay as they told him to. While he was lying there, the people whispered secretly to each other and agreed on what to do to him. Some of them said to the hyena, 'All right. When you get your markings you hold your hands tightly over your eyes so you won't see anything. Cover your face and lie still.'

So he kept on lying there as he was told. 'Now lift your leg. We've already done this same thing to the zebra and he's all finished. We laid down stripes on his rump just like the ones we're going to give you.' The hyena thanked the people and lay just as they said. He covered his face and lay there. Then they took the iron out of the fire. They thrust it into him right below the buttocks. It went 'sh-sh-sh!' as it burned him. They screwed it in even further. 'Khoa-u-u-u-u N=ao!' He defecated all over everyone and ran off.

Now they had already collected together a bag of old bones. When the hyena jumped up and ran off, they took the old bag and threw it after him. The bag hit him in the head.

'Be gone!' they cried. 'Go off and gnaw on these old bones. Eat like a hyena should and gnaw on bones. You're a hyena and nothing else.' So the hyena ran off with the old bag around his neck.

At the fire the marking of the animals went on. All the animals came and received beautiful designs. The giraffes came, and they were branded. The people drew giraffe designs on them and drew them until all the giraffes were done.

Then they took the kudu and stood the kudu by the fire.

They branded the kudu with designs and then they said, 'Mm, this one will be the female kudu.' And they stood her aside.

Then they marked the male kudu. They marked him and drew upon his hide, and then they stood his horns upon his head. Next, they branded the little stripes that run down his sides. The little stripes you see there today are the ones they made.

And they said, 'Mm, this one will be the male kudu.' And the male kudu stepped from the fire and went to stand off to one side.

Then they made the wildebeest. They marked him and marked him and put a little beard on him. They made horns for him. They created the wildebeest, and then they said, 'Mm, now this one is the wildebeest.' Then the wildebeest got up and went and stood to one side. The people built up the fire and got ready to mark some more animals. The springbok came up to the fire. The people worked on him and drew his colours on him. They drew lovely stripes on his face. Then they said, 'Mm, here you are, you're the springbok. You're finished – now go and stand over there.'

Then the gemsbok who had been standing there all this time approached the fire. The people said, 'Oh, yes, come right over here and let us brand you.' The gemsbok came up to the people, and they gave him his markings. They drew upon his beautiful forelegs. When he was done, the gemsbok left the fire and stood aside. The people said, 'Mm, that's the gemsbok over there.' Everyone went to look at the gemsbok and many people said, 'This animal is certainly beautiful'. When the gemsbok was

finished, the hartebeest came to the fire. Then they marked the
hartebeest's hide with the colours you see on it today. They told
the hartebeest that his horns would be shaped the way a
hartebeest's horns should be. When he heard them, he walked
up to them and had his horns placed on his head. Then he was
finished, and he went to stand aside. The people said, 'Mm,
aren't all these animals beautiful?' Every single animal came
and was branded that day with the fire. The tsessebe too – they
branded the tsessebe's face, just as they had burned the
hartebeest's face, they burned the tsessebe's face too. Then they
made his rump, and it was black. His forelegs they made black
too, and they cut the black sharply at his ankles so that his legs
were very beautiful. Then the tsessebe left the fire and went to
stand off at one side. He stood up tall and proud. Everyone said,
'Yes, we've done him just right.'

So they kept on making animals and marking them with fire.
The duiker came, and they marked him too. Then he jumped
back from the fire and walked away. His horns stood up stiffly
on his head: he was a male duiker and he walked proudly away.
When he was finished the people said: 'Mm, all these animals
we've made are fine ones'. The female duiker came and they
gave her markings too. Then she turned aside from them and
walked away. 'Yes, these are surely fine animals,' they said.
Then the little steenbok came up and they branded the steenbok
with his red coat. When he left the fire, he paced a few steps,
lowered his neck, paced again, and ran away.

So they branded and marked the animals until all were done.
Then the kori bustard came up and said, 'Yau! Since you're
marking all these animals, so very many of them, won't you do
me as well?'

'Come here,' they said. 'Come here and we'll give you
beautiful colours and markings like the others.' The kori bustard
came forward. 'We'll mark you too.' So they made the kori
bustard's feathers. They made feathers and stuck them all over
him. Then they made his little kori bustard head-feather, his
topknot, the long, slender feather that hangs over the back of his

neck and waggles when he walks. They fastened the topknot on him and as he walked away it bobbed up and down gracefully. *'Yau!'* said everyone. Isn't he beautiful?'

Then the python came. The python walked forward and sat down. So they fixed the python and painted her skin and the python came out just fine. As she walked around she undulated smoothly and all her markings shone. The people exclaimed *'Yau!* This is a fine woman we have before us, so beautiful with all her stripes.' The python glided around the fire, arching her back so everyone could see how pretty and striped she was. She undulated back and forth and then went to sit down.

The people kept on marking the other animals. Pretty soon the ostrich stepped forward. *'Yau!'* he said. 'What's going on here, what's this, what's happening?' *'Yau* yourself,' answered the people. 'What kind of animal is this who has come up now?' they asked themselves. They refused to mark him, saying, 'We're not going to brand a person like you. You might just as well go away. Go on, scoot! Just run away and be an ostrich.' So the ostrich left them and ran clumsily away. He ran away with the people crying after him, 'Be gone! Run away, and may you break your foot on a stick. Go away and become an ostrich and go about doing what ostriches do.' That's what the people said. 'Go and be an ostrich and do ostrich things, and walk about like an ostrich.' So the ostrich jumped away from the fire and ran away and became an ostrich.

They marked the other animals and branded them until they were done. 'Mm, yes,' they said. 'These pretty ones are the ones who will turn into meat animals. They will be good meat animals.' And since then the meat animals have spread out into the land. People go about naming them. When people get together and talk, they say, 'Yes, these are the meat animals, and we will kill them and eat them.

Told by Tci!xo N!a'an, G!oce, Botswana, 1972

DISCUSSION: MALE VISIONS OF ORDER

Kaoxa's magical fire, as we have just seen, is linked in the male
initiation story with the central fire of creation. Male control over
weather and carnivores is also symbolically connected with male
control over hunting. 'The Branding of the Animals' forms a link
between the young boy's ceremony of the First Killing and Ju/'hoan
beliefs about the original creation of all the animals. Their old people
tell the Ju/'hoansi of today that when the world first began, the
animals were people, with people's names. Then Kaoxa, through the
agency of his servant the kori bustard, changed all the people into the
different animals by branding markings on them with fire. The kori
bustard's huge wings, the feathers of which Ju/'hoan use today to
fan their own fires, are used in this story as a bellows to blow on the
fire of creation. (The word for fire-fan, !uih, is the same as the name
of the bird.) Irons heated in the fire are used to give the animals their
distinctive markings. The verb for this branding process, n=om, is the
same as that for the scarification of boy initiates at their first-kill rites.
It means 'mark, form, create'. The man-made scars are called ='usi –
which is also the word for animals' markings and stripes.

Important in the story is the brown hyena, a despised scavenger
believed by Ju/'hoansi to have been created last of all.

In some versions the black-backed jackal, another scavenger, also
goes through a travesty of initiation. It is in the episodes concerning
these two animals that the connection with hunting ritual is firmly
made, since each brings, as an initiate, a freshly killed buck so that he
may receive his scarification of manhood. Sometimes there is a close
association between the branding story and the one that follows, the
women's story of the python and the jackal. The central fire and
central spring, fire and water, male and female visions of the beginning, are 'twinned' in many storytellers' minds. Considering the
factors which link the first tale to boys' hunting initiation and those
linking the second to girls' menstrual initiation – production and
reproduction – it is appropriate that in some performances the two
are told as a single story.

In real life brown hyenas' hind legs are peculiarly fashioned, and their gait is peculiar, traits which seem to be 'explained' in the branding story. But this aetiological outcome is the least important one in the branding story. The significant event is that the animal world is divided into its categories. The scavengers are banned forever from the august company of meat animals. Similarly, boys who do not successfully complete initiation (note that the hyena does not kill the required large buck but only a steenbok) are likened to carrion-eaters and do not enter society.

'The Branding of the Animals' is the story, then, of the origin of animal species. Before the time of this story, the animals had undifferentiated bodies, and in fact were indistinguishable from people. Afterwards, they had marks to show which animals they were, and species names. Socially, the story links the differentiation of 'species' or categories of human beings, by the markings they receive at initiation, to this differentiation among the animals. Boys become hunters when they make their first kills and their arms, shoulders, and backs are scarified. Their separation from women is further enhanced by the way girls are scarified in Ju/'hoan society. 'To make themselves beautiful', Ju/'hoan girls say, they imitate the stripes of the zebra on their thighs and on their cheekbones, 'because the zebra is the most beautiful animal'. Thus women are likened to the zebra, an animal whose meat is fastidiously avoided by the Ju/'hoansi. In contrast, men are likened to the desired meat animals by the markings they receive. This symbolic division is yet another reverberation of the basic distinction in Ju/'hoan society between the hunters and the gatherers.

Next we look at several versions of the women's story of the creation of the world as Ju/'hoansi now know it. These stories involve two female creatures, a python heroine and a jackal villain, in a tale of initiation which is at the same time a tale of origin.

THE CREATION OF THE WORLD

VERSION I

The kori bustard refused the jackal and married the python instead. The kori bustard said, 'All right now, everybody, I'm the kori bustard and I'm going to marry this girl, the python.' So the kori bustard married the python. They lived together for a very long time. But the jackal was saying to herself all this while, 'Oh. Here's this man with such a wonderful headfeather. I wish my older sister would die so I could marry her fine husband.' Then one day all the women went gathering. But the jackal refused to accompany them, saying to the python, 'Sister, let's go draw water from the spring. Your husband is away, so let's go fetch water and bring it home.' So the two of them walked to the spring. A big $n=ah^3$ tree stood near it. Its broad shadow fell over the well, and one of its branches was stretched out above the water.

This was the branch that broke and fell into the spring that day, carrying the python along with it. The jackal and her older sister arrived at the spring. The jackal said, 'Climb that tree and knock down the fruit. If you fall, I'll catch you.'

But the python said, You're a strong girl, climb the tree yourself and knock down the $n=ah$ so we can eat. You're a young girl, a child – go on, climb the $n=ah$ tree and shake down its fruit so we can eat.'

'No!' said the jackal, 'you're the one to do it; you're soft and slippery, and you can slide along the $n=ah$ branches as well. Go on, you climb it. Do you think so badly of me as to imagine that if you climb and fall I won't catch you? I'll watch you and run back and forth beneath you as you climb and then jump to catch you as you come down.'

At last the python agreed. She slithered, and climbed, and slithered beautifully up the tree. When she came to the branch lying over the spring she went out on it to knock the fruit down. She shook the branch, and the $n=ah$ fell down on the ground.

The python ate some of the fruit up in the tree, and the jackal ate the rest down on the ground. Then the python began to move out upon the branch so that she could reach another branch. But she lost her grip! Her smooth body slipped off the branch and she fell into the spring; 'G!o-ae!' was the sound she made.

Her sister the jackal ran home to their camp. She went to her sister's husband and said, 'Come and see! My older sister has fallen out of the *n=ah* tree.'

At that, everyone wailed, 'If she has fallen out of the *n=ah* tree, what will we do?' When night fell, everyone just went to bed. The python's husband went to his house, and there was the jackal, pretending to be his wife. The kori bustard told her to spread out their sleeping-skins for the night. Secretly he stood bone arrows upright in the sand beneath her sleeping-place. She lay down on top of them, and began to complain that the place was thorny. But her sister used to sleep in the same place, so she had to be content. An arrow pricked her and she died in her sleep. Her anus protruded from her and stood out from her back. The kori bustard said, 'Hey, everybody, what's happened to the good wife I married recently? Why is it that today so many *n=ah* seeds are sticking in her arse?'

He stood beside the dead jackal crying for his lost wife. He mourned for her loud and long. The people said, 'Get together, everyone. Let's go and pull his wife out of the spring for him and bring her home. What makes you think we won't be able to get her out?'

The kori bustard said, 'How can she possibly get out? I'm just never going to see her again.'

But the others said to him, 'Gather lots of people together, tell everyone to come together and help you get her out. Call the wildebeests, call all the animals, whatever their names are. Gather them all together so they can work on trying to get her out.'

The kori bustard said, 'How can they help? Who will be able to reach her? All of us are too short: everyone's legs are too short to reach her, since she's so far down. Who will be able to get to her? If you go down that far, you'll never see the sky again.

You'll go right down to the bottom and never come up again. A person might never see daylight again! That's how far down the python is.' But the next morning the kori bustard got up and went to the spring. He gathered all the animals together: the giraffes, the wildebeests, the springhares, the gemsbok – all the many animals, all the animals there are. He called them together, and told them to come to the spring. He called the female animals and he called the male animals. He told them that yesterday the python had sunk to the bottom of the water. He gathered them together and called and gathered them, and there were female animals and male animals who collected at the spring. As many as there are animals came, and they spread as far as the eye could see. The sight of them was something to behold.

Then one by one they came forward to try their luck. Each one would stick in his leg and reach down into the spring. But each one failed to go all the way to the bottom, and they all drew back their legs about half-way down. Each one said, 'I can't figure out a way to do it.' The gemsbok stepped forward and put in his leg. It went down, down, down – and he almost fell in. So he pulled back his leg and stepped aside. Then the wildebeest stepped up and tried it.

But he, too, nearly fell into the water. So he drew his leg out too. The kudu tried next. He put his foot in and nearly tumbled in himself, so he pulled it back out again. As many as there were animals, as many animals as have names, that's how many tried and failed.

All this while the giraffe just stood there, and so did the ostrich. The ostrich came forward then, and put in his legs. He sat down at the edge of the well and stretched his legs down and down and down. With the very tip of one claw he was able to scratch the python.

'Mm,' he said, 'I got pretty close to her. It felt to me as if my fingertip was touching something. Why doesn't that long fellow over there come forward and find out if it's really the python I'm feeling?' At this the giraffe drew himself up very tall. 'If that guy tries it,' said the ostrich, 'he's bound to get the woman out. That woman will get out if the giraffe reaches down for her!'

Then the kori bustard said, 'Mm, the rest of us will go back to camp to look for things to spread out on the ground to receive her. We'll spread mats from the well to the village.'

So he and the others went to do that. Many of the animals said, 'Aah, this will never come true.'

But others replied, 'Don't talk like that. Just be silent. They've gone to fetch mats and they'll come back and spread them out. Then you'll see what the giraffe can do.'

No! The kori bustard didn't call for mats to be spread first. *First* the giraffe stuck his foot into the spring. Down, down, down, down, it went. At the bottom it reached the python. The giraffe took hold of her and felt her all over. Then he withdrew his leg and said to the others, I've put my leg all the way down and it feels like there's more than one python down there.' The python had given birth in the bottom of the spring. 'Now go to the camp,' said the giraffe, 'and find something to spread out on the ground. Then bring them back here and fix them nicely.'

When they heard the giraffe's words, everybody laughed and grabbed each other in delight and fell to the ground. 'How has this fellow managed to do it?' they asked each other.

Then they ran back to the camp and began to spread mats from the camp to the spring. Then the giraffe stepped out of the crowd again. He rocked backwards and forwards on his long legs as he approached the spring. He reached in with his leg, and reached and stretched right down to the bottom. He grasped the python and shook the mud off her while she was still down there. Then he opened his mouth and laughed! He began bringing her up and up and up toward the surface. It was a very deep spring! It was a fearsome spring, and a deep waterhole. As the python came near the surface, the other animals saw her and hugged each other. They fell to the ground laughing. The giraffe brought her up, and lifted her to the surface. At last he laid her on the ground. She lay there and vomited up water. Then the giraffe pulled a baby python out of the spring and laid it beside its mother.

The animals were so delighted that they embraced each other and rolled on their backs on the ground. Here's our beautiful girl again,' they said, 'What the jackal did was a terrible thing.'

Then they brought a whisk to wipe her face.'G!a!' it went across her brow, and they said, 'Yes, isn't this the woman we were looking for the other day? And today she's come up out of the spring, and here she is.'

Then they greeted her and embraced her and exclaimed over her. 'Yes, this is a very good thing the giraffe has done for us.'

Then the python walked on the trail of mats with her child back to the camp. She walked beautifully and gracefully back home to her own house.

'Yes. It's our own daughter again,' said the people of the camp. 'Here she is, and that jackal over there is dead, and good riddance.' The kori bustard greeted his wife and said, 'Oh my good wife, today you've come home to me!' She glided regally and smoothly like she always had, and she sat down before her house and looked around at everyone.

Later she took her child to bed and they both slept well for a long time. The people said, 'Mm. This is the right woman. This is the daughter of our camp for sure. She fits in with the camp so well, and she's so very beautiful.'

So the people lived there together. After a while they separated and travelled around to different places. The kori bustard's heart was so happy that he ran about tossing his head feather. He ran and tossed his head feather in praise of his wife. And the two of them went on living. Mm, yes, that's how it was. My friend, that's how it happened.

Told by Tci!xo N!a'an, G!oce, Botswana, 1972

VERSION II

The older sister, the python, was pregnant. She and her younger sister, the jackal, went one morning to fetch water. People were drinking at that time from a rock spring, and they went to draw water from it. In the well was a *n=ah* tree with ripe fruits on it.

The python said to her sister, 'Climb up and shake that *n=ah* branch, so we can have *n=ah* to eat.'

But the jackal refused. 'Uh-uh,' she said. 'Older sister, climb up yourself and shake down something for us to eat.'

So the python herself had to climb the tree. She was pregnant and heavy. When she was up in the tree, she reached for the branch she wanted to shake. But she missed her grasp, and fell into the water. She went down into the spring. She tried to climb out but the sides were too steep. She had to remain in the spring. She gave birth down there. The python's in-laws looked up and saw the jackal come running from the spring. She ran with a funny gait, wobbling from side to side. The in-laws sat and watched her come into the camp.

'*Yau!*' they said. 'Where's our beautiful daughter-in-law? The jackal has come back alone; we thought our daughter-in-law had gone with her to the spring. What has this jackal done with her older sister?'

When the jackal came up to where they were sitting, the in-laws took a whisk and drew it across her face. That was what they were accustomed to do to her older sister. They would draw a whisk loaded with fat across her face, so that her face would be smooth and shiny.

But the jackal misunderstood: 'Fat! Fat! There's fat dripping on my face,' she yelled, and she began to drink it. The people said, 'We were right, you are certainly not our daughter-in-law. What have you done with her? What do you think you're doing coming back without her and pretending to be the beautiful python?'

Now all this while the kori bustard, the husband of the python, had been off hunting. When he came home he saw the

jackal and said, 'Where's my wife?' (The jackal had told the
people nothing of how her sister had fallen into the spring. She
just kept quiet.) As the jackal was still walking about from fire to
fire, the kori bustard went to prepare their sleeping place. He
took porcupine quills and stuck them upright in the sand
beneath the jackal's sleeping-skins. When the jackal lay down to
sleep, the quills stuck in her ribs. They pierced right through her
skin.

'Hey!' she yelled. 'Get rid of all these spikes!' But the kori
bustard pretended not to hear. Finally the jackal was quiet. The
porcupine quills killed her. She died, and continued to lie inside
the house.

In the morning the kori bustard got up and went off. The
jackal's little sister was told by her grandmother, 'Go and see
what's happening about your sister. Is she staying inside the
house because she's menstruating? What is she doing sleeping
so late?' The little girl ran to see. The jackal had died and the
n=ah seeds were protruding from her anus. The little girl saw
this and called to her grandmother. 'Granny! N=ah seeds have
dried-dried in older sister's arse-arse.' The grandmother called
back, 'Granddaughter! Did you say I should bring a pubic apron
to tie on her?'

The granddaughter shook her head and called a little louder,
'Uh-uh. Older sister, for heaven's sake, died in the night and the
n=ah has dried in her arse-arse!' 'Did you say I should bring a
cloth pubic apron and tie it on her?'

Well, they shouted back and forth for a while. The little girl
said again, 'N=ah seeds-seeds have dried-dried in older sister's
arse-arse!'

Finally the old lady came to see. By this time her
granddaughter had broken off the n=ah that was protruding
from her sister's anus. The grandmother came over and said,
'Oh, is your sister dead?' and then the two of them ate her. They
roasted the jackal and ate her.

Meanwhile the kori bustard had gone off to gather all the
animals together. He called the giraffe, the elephant, the

gemsbok – all the animals. They all walked until they were together at the spring. One by one they stuck their legs into the spring. But their legs weren't long enough – they only reached half-way. The eland put in his leg. But it didn't reach. The gemsbok came up and put in his leg. But it didn't reach either. The wildebeest stuck his leg into the spring but failed to reach the bottom. All the animals – kudus, steenboks, duikers, tortoises, turtles – all gave it a try. Hartebeests, lions, everything – all tried to reach the python, but their legs weren't long enough.

'Who will I call to help me?' asked the kori bustard.

'Call the giraffe,' said someone.

'Yes, I'll call him.'

The giraffe came forward and put in his leg. Now the python had given birth down there in the bottom of the spring. She had her child with her and they were together at the bottom of the spring. The giraffe put in his leg and felt about. He said to the python's husband, 'She's carrying a baby. She has given birth and she's down there with her baby and I can feel both of them.'

So the kori bustard sent someone off to the camp to fetch mats to lay on the ground. They brought the mats and laid them all the way between the spring and the camp. Again the giraffe put in his leg. He pulled out the python and her child. The two of them went to sit on the mat. Then her in-laws came to take her home to their camp. They all embraced her and sat down on the ground together joyfully. Here's our dear daughter-in-law we've been searching for, here she is, most certainly.' Then the kori bustard and his wife and child walked slowly and gracefully home along the line of mats.

These are things that were told to me by the old people. They told them and I listened. Would I be lying?

Told by /Asa N!a'an, Kauri, Botswana, 1971

VERSION III

G!kon//'amdima and her younger sister went to the spring.

G!kon//'amdima fell in and her sister left her there and ran home. When she got back to the camp, the kori bustard looked surprised and said, 'My wife ... where's my wife?' He saw that only one girl had returned from the spring. To test whether she was his wife he passed a whisk across her face. Where there should have been the smoothness of his wife's face he felt only hairy jowls, for the younger sister was a jackal.

Fat dripped from the whisk and the jackal licked it in glee.

'But if this were really G!kon//'amdima,' thought the kori bustard, 'she would have just let the fat slide over her smooth skin as she always does. This must be my wife's younger sister instead.'

Well, the jackal, trying to imitate her sister's walk, managed to slide sedately to their grandmother's fire. While she sat there, the kori bustard was arranging their sleeping place. He spread out skins and then took arrows and stuck them upright in the sand beneath the place where the jackal was going to sleep. Soon she came to join him. She tried to lie down but something stuck in her back. 'What the ... why do I have to sleep in a spot that feels like this? It's all thorny here.'

But the kori bustard replied, 'Oh, let's just go to sleep. My spot feels just as bad as yours, and I'm not complaining.'

In the night the jackal died from the arrow poison.

The next morning her little sister came to see about her: the sun rose higher and higher and hung in the sky but still she did not come out of her house.

'Granny,' called the little girl when she found the dead jackal. '*N=ah* seeds have dried in older sister's arse-arse.'

'Did you say that I should come and put a beaded pubic apron on her?'

'No! I said *n=ah* has dried in older sister's arse-arse.'

Finally the grandmother came to see for herself. She picked up the dead jackal and carried her out to the fire. Then she gathered wood and built up the fire to roast her. She spent the rest of the day eating the roasted jackal. She would eat, then rest a while, and eat again.

Meanwhile everyone came out of the bush and gathered at the spring. Everyone – the gemsbok, the eland, the giraffe, the zebra. First one, and then the other of them would stick his foreleg into the opening and try to reach G!kon//'amdima.

The eland came forward and tried but he couldn't reach her.

Then the gemsbok tried, but his leg wasn't long enough. One by one they came forward and stuck their legs into the spring.

But no one could reach her. At last the giraffe came up and put in his leg. And it reached right down to where she was.

So the kori bustard called for skin mats to be spread all the way from the spring to the camp. Then the giraffe drew G!kon//'amdima out of the spring and sat her down on a skin. She sat there and dried out. Then they brought her back into the camp and sat her down there.

That's the story of G!kon//'amdima. The jackal fooled her brother-in-law into whisking her face, but he discovered she wasn't his wife at all. G!kon//'amdima and the kori bustard were so happy to see each other, and all the people said, 'Yes, here's our niece at last: that other girl was the wrong one all along.'

Told by Di//xao, Kauri, Botswana, 1972

DISCUSSION: FEMALE VISIONS OF ORDER

The 'female' creation story centres around a lovely python girl who is sometimes called G!kon//'amdima, the name of the central Ju/'hoan heroine. The jackal character acts as a foil for the womanly grace of this python. In many versions of this episode great attention is given by the storytellers to colourful verbs differentiating the python's behaviour from that of the jackal. The python walks-and-shimmers, walks very slowly, sparkles like the sun, glides like a grand person, =xain=xani-n=haoh ha /'ae, undulates slowly along, =xani-=xani-n/ang, sits down gracefully or undulates to a sitting position. The jackal on the other hand kainkain, wobbles, or bounces, making a sound like !khu !khu !khu! She laughs harshly, //ka //ka, //ka! and speaks in a rough voice, going wa wa wa! The whisk, which made a sound like g!an across the python's smooth face, instead goes //ae //ae (a rough sound) across the jackal's dry and hairy one.

The python is all a woman should be – slow and sedate of gait, acquiescent and helpful, beautiful, sophisticated, quiet, married, and pregnant. In some versions it is stressed that she smells sweet and has beautiful clothing and ornaments, and knows how to wear them. The jackal, in contrast, is contrary and treacherous, awkward and bouncing in her movements, ugly and hairy rather than smooth-skinned, easily excitable, naive, noisy – and single. She is an inverted creature who in some versions puts on her sister's clothing inside out and backwards: she laughs harshly, and she smells bad. Instead of giving birth to a child, she produces out of her body only the n=ah seeds that protrude from her anus.

The jackal is the opposite of a woman. She is not a man, though, but a tci=xei=xei (worthless, bad thing, barren or abnormal person). She does not have a husband of her own and so strives to get her sister's husband away from her by treachery. Her infertility is underscored by the questions put by her hard-of-hearing grandmother about her menstruation in the various other versions:

'Is she staying inside the house because she's menstruating?'

'Did you say I should bring a pubic apron to tie on her?' 'Did you say I should bring a cloth pubic apron to tie on her?'

'Should I bring a beaded pubic apron?'

There are clear indications that the jackal is going through the first menstrual ceremony. During and after this ceremony, the girl is not supposed to talk to other people 'even if people give her food or are laughing,' one old grandmother told me. The girl who is menstruating for the first time lies curled under a blanket. An old woman who may be her grandmother anoints her with fat and brings her food to eat. When she leaves the hut 'to urinate or defecate, she is carried on the back of a kinswoman' (L. Marshall 1959:356).

The grandmother's questions, then, emphasise the ridiculous inappropriateness of the jackal as a substitute for her fecund sister. Not only has the python made the most of her time in the spring, lying there quietly and giving birth, but as one informant said, 'that was why her husband had gone off hunting in the first place, because his wife was pregnant and her heart wanted meat'. The jackal cannot even manage to menstruate: she is in the seclusion house after sunrise merely because she is dead.

While the python is going through a kind of birth-seclusion[4] which brings about an augmented restoration of the social order, the jackal has a hollow mockery of a menarchal seclusion (L. Marshall 1959:336) which culminates in her being eaten by her own grandmother and sister. This act of cannibalism is the opposite of the loving, protective relationship which should obtain between grandmother and granddaughter, especially during the granddaughter's first menstrual ceremony.

In the story, the jackal is not only raucously talkative but in some versions she makes an egregious mistake about the liquid fat with which her 'husband' greets her. When she lies curled under a blanket she does so not because she is menstruating but because she is dead. Far from carrying her out so that she will not foul the hut, her kinswoman discovers she has already defecated there, and proceeds in some versions to eat the faeces.

Though in some versions the grandmother is referred to as 'the old jackal lady', in a version collected by Richard Lee[5] she is a dung beetle named //Uce who is glad to see that faeces have dried in her granddaughter's anus: 'Praise, praise, she did well to die,' she cries. The old lady builds a fire and roasts the jackal, eating her afterwards, as reported with great detail, for instance, in the tale told earlier in this book by the Old Ostrich Lady.

Besides the themes of correct and 'inverted' femininity, the 'female' creation story also contains allusions to male concerns. The jackal dies because she is pierced by bone arrows or by 'porcupine quills' (from which Ju/'hoan men make arrow shafts). It is clear the jackal's death is caused by the effects of arrow poison. Usually it is arrows which are stood in rows in the sand by the kori bustard and covered then with the jackal's blankets. In most versions of the story, in fact, it is quite specifically /omn//asi, bone arrows, which are used. Ju/'hoan hunters say that symptoms of arrow poisoning include feeling like one wants to defecate all the time but not being able to (Marjorie Shostak, personal communication, Dec. 1970). Furthermore, the way the arrows are stuck in the sand in the stories (usually pantomimed by the storytellers) corresponds exactly to the way arrowheads are stuck in the sand at an angle by the hunters today to hold them upright while they are being poisoned:

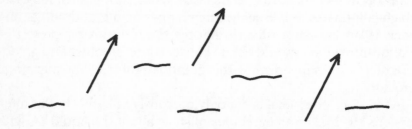

There are other indications of the relevance of hunting themes to this 'women's story.' For instance, Richard Lee's version is immediately preceded in his field notes by a statement that the main male characters 'were dancing Eland one night and the next morning they went out and killed eland.' The dance of the Eland Bulls is only performed at a girl's menarchal ceremony, and the girl is specifically to avoid eating eland meat. But when she is anointed by the old woman it is preferably eland fat that is used. In a story collected by Elizabeth

Marshall Thomas (17.1.53), men come home with eland meat just before the jackal tricks G!kon//'amdima into falling into the spring. The theme of the men's hunting and also what they are hunting thus bears a close relationship to the female themes of menarche and marriage. Men's activities are shown to be complementary and indispensable to those of women.

When it comes to retrieving the python girl from the spring, it is her husband who organises the rescue operation.

Only the tall, obliging giraffe can reach her with his long legs. The other animals try, and fail.[6] The giraffe, portrayed as gracious and graceful like the python herself, 'comes forward undulating like something tall'.

In Lee's version he is named Zarudum or 'Pipe Gullet'. When he triumphantly brings up the beautiful G!kon//'amdima, the python girl, and her newborn child, all the animals and people are there to celebrate the occasion. Rightful order is restored. In one version, 'the kori bustard's heart was so happy that he ran about tossing his head feather. He ran and tossed his head feather in praise of his wife. And the two of them went on living.'

However, in the version of this story collected by Lee there is a sobering anticlimax; this world-ordering outcome is implied by the events of the story but is not enunciated by all the storytellers.

> ... But when they came back to the village, Python's father, Old Elephant, was grave.
>
> 'Oh, what has that trash Jackal done to my beautiful daughter, since she no longer sparkles as before?' He got all his medicines and washed her and cleansed her and blew in her eyes and blew in her ears to erase the awful memories of the evil that she suffered at the hands of Jackal in the cold darkness of the well.
>
> After the cleansing, Father Elephant called everyone together and became very serious. 'This Jackal affair has spoiled my heart. You, Kori, I trusted my daughter to you and you let her get into this mess. Now go away and just be a bird who flies around and eats gum off the bark of trees. And you, my

daughter Python, who used to be so beautiful, you will just be a
snake and lie around coiled in the shadows. And I too, will just
go away and be an elephant tearing up and throwing up trees
looking for food to eat. Let this camp be split up forever. Let us
all live separately. We are no longer related.'

And so they all split up, went their separate ways and
became the animals they are today.

Lee's ending makes it clear that the import of this story as a fall from
grace is similar to that in 'The Branding of the Animals'. From this
day at the spring, paralleled by the day at the branding camp, animals
are just animals and no longer have human characteristics. From then
on they have gone their separate ways. The initiatory theme of the
menstrual rite in this story is similarly echoed in the branding story:
'These pretty ones are the ones who will turn into meat animals.' The
branding deals with the young boys' structural equivalent of the
menstrual rite, their ceremony of the first kill. Both stories stress the
themes of individuation and right relationship to the adult social
world that are so important in the initiations for both sexes. Etymo-
logical connections between the words used in both contexts are
evidence, further, that initiation, the process of becoming full human
beings, is symbolised in both these stories.[7]

Fully adult men thus have their origin in fire. Before they are
branded with fire they are little boys. Afterwards, they are hunters,
with all that this implies of adult social responsibilities. Women, on
the other hand, originate in water. Their fecundity is connected with
seclusion in a watery place, and as they emerge from this place as
established childbearers the social world around them falls into its
rightful order.

III

The Heroine

THE ELEPHANT GIRL
VERSION I

There were a man and a woman who had a son. The woman was also pregnant with another child. Now the son requested the elephant girl in marriage. He married her and went to live with her at her parents' camp. They lived there for a while, until the elephant girl gave birth to a child. She bore a girl-child there at her parents' camp. Then her husband left his wife and child safely with her people and went to visit his own parents. He went to them to ask for gifts for his child and for his wife.

By this time his own mother's stomach had grown very large. She was about to give birth. But she gathered together the gifts her son wanted, and she ground ochre and spread it on him because she was glad of his successful marriage. All the while her second child lay in her stomach.

As her son was making ready his things to leave, the second child all by himself popped out from her midriff. He jumped out and said, 'Here I am, Mother. Now rub my head with ochre too so I can go with my older brother.'

Well, the people were very surprised. They said they had

139

never seen such a thing. Then one of them cautioned the others not to talk like that.

He said, 'Obviously this is a sky-thing, a child of G//aoan. Let's agree that we've never seen such a thing and just do what he says. A normal child doesn't jump out of his mother's stomach and start to speak. Just rub him with ochre, and let him go with his older brother.'

This is how the people talked about it. So the mother came with more ochre and she rubbed it on the child. Then she asked her older son to bring his wife back with him when he returned, so that they could all see the new granddaughter.

He agreed, saying, 'Yes, I'll bring her back for you to see. My wife gave birth to a child and the child has grown and I will bring them both to visit you.'

So he left, and he took with him his new brother. They walked and walked until they came to the camp of the elephant girl's parents. They slept a night there. In the morning the two brothers and the elephant girl and her baby daughter left to return to the other camp.

As they were walking back to the brothers' people's camp, they came to a place where there was a termite hill. Suddenly the younger brother cried, 'Ouch! /'ang-/'ang'-/'ang-/'ang'! The others came up to him. He was crying 'Ouch!' and rubbing his foot.

Then he said 'Yau!' and took off his shoe and threw it away. He cried, 'Go and turn yourself into a vulture.' He threw away both his shoes. Then he turned to his older brother and said, 'Run, brother, run after the vultures and they will lead you to meat. Why should we remain so hungry?' So the older brother ran away after the shoes. Then the younger brother said, 'This thorn in my foot is killing me. Wife of my brother, come and take it out for me.' The elephant girl agreed, and took out her awl. She had an awl stuck into a well-sewn piece of skin, an awl like a great, big needle. She said she would try to take out the thorn with it. But the boy said, 'First give the awl to me and I'll point out to you where the thorn is. Just take it out and give it to me.'

So the elephant girl pulled out the awl and handed it to him.
Before she knew what was happening, he had stuck the awl into
her and she was dead.

Now the elephant girl had already warned her grandmother
that something might happen to her. She had said, 'A thing
which jumps out of its mother's stomach ready to accompany its
older brother is a thing that I don't understand. I am shocked by
it; my mind is unsettled. So you watch well: a little wind will
come to you. The little wind will come to you with something in
it. It will bring you some droplets of blood. The blood will come
to lodge inside your groin. Take that bit of blood and put it into
a container. Don't let on what you're doing – just take it and put
it into something. Something like a little dish or a little bottle.'

Then they all left the camp, and it happened just as the girl
said. A little wind came back to her grandmother. The bit of
blood came to lodge in her groin.

The grandmother saw it and said, 'Didn't the child tell me
something like this would happen?' She didn't speak aloud, she
just said this in her heart. She took the drops of blood and put
them in a bottle.

[Aside:] Did you suppose that events of long ago, the things
that Hoe and all those people did, were nice?

Then she sat and thought, and asked herself, 'Should I go and
see what has happened to my granddaughter? No; it has
already happened just is she said it would, so he must have
killed her already and there's no help for it.'

She turned it over and over in her mind. Then she went to
some of the young men, the girl's older brothers and younger
brothers, and said, 'Hey! Aren't you going to see whether these
people have arrived safely at their camp with your sister?'

Meanwhile, the older brother had failed to find meat by
following the vultures. The younger brother had killed and
butchered his brother's wife and was waiting for his brother to
return. While he waited he started a fire. When it was burning
well he began cutting off and eating bites of the elephant girl's

fat. He stood by the fire and cut off pieces of fat and ate them.
The elephant girl's daughter was standing right there watching.

When the older brother came back he said to himself, 'Yau!
Where's my wife? Why is the child standing there all alone?
What has happened – why has my brother made such a big fire
and why is he cutting and eating fat?' He came up to his brother
and said, 'What foul thing have you done? Where is my wife?
Where does that meat come from?'

The younger brother said, 'Oh stop giving me this business
about what kind of meat it is; just take a bit and taste it. Why do
you look at a piece of meat and start calling it a woman?'

But his brother said, 'You big-penis … you've ruined me.
How do you think I can go on living? Do you just want to kill
me? Did you pop out of my mother's stomach just to kill my
wife for me?'

The younger brother said, 'Oh, take some meat and shut up
and just have a taste of it, will you? It's just eland meat,
obviously; not human meat. Just take a taste of it and leave me
alone. Won't you just try it and talk later?' Finally he tried some,
and he found that it tasted like plain meat. So they ate together.
But then the older brother began to regret what he had done. He
asked, 'Is it possible that we will go on living after doing a thing
like this?'

The younger brother answered, 'What is there that will kill
us? We aren't going to die – I know better. There's nothing in
the world that can kill us. Stick with me. I'm the one to stick
with.' But this didn't make the older brother feel any better
about it.

Just then they saw the young men approaching, the ones who
were sent by the elephant girl's grandmother. They were
tracking the two brothers. As they were coming nearer, the
younger brother said, 'Quick! They're coming. I'll do something
for you so that they won't see you.'

His brother agreed. 'Yes, hide me; I have no other escape. I
don't want my wife's brothers to come and kill me.' So the
younger brother got up and went to the termite hill nearby. He

said to it, 'Termite hill, open and let my brother in: a fight is coming. I'll stand alone outside.' And the termite hill opened. It opened wide, and the older brother went inside. Then the younger brother said, 'Now close your door.' Click. The termite hill came together again.

The younger brother stood outside and watched the brothers of the elephant girl as they came closer. As he watched he cut and ate pieces of her fat. When they came up they said, 'Without a doubt this person standing here is eating our sister. There's her child, right over there.' They came right up to the termite hill. Quickly the younger brother turned himself into that bird the Narons call //'omhaea.[8] The young men tried to spear it. '//'om!' The bird perched on the points of the spears, so they couldn't spear it. '//'om!' It perched on their heads. '//'om!' It perched on their noses. They stabbed at it and missed, but the bird eluded them. '//'om //'om //'om...' They thought they could spear it, but they stabbed and missed over and over again. Finally they stopped, completely baffled. They said, 'Where will we see this person's face clearly, so we can kill him? We can't kill him, so let's go. He has defeated us.'

They left him and went off. Then the older brother came out of the termite hill. He and the younger brother packed up all the meat and took the child and went home. When they got there, their mother said, '*Yau*! What have you done to your wife?'

The younger brother answered innocently, 'Wife? What wife? This is some meat I cooked, and we two have been walking along with our stomachs full of it.'

His mother said, 'Don't talk that way about your brother's wife, *yau*!'

But he persisted. 'This is just meat that I'm holding. How could it be a person? Besides, here's the child you wanted to see – we've brought her to you. Here, take her.'

The mother refused, saying, 'No. I know that you two have done something really bad. Tell the child to go back to her people. I am in pain about what you have done. When they had finished talking, the child went back to her mother's people

and stayed there. Meanwhile the bit of blood was growing. It
grew and grew until it was too big for the bottle. Then the
grandmother took it out and put it in a skin bag. It grew again
and burst the bag, so the grandmother put it into something
bigger. Then it grew some more and broke that. Only the
grandmother knew about it. No one else knew that she had the
elephant girl and was restoring her to life. She kept it a secret.
She had the bit of blood and it grew and she fixed it, and it grew
some more and she fixed it.

When it had grown completely it was a woman again. She
looked just like she had before.

One morning when the camp awoke, the women decided to
go gathering n/ang. They got up and went off picking n/ang. The
elephant girl's little daughter went with them, saying, 'Today I'll
accompany my aunts and eat n/ang.' The old grandmother said,
'Go ahead, go with them.' So the elephant girl's mother and all
the other women went gathering. The old woman stayed home
alone. She spent the day quietly. In the afternoon she took a skin
and spread it in the shade, spread it in the late afternoon
shadows. Then she took out the elephant girl and sat her upon
the skin. She ground ochre and spread it on the young woman's
face. She replaced her old rags with soft, new skin clothing and
hung her all over with ornaments. Then the old woman tied
copper rings in her granddaughter's hair the way people used to
tie them long ago. She fixed her up so that she was the beautiful
elephant girl again.

Later the women came back from gathering. Towards sunset
they returned. The old woman was telling funny stories and the
elephant girl was laughing, '/ae-/ae-/ae-/ae-o'. As they approached
the village, her little daughter said to the others, 'Who's that
laughing just like my mother in the village?'

Her aunt said, 'How can you be so crazy? My older sister
died a long time ago. Don't you go saying you hear her laughing
somewhere.'

Another woman said, 'My aunt is certainly dead: this child is
crazy.'

So they came closer, listening. The elephant girl laughed
again. This time they said, 'Can it be? Whose laughter is this?
When we left there was nobody but the old woman in the camp;
we had all gone gathering. What young girl can that be whose
laughter sounds just like our sister's?'

When they came into the camp they saw the elephant girl
sitting there with her grandmother.

Her daughter cried, 'Mother, mother, mother,' and ran to her,
flopped down, and began to nurse. When her mother had died
she was still nursing, so she flopped down and began to nurse.
The others cried out and said, '*Yau!* Who has accomplished
this?' The young woman answered softly, 'Granny, of course.
Granny lifted me up. Granny spoke the word and I sat up and
was alive. If it had been up to you others alone, I wouldn't be
here. Long ago Granny took me and sheltered me in a skin
pouch and now I am alive again. That's how it was. The old
people give you life.'

Then one day the ones who had killed her, the two brothers,
came to the camp. They saw her and were very much afraid.
They decided to take her back again. Then her people began to
question them about the murder. But the old woman stopped
them. 'No,' she said, 'don't talk like that. I'll just give her back to
them. Just get up and let her get ready. She'll fix them herself.'
She got up and began to prepare her granddaughter's departure.

The people said to the brothers then, 'Here's your wife; you
shall certainly take her with you.' They talked together and the
elephant girl's people agreed that she should go away again
with her husband.

That night the husband and wife slept together. In the
morning he said, 'Now we're going to go home to my camp.'

The elephant girl said to her people, 'This man says he's
going to take me away with him.'

Her people replied, 'Yes. You will go with your husband.
What can be wrong with that?'

The old grandmother took out a =u and gave it to her
granddaughter. [Even long ago the Ju/'hoansi had this thing, a

gemsbok horn to blow upon just like the one old /Ukxa uses today. When you blow on it, it goes 'odi, odi, chodi' – that is how it sounds.] She gave the horn to the elephant girl, and said, 'Take this. Conceal it well. And leave with them. When you have walked and walked and are close to the camp, tell them to enter the camp ahead of you. Say that you are going into the bushes for a moment. Say that you have to go into the bushes and will come in after them, that they should go ahead. When they have entered the village you blow the horn, so that everyone in the camp falls dead. Then you can return to us.'

The elephant girl packed up her things and her grandmother helped her. The old woman fixed her up and got her things ready. 'The child will stay with us but you will go,' she said. The brothers agreed, and so they left. As they were walking to the other camp, the elephant girl kept asking them how far it was to the next hill. Sometimes they would be travelling along a valley of soft sand and sometimes they came to a hill. They would answer her, and tell her how far it was. She said, 'Tell me how the hills lie, tell me how far it is between them. And when we get near the hill near your camp, let me know. I want to stop before we come into the camp.'

They continued to walk. She asked them again about the hills that lay between them and the village. They said, 'Here is one hill. Beyond it lies a valley of soft sand and then another hill and then another valley. Then there's another hill, another valley, and then comes a hill that lies green.

'Near the green hill is our camp. You'll see houses, and children running about with clean tummies and playing. That's our camp.'

She said, 'All right,' and remembered what they had said.

They came to a hill and she asked, 'Is this it?'

'No, it's still far ahead,' they said.

'All right, then we'll keep going,' she answered.

A while later she said, 'Is it this one?'

'No,' they said, 'that's the wrong hill.'

They walked and walked and when they got to the green hill
she asked, 'This one?'

'This is the hill next to our village,' they answered.

She looked, and there were children standing about in the
camp with clean tummies. *'Yau!'* she said, 'now you two go on
in. I'm going to powder myself and then come into the camp.'
The brothers went into the camp ahead of her. The elephant girl
took out the horn and blew it. She blew down the brothers and
blew down their people, and the camps of their people were
simply flattened. She flattened them all and left them lying there
just as her grandmother had told her to do.

Told by !Unn/obe N!a'an, Kauri, Botswana, 1972

DISCUSSION: WOMANLY POWER I

Here is the tale which echoes the structure of the /Xam story
presented at the beginning of the book. It features the journey of a
newly-married woman caught in the conflict between her family of
birth and her new in-laws. It explores the strengths of women by
pitting a virtuous heroine against male assailants. The story centres
around a marvellous girl named G!kon//'amdima who sometimes
appears in the form of an elephant. The name G!kon//'amdima was
sometimes applied as well to the beautiful python heroine of the
central spring.[9] But usually it was reserved for the central character
in this longer cycle of tales. In this cycle the heroine is a human or an
elephant, never a python.

However, Ju/'hoansi make a close symbolic association between
pythons and elephants. One of the respect words for python is, in
fact, 'elephant'. This association has important ramifications, as we
will see when we look into the structure of these tales.

Emotional attitudes taken towards the heroines of both groups are
also strikingly similar. They are always described as courageous
young married women, often with a young child or children, who
are beautiful and resourceful and the pride of their kin and in-laws.

Portrayed as virtuous and fertile, they are attacked or tricked by
envious little sisters or vengeful younger brothers-in-law. They have
animal aid and supernatural recourse, and no matter what trials they
are put through they get off scot-free and come up shining.

The name G!kon//'amdima which appears to link the python with
the other female heroine is not just a proper name but also a generic
one. It has the general meaning of 'beautiful and honoured woman'.
The -*ma* ending is a diminutive: several times the heroine is referred
to merely as G!ko//'amdi, -*di* meaning female or woman. An analogous name is used by her in-laws in one version: they call her
e/'uidima, 'our little female affine'.

The first two syllables of the name G!kon//'amdima are much more
difficult to pin down, especially as many informants slur them
together and even change the clicks. The first syllable is the word for
termite(s), but informants say this is not significant. The heroine has
much to do with elephants in the main cycle of stories: her father is
an elephant and she marries an elephant. Sometimes she is an
elephant herself and is called !Xodi 'elephant girl'. In any case, she is
always described as beautiful, and specifically as fat, with the smooth
skin that comes of having plenty of fat under it. In this connection
Winifred Hoernlé (1918:71) reports of the Khoikoi that 'one of the
chief things required of a girl in the [menstrual] hut is that she should
get fat, with smoothly shining skin'.

In the field, having heard these stories for months and months, I
began to notice a strange similarity between the way G!kon//'amdima
as a python was described and the way G!kon//'amdima as an elephant girl was described. There was great concentration on the fat,
smoothness and beauty of each, and the idea was often repeated. I
felt there was a kind of luminous equivalence – that is the only way
I can put it – about the attitudes held toward the physical beings of
these animals in their roles as heroines. I felt it so strongly I was about
to burst – or burst out with a question. Then one day, one of the
storytellers made a 'slip'.

She had been telling me the story of the 'elephant girl'.

When she came to describe how the girl's grandmother made her
beautiful again after she had grown up in a bag, she said, '...fixed her

and fixed her, certainly she was a beautiful woman, the python girl
– er, elephant girl.'

I said, 'She was a python girl, huh?'

'Elephant girl.'

'Didn't you just say she was a python girl?'

'No, I made a mistake. She was the elephant girl. The python girl
was the one that got killed and *n=ah* seeds-seeds dried in her arse-
arse. That one was the python girl. And this one is the elephant girl.'

Some weeks later another storyteller made a similar connection for
me, this time an explicit one. Telling the story of the python and the
jackal, she said, 'She glided beautifully along and sat down, because
she was a person, an elephant girl. Because a python is an elephant.'

I asked, 'How can that be? I thought a python was one thing and
an elephant was another thing.'

'Yes, that's true, but people say that a python is an elephant anyway.'

I was intrigued. The metaphoric equation of woman and hunted
meat animal made by Ju/'hoansi led me to investigate Ju/'hoan
attitudes toward eating these two animals. As it turns out, python
meat is well liked by most people, particularly its abundant fat. But
a range of attitudes is to be found in Ju/'hoan society toward elephant
meat. Some people eat it gladly, while others regard it with distaste.
I tried to discover more about attitudes toward elephant meat in
terms of its colour categorisation.

'Elephant meat isn't red, or black, or white,' said one man. 'Elephants have all three.'

'Really?' I said.

'Cut an elephant open, walk inside, and you see hanging down in
great sheets meat of all three colours. Black meat is there, and red
meat, and white.'

Someone else said, 'There's human meat there, and gemsbok meat,
carnivores' meat, eland meat, every kind of meat, red, black, and
white. It's very fat. When it's dead, an elephant smells bad like a dead
person.'

Whenever the subject of elephants or their meat came up, people
got excited about telling me and each other how strange it all was.
'Its fat hangs down all around you – there's so much fat!'

'It has all the kinds of meat in it – eland, human – it's the father of meat.'

'Elephant? I don't eat it,' said /Ukxa N!a'an. 'Nobody now does. It's got people's flesh and bush-animals' flesh, all hanging down. It's a *koaqkoaq* [thing to be feared], *tci dore* [bad, strange thing].'

'You don't eat it because it's like a person. The female has two breasts and they are on her chest like a woman's. When she's young they stick out and when she gets old they fall. Also, her crotch is like a woman's with long labia.'

'The males have penises like people. They have only penises and no balls.'

'Their balls went up inside their bodies because they were afraid of lightning. They have an arse like a person's arse.'

'When they run, their breasts flap. Their eyes are small like a tortoise's eyes.'

'You don't use elephant hide, because it's *tci dore*, like human skin. Besides, elephants have two backbones.'

'We found a dead one once and it took five people to lift its penis.'

'If an elephant kills you it buries you and puts logs over the top of the hole.'

'When they run, elephants really get into the swing of it and begin to dance, just like people.'

Many people said they would only eat the red or black elephant meat but not the white, 'because carnivores' meat, lion meat, is white.' As far as I know, elephant meat is the only meat not distributed by Ju/'hoansi along the usual lines of sharing. 'There is so much there, you just walk up and cut off what you want.'

A number of considerations thus make elephant meat out of the ordinary. The main problem with it is that it is 'like' human meat. This characteristic distinguishes it from python meat: here is the reason, I believe, why the heroine does not appear in python form in the vengeance stories. She appears as elephant or as human, and killing her for her flesh will in both these cases generate very grave consequences. To see the consequences of eating the human-like elephant, let us turn to a G/ui version of the elephant story collected by Lorna Marshall:

'... brother, come near. Taste what I am eating, then you can kill me if you wish. You are a lazy man. You are married to meat and you think it is a wife.' When Pishiboro came up to his brother, the brother gave him a piece of the breast he was eating. Pishiboro ate some and said, '*Ehay, ehay, ehay*. This is good. You are right: I was married to meat and thought it was a wife.' The day they had left home, the elephant had told her parents that she married a man whose people might eat her...[10]

The younger brother, after eating the dead wife's breast (an anatomical feature which does appear to link elephants closely with human beings), cuts open her uterus. The foetus walks out, accompanied by a flood of uterine fluid. The trickster, Pishiboro, fearing that the fluid will go to warn the elephant girl's parents, tries to catch it by digging a hole. But it flows past him and indeed continues on to alert his in-laws that their daughter has been murdered.

Inappropriate 'eating' of a woman has led to an inordinate release of female essence, the uterine fluid. The plot of the story is advanced one more step as the pendulum swings from male aggression to female retribution.

The battle lines are drawn in this story between i) the wife and her people and ii) the husband and his people. Where the python and jackal story explores the relationship between rivalrous sisters, the vengeance stories involving G!kon//'amdima deal with that between the young married woman and her new affines. It uses the problems of this relationship to probe themes of bride-service, marriage, and residence, of insults, murder, and blood-vengeance, of sex, birth and the origin of meat, and of the balance of power between men and women.

As in the python stories, the virtuous heroine is continually put upon by an upstart younger sibling, but in this case not her own. Instead, it is her husband's younger brother who is her antagonist. She is tricked, killed, and eaten by this younger brother. Her husband is tricked by him into cannibalising upon his own wife's flesh. The heroine reacts to the aggression of her young brother-in law by seeking refuge with her grandmother. But she is only taken away

again by her killers. At last she vanquishes the killers and all her
in-laws by magical means given her by her grandmother.

The principal conflict could appear at first glance to be one between
the new wife and her affines. The affines are portrayed as somewhat
uncanny: they have a child born under strange circumstances who
proceeds to undo his older brother's successful marriage. But it is not
really the affines in general who are the heroine's antagonists. Her
mother-in-law quite specifically is not responsible for the strange
birth, and she abhors its murderous consequences: 'I know that you
two have done something really bad,' she says. 'I am in pain about
what you have done.' The antagonist is not really the husband, either;
he is tricked into eating his wife and regrets it as soon as he does. The
principal channel for aggression can be narrowed down, then, to the
relationship between the younger brother and his sister-in-law.

The younger brother's aggression takes the form of a mistake
between the literal and figurative meanings of the word 'eat'. He does
not differentiate between these two senses of the word, so he wrongly
transposes a sexual object into the realm of food. His main attack on
the heroine, then, consists of an elaborate equation he makes between
her and animal game. She reacts in three different ways: escaping,
being magically reconstituted, and destroying her assailant and his
people by magical means. The equation of a sexual object with a
hunted object, as we have said, is one which emerges over and over
again in Bushman folklore, as it does in the metaphorical systems of
numerous peoples throughout the world.

Everyday Ju/'hoan language use attests as well to this equivalence. 'To eat meat,' 'to drink fat,' and so forth, are common
metaphors for intercourse. Two men who sleep with the same
woman *'m-'aankhoe,* 'eat-share' her.[11]

The heroine's answers to this sexual aggression are characteristically assertive. In one, her blood escapes murder and grows in
a bag to result in a full-size woman as before. Cared for by her
nurturant grandmother, she goes through a second period of time 'in
the womb'. In this she acts in a diametrically opposite way to her
assailant: instead of returning to the womb, he has emerged from the
womb prematurely. In a sense, they have opposite 'magical births'.

The heroine's return to the womb has parallels with the python girl's fruitful seclusion in the spring. In some versions much is made of the charming babyhood of the girl as she is growing in the bag and is occasionally taken out to crawl and play. Much is also made of the beauty of the full-grown woman when she finally emerges. In a sense, both child and woman emerge as from the python's spring, making a return which enhances life. She is washed, rubbed with ochre, dressed freshly, hung with ornaments, and placed upon a skin mat as a young bride would be, or a girl freshly emerged from her first menstrual seclusion. Lorna Marshall (1959:356) has commented on the symbolism which appears to link the ceremonies of marriage and menarche among the Ju/'hoansi. The close merging of the two themes in the folklore seems to corroborate her observation.

Like the python when she is rescued, G!kon//'amdima is set grandly on a skin and celebrated by doting kin when she emerges from the bag. Happiness reigns in the camp. 'The old people,' says G!kon//'amdima in our text, 'give you life.'

The younger brother's repeated attempts to devour this desirable heroine and wrest her from her grandmother and kin trigger a series of events which lead to a vengeance foray.

The girl's people are informed by the uterine fluid about this male aggression, and they turn out (in 'female' retaliation) against the cannibal mistake. There seems to be a connection between the motif of the uterine fluid flowing away to bear witness and that of the heroine's blood flowing away on the wind to her grandmother. Both are red female substances and both contain information about death and the essence of new life. In a further episode of the G!kon//'amdima cycle, another woman's death is discovered by means of blood which flows from her corpse all the way to the fire.

It is possible to see in these motifs an echo of the *guri =ab* (yearly killing) sacrificial rainmaking practice of the Nama Khoikoi in which pregnant cows or ewes were slaughtered. The old men of the tribe who are good at prophesying take the uteri, writes Schapera (1930:379), and 'hold them over the fire and pierce them with sticks so that the uterine fluid flows directly through the fire and down the river. At the same time milk in plenty and fat from the animals are thrown on the fire, so that liquid really flows, and great clouds of smoke rise into the sky.' In an account of a similar ceremony, Vedder (1928:131) writes that blood from a cow pregnant with her first calf was poured over the fire, extinguishing it and causing the smoke to rise abundantly. Prayers for rain, plant food, and good grazing were said. Pregnancy, prophesy, and rain were linked, for the Nama then, at this nexus where uterine fluid or blood met the fire. Lorna Marshall (1957:234) points out about this yearly killing ceremony that

> the uterine fluid, the fire and clouds of smoke rising into the sky, and the association of the ceremony with rain are the elements in the Hottentot (Nama Khoi) belief which are similar to the elements in the !Kung Bushman belief of *n!ow*.

Sexual progress (pregnancy) and progress toward good weather (rain) are furthered in both Khoikoi and Bushman belief by the mediation of hot and cold, male and female, dry and wet which occurs when women's substances meet the substance of men's fire. Clouds of smoke thus produced link earth and sky into fruitful collaboration. The great split between a parched earth and the water-withholding sky is, for a time, healed. Fire and its associated powers – 'hot' *n!om* for curing; 'hot' arrow points, spears, and poison for hunting; 'hot' sexuality for impregnating women – meet wet, cold, female powers – uterine fluid, blood, foetuses – and combine with them, creating a dynamic movement toward desired ends.

The male and female antagonists in our story, G!kon//'amdima and her young brother-in-law, are balanced against each other just as these male and female oppositions are balanced in ritual. A further set of episodes in G!kon//'amdima's stories beginning with the insulting equation of a man's testicles with plant food bulbs reinforce this theme of male/female balance. In these episodes G!kon//'amdima is pitted not only against her brother-in-law but directly against her husband.

VERSION II

G!kon//'amdima's mother was living with her daughter and her
daughter's husband in the bush, and the husband was having
luck in hunting. One day he killed a duiker. It was raining, and
he killed a duiker. He left the camp that they had together, and
went off and killed it. In the morning it was raining, and he
went out and killed the duiker.

When he came back with the meat, G!kon//'amdima said to
him, 'Since you have been killing all these duikers, aren't we
about ready to go back to join the rest of our people? Isn't that
what we agreed to do?'

But her husband answered, 'No. I don't want to return to
them yet. I want to keep on hunting these duikers so I will have
plenty of meat to give your mother. I want to hunt for your
mother's people and come home with plenty.'

'All right,' said G!kon//'amdima. 'You are certainly talking
sense. You will hunt some more and kill animals and soften
their skins. My mother will have meat to eat, and when you
have softened the skins, you can sew her an apron from them.'

When they had agreed upon this plan, the husband went
hunting again. Well, what should happen, what should happen,
but that he should kill another duiker! He set out in the morning,
and he chased the duiker and chased it and chased it until finally
he killed it. Now at that time the *dchuun* had come up and was ripe
and pretty. It was mature, and its bulbs were swollen and ready to
be eaten. The duiker led the husband a chase across the *dchuun*
patches far off in the bush. When he went back to the camp he said
to his little daughter, 'Yesterday when I was following a duiker, I
saw a patch of *dchuun* bulbs, all ripe and ready to be gathered.
Why don't you and your grandmother go and pick them?'

'Yes!' said the little girl, 'that's just what we'll do. Mother can
stay home and granny and I will go to pick *dchuun*.'

So the old woman and her granddaughter set out. They
walked and walked until they came to where the child's father
had been chasing the duiker.

When they got there, the bulbs were ripe and round as a
man's testicles. The child saw them first. She cried, 'Here we are!
Is this the place my father meant? Granny, come and dig up
these nice *dchuun* bulbs.' When the grandmother saw them, she
exclaimed, '//hoi-//hoi-s-a-ka-//hoi, hui-hui s-a-ka-hui! Was it here
your father chased the duiker yesterday, so that his balls have
fallen upon the ground?'

'*Yau!*' cried the child. 'What are you saying, granny? Are you
saying that where my father yesterday...are you insulting my
father? Are you insulting my father and saying that his testicles
are lying on the ground here?'

'What do you mean, child? Stop talking such foulness! What
do you think you're doing talking like that? Don't you know
what you're talking about, don't you see that he's my son-in-law
and I fear him and respect him? Knowing that, how can you talk
like this?'

So the child said only, 'Granny, come and dig up these bulbs
we were talking about. Come and dig up these bulbs.' So the old
woman went to her and dug up the *dchuun*. She dug them and
dug them and then she looked at what she had dug up. 'O!' she
cried. '//hoi-//hoi-s-a-ka-//hoi, hui-hui-s-a-ka-hui! Yesterday my
son-in-law was chasing a duiker and his balls have fallen on the
ground. Hee-hee! This is how his balls look. This is what the
tops of his balls look like!'

'Granny!' cried the child again. 'Are you insulting my father?'

'Stop talking like that!' answered the old woman. 'Are you
saying I don't have respect for other people? Stop this kind of
talking – what's got into you today?' So they dug and dug, and
then they started home.

On the way the little girl said, 'I'm very hungry. Let's go
home and you can roast the *dchuun* so I'll have something to eat.'

'All right,' answered the grandmother. 'You can go on into
camp while I collect some firewood.' They walked and walked.
As they neared the camp, the old woman picked up pieces of
firewood and put them in her kaross. She gathered wood until
she had a load.

The little girl went on ahead. When she came into the camp she saw a dead duiker. There was her father; he had already killed a duiker and returned to camp to skin it. The little girl ran up to him. 'Father! Granny and I went out together and she insulted you to death! She killed you. She said that a certain place was where you had been chasing a duiker, and that your testicles were lying together on the ground.'

'*Yau*! What on earth! What can you be saying! What kind of talk is this?' exclaimed her father. But he went on skinning the duiker. He skinned it and opened it up and took out its intestines and hung them from a tree. Then he took out its stomach and dumped out its contents. Then he filled the stomach with the duiker's blood and hung that in a tree. All right now, I want you to take the intestines and give them to your grandmother. She'll cook them and both of you can eat.'

'What? She's insulted you to death and you want me to take her the duiker's intestines?'

'*Uru-u-u*! What's wrong with you, child? Don't you know there's such a thing as respect for other people? What do you mean, saying your own grandmother has insulted someone?' But the child said, 'I just won't do it. If she hadn't insulted you I would have taken her the duiker's intestines, but she insulted you to death.'

'Oh, all right, I'll take them to her,' said her father. He took the intestines down from the tree. Then he took a kaross and wrapped it around himself. He picked up his axe, a Goba [Bantu] axe that was big and sharp and hid it inside the kaross in an inside pocket. Then he went across to his mother-in-law's fire.

'Here, take the duiker's intestines. I've brought them to you myself, because your grandchild refused to.' He took out the intestines and gave them to her. Then he said, 'When you receive a gift of meat you should bow your head.' She did so, and her neck was exposed as he stood above her. '*Dzop*!' He chopped her head off with the axe. The blood spurted from her: it was simply horrible.

G!kon//'amdima was not there to see her mother die: since
early morning she had been off gathering somewhere else. So
her husband was able to arrange the body in secret. He dragged
it out of the pool of blood. He took its arms and pulled it into a
hut. There he covered up all signs of foul play. But since the
bones of the corpse's neck were broken, there was no stopping
the flow of blood. He went away, but the blood kept on
dripping.

G!kon//'amdima's husband went back to his own fire; he
hung the duiker's intestines by his mother-in-law's hut and
went back to sit by his own fire. All this while, G!kon//'amdima
was off in the bush eating and gathering. She ate lizards, mice,
all sorts of things. She ate some and gathered some. She
collected them and stowed them in her kaross to take home.

Then she gathered a load of firewood and put that in her
kaross, and at last she headed back to the camp.

Her child and her husband were sitting by their fire when she
arrived. Her husband was cooking the duiker. G!kon//'amdima
glanced toward her mother's hut. Her mother appeared to be
lying inside asleep. '*Yau!*' said G!kon//'amdima. 'What's wrong
with mother? Why has she come home and gone straight to
bed? Why doesn't she blow on her fire and cook something so
she'll have something to eat? All she'll have to do is sit up and
roast it. Why should she have to sleep on an empty stomach?' So
she divided into piles the food she had brought, the mice, the
lizards, and all the other things. Then she said to her little
daughter, 'Go and give these to your grandmother so she can sit
up and blow on her fire and roast herself something to eat. Why
is she still lying down?' But the child answered, 'No, I won't.'

'You won't?' said G!kon//'amdima. 'What do you mean you
won't?' As she said this, G!kon//'amdima knew in her heart
what had happened. So she walked across the camp. She could
see the flow of blood where it had gushed out and dried.

'Yes, I knew it,' she said to herself. 'I already knew it. Well, I
won't let him know that I know. I'll just set down the food I've
brought and go back to my own fire.'

So she left her mother's hut and went back to her own.

She heaped wood on her fire, and it began to smoke. The wind blew the smoke first one way and then the other.

G!kon//'amdima changed her sitting place each time the wind changed, so that she could sit in the smoke and cry unobserved. Her face was covered with tears. Her husband said, 'Yau!' What are you crying about?'

'Uru!' she answered loudly. 'Why on earth should I be crying? Why do you think I'm crying when it's only the smoke in my eyes? This fire is awful – it just keeps smoking in my eyes. I don't have anything to cry about. Can't you see this fire just keeps smoking in my eyes so that they keep on watering?' Every time her husband asked her why she was crying, she would say it was only the smoke in her face. Finally, it grew dark and they went to bed. The husband lay down right away, but G!kon//'amdima remained sitting up in her blanket and nibbling on the food she had brought. Her husband dropped off to sleep, but she sat on into the night thinking.

'Oho. Just you wait.' she whispered to her sleeping husband. 'I'm going to get you. You killed my mother and so I'm going to kill you.' G!kon//'amdima turned these thoughts over and over in her mind.

'Kuru!' she said to herself. 'If I take a spear from this pile of short spears he has and try to kill him with it, will I manage to stay alive myself?' She thought the matter over.

Then she pulled out a spear from the pile. But as she did, the spearheads rattled against each other. Their rattling woke her husband.

'Yau! What are you doing rattling spears together?'

'Yau!' she retorted. 'What would I be doing with spears? Those spears you hear are my brothers' spears; they are on the move tonight. Why do you think I'd want to have anything to do with spears?'

In this way she meant to soothe his fear so that his watch-fulness would no longer hinder her plans.

'Just wait,' she said to herself, 'as soon as he's off his guard,

I'll kill him.' But he stayed awake, and she had no chance of reaching for a spear a second time. Then a fresh thought struck her.

'There's no point in his going on living when I'm wearing a knife. That's what I'll use to kill him. He killed mother; now I'll do the same to him.' Then she slowly and carefully drew out her knife and laid it in the fire. It lay there and grew hot. It heated up until it was red-hot. Then G!kon//'amdima did to her husband the same thing he had done to her mother. Yes, she killed him. When his body lay still, she went to sleep.

In the morning, she gathered up her mother's blood into a ball and stuck it in the left side of her groin. Then she gathered up her husband's blood and stuck it in the right side of her groin. She dumped her husband's body in the bush.

Then she came back and fetched her mother's body and dumped it in the bush as well.

When she returned, she found a group of people sitting with her children in the camp. They were eating together.

Her husband's younger brothers had arrived while she was busy in the bush. 'What have my brothers-in-law come for?' she wondered. 'What are they going to do to me?' Just then her little son ran across to one of the men. 'Uncle, Uncle,' he said.

G!kon//'amdima knew that he was going to say, 'Mother has killed my father! Now you know.' So she grabbed the little boy and turned his attention to something else.

Then the brothers were ready to leave. They told G!kon//'amdima to pack up her things, that she was coming with them. So she packed up all kinds of thorns, morningstar thorns, g//amig//ami (devil's claw) thorns, everything, and was ready to go. But she did it so quickly that she was ready before they were.

Thus she fled the camp and ran off in the direction of her own people's camp, where her mother's people, her father's people, her older brothers, and all their children were living. Meanwhile, vultures had begun to gather in the sky. The husband's younger brothers said to themselves, 'What are these vultures after? What on earth can be making them all gather together like this? Ooh! Just look at them flapping their wings.'

The vultures began to drop out of the sky. They came down on the body of G!kon//'amdima's husband, and they came down on the body of her mother. The brothers ran to where they came down and found them feasting upon the bodies. '*Kuru*!' they cried. 'Is this what she's done? Here's what that child was trying to tell us about her mother – that she had killed her father! But he didn't manage to get the story told. Now we'll have to leave the child's father and come back to bury him later.'

Now that they knew what had happened, they lost no time in getting out to pursue G!kon//'amdima. They tracked her and tracked her, and soon had begun to catch up with her. But her child gave her some help. G!kon//'amdima said to the child, 'My brothers-in-law are following us. Won't you help me watch out behind for them; won't you look for them and tell me when you see them? Otherwise, they are going to come up on us and kill us.' Then G!kon//'dima began to strew morningstar thorns in the path behind her as she fled. When the brothers came as far as that place, they ran into the midst of the thorns. The thorns stuck into their feet and pierced their feet – it was just terrible for them. They stumbled around looking for a way out of the thorns. Meanwhile, G!kon//'amdima and her child ran on ahead, far into the distance. The brothers' feet were pierced over and over again by the thorns. Finally, they managed to extricate themselves. They made a wide circle around the thorns and began to follow G!kon//'amdima's trail again.

Now G!kon//'amdima's daughter was a little guinea fowl. She was watching to the rear for her mother. She saw the brothers catching up again, so she cried (in guinea-fowl language), '*Kasasaa-a-/oe-/oe.* They're almost upon us. /*oe-/oe*!' she cried.

'What shall I do, what ever shall I do? I'm about to die, with nobody to help me,' said G!kon//'amdima. Then she scattered her big *g//amig//ami* (devil's claw) thorns that had very long spines. When the brothers came to where the thorns were, they

ran right in among them. The thorns were so big that they broke
the brothers' shoes to pieces.

G!kon//'amdima and her daughter ran on. The sun beat down
upon them. They struggled to keep running. Now, a single
cloud hung in the sky. G!kon//'amdima spoke to it, saying 'Why
is it that I'm about to die and you're not helping me at all? Don't
you see what's happening, don't you see that I'm going to die?'
Well, the cloud did help her. It waited until her brothers-in-law
had stopped at their camp for the night. When they were inside
their houses with their children, the cloud sent down a rain so
hard it nearly killed them all. In the morning they came
shivering out of their houses to build fires to warm themselves
by, and again the cloud dropped a drenching downpour upon
them. All they could do was to stand around and shiver.

Then do you know what those young men did? They said,
'Why doesn't our grandfather send us after her again? Come on,
let's go. Why should G!kon//'amdima remain alive when she has
killed our brother? Let's be sure to get her this time. When
someone as important as an older brother gets killed, someone
else will die for it later.' So the brothers left their camp and
walked until they came to the waterhole. They planned to kill
her there. They sat down in the bushes near the waterhole and
waited for her to come. While they were waiting there, some
other people came down to the waterhole to fetch water. They
saw the brothers and hurried back to G!kon//'amdima with the
news.

'Your brothers-in-law have come after you. They have
already come to kill you. Be warned.' 'Yes,' she answered, 'do
you think I don't know? Of course I know already ... I know
they're there.'

To her grandmother she said, 'When I leave here, granny, do
you know what I want you to do for me? Well, something is
going to fly to you from the direction of that waterhole. It will
fly to you and perch at the top of your spine. That something
will be my heart's blood. Now when that happens, you must

hurry and put it in a pouch. Yes, I want you to put it in a pouch for me.'

Then G!kon//'amdima went down to the waterhole. The brothers put a dipper into the waterhole and brought up, not water, but mud for her to drink. '*Yau!*' she said. 'If you're going to kill me, at least give me good water to drink so my blood will flow clean. What do you think you're doing?' So the brothers dipped up good water for her to drink. Then they took out their knives and stabbed her.

Her heart's blood sprang from the top of her spine and flew to fling itself – '*g=ari!*' squarely at the middle of the top of her grandmother's spine. The grandmother hastened to take hold of it and put it into a pouch. Once inside the pouch it began to grow. It grew and grew and grew until it was a grown person again. But still it lived in the bag in secret.

Now one day all the women in the camp, except the grandmother, had gone gathering. When they were returning they heard the sound of *n=hang* being pounded into powder in the camp. 'Hey, everybody,' they said, 'who's pounding *n=hang*? Who can that be pounding *n=hang* in our camp? We're almost there: let's hurry and see who it is.' When they came into the camp they cried, 'Ooo! Where has such a beautiful woman come from? Why, it's our older sister, our aunt, our what-have-you – greetings to our relative. Here's our relative returned to us again!' And they greeted her and embraced her happily and she lived quietly with them for some time.

But one day her husband's younger brothers made a new plan. 'Let's marry her this time – come on!' they said to each other. 'Let's not talk any more about killing her, because she's so very beautiful. Such a person you don't kill, you marry her instead.'

But one of the brothers disagreed. '*Yau!* She's beautiful, but was our older brother ugly? He was beautiful too, and she killed him: why do you say we shouldn't kill her but should marry her instead?'

The brothers argued back and forth. 'Let's marry her!' 'No:

let's kill her!' they shouted to each other. But finally they
decided to marry her. So they all left their camp and went to get
her. There were many of them, and they brought her home with
them to their camp.

When they arrived at the camp, she took out her medicine
horn, the kind that kills people. Then she blew: 'N!*aaaaa*! What
do you think you're doing, *yau*? First you kill me and now you
think you're going to marry me? What kind of marriage did you
have in mind? If this is what you're going to do, I'll see that all
of you die! Not one of you shall have me.' And that's just what
happened. With her magical horn, G!kon//'amdima flattened
them all. Every one of the brothers died. They were finished,
dead, and did not come back to life again. G!kon//'amdima went
home to her own camp. Now you've seen what things were like
in the long-ago time.

Told by //Xukxa N!a'an, Dobe, Botswana, 1971

DISCUSSION: WOMANLY POWER II

Though these heroine episodes, too, form a 'women's story', they begin with a reference to hunting. G!kon//'amdima's husband is killing duikers. In other versions, too, this element regularly appears – the hunting is not a mere aside. A 'women's story' is never separate unto itself: it is necessarily grounded in what the men are doing. The hunting of the duiker is connected to the ripening plant food bulbs at a specific season good for both duikers and the specific species of bulb (*dchuun, Walleria nutans Kirk.*). The two activities, hunting and gathering, together occasion the insult which begins the conflict between in-laws. The duiker's meat becomes a literal bone of contention which leads at last to violent confrontation.

Concern with the tensions of bride-service and marital residence is strongly etched in this story. Bride service among the Ju/'hoansi consists of living with and hunting for the bride's parents for the first several years of marriage. Lorna Marshall (1959:352) writes that the service is 'one of the most rigid social rules the !Kung have', and that it continues 'long enough for the boy's youth to have turned to manhood and for him to be looked upon as an able, responsible head of his family'.

Before they marry, too, boys must prove their ability to support a wife by killing one of the great meat animals. A boy's ceremony of the first kill precedes and is symbolically linked to that of his wedding. At the wedding itself the husband must bring an animal he has killed to his bride's parents. Informants told Marshall that 'a boy who never killed any large meat animal would not be given a wife' (L. Marshall 1959:352). Male identity and success are thus linked very closely both with hunting prowess and with the acquisition and maintenance of a bride and affinal family.

A great deal depends on a Ju/'hoan man's being given a wife by her parents. For the parents, the arrangement means meat, skin karosses, knowledge that their daughter is well cared for. The women who 'like meat' provided by a young husband include not only his new wife but his mother-in-law. For the in-laws, as Marshall (1959:351) points out, 'since they are related, both the sexual and the hunting powers of the young man can be captured at once with a bride'. The relationship of a man to his wife's parents is thus one of enormous interest to the Ju/'hoansi.

There is great expectation put upon the young man by the older people. Lorna Marshall (personal communicaton, Oct. 1974) noticed that new Ju/'hoan husbands tend to act in a very quiet, subdued, almost passive manner. They must be careful not only to provide well for their wives and their parents, but also not to violate any of the in-law avoidances that are newly required of them. It is easy to see how buried conflict could develop within a relationship so exacting and so important. It is not surprising at all that these tensions should turn up in the folklore.

As the story begins, G!kon//'amdima's husband is killing duikers and it is raining. He sees that the *dchuun* bulbs, which ripen in the rainy season, are ready to be gathered. The hunter's mother-in-law goes out with her granddaughter to gather them. So far all is well. But the peace is broken suddenly by the old woman's reference to her son-in-law's testicles. The drama has begun.

In speaking thus, the old woman assaults not only her son-in-law's ability to hunt but his very maleness. 'Was it here your father chased the duiker yesterday, so that his balls have fallen upon the ground?' The similarity of the *dchuun* bulbs to a man's testicles provides both the humour of the metaphor and the ambiguity which allows her to put the blame for her statement upon her innocent granddaughter. The suggestion that a mother-in-law might actually see her daughter's husband's private parts is deeply shocking, considering the avoidance relationship supposed to prevail between them.[12] But the further implication that she should see them after they have fallen off him is serious in yet another way. When Ju/'hoansi ridicule a man for laziness, they may say humorously that he sits around so much that 'his testicles are growing right into the sand'. Thus laziness (which in a man's case means lack of success in hunting) is also implied by his mother-in-law's insult. And if the hunter has left his testicles out there in the *dchuun* patch, he certainly has not got them any more. Thus the insult contains by implication the message, 'my son-in-law is not a man'. The old woman's bit of fun is thus a very dangerous social and sexual aspersion. Ordinarily, sexual joking of this sort would not go beyond the confines of the single-sex group of women gatherers. But the young child takes the insult home to her father. Children often function in Khoisan folklore as noticers and reporters of social breaches and other untoward situations. They act as a sort of chorus of shame, commenting on their elders' behaviour. This particular child, in her role as upholder of right relationships between in-laws, advances the plot by refusing to carry the meat of the duiker's intestines to the woman who has insulted her father. Ordinarily, children do perform this kind of small errand in a Ju/'hoan camp: they are usually the ones who are already on their feet, with unencumbered hands. They do it easily and without resistance most of the time, but when they do not want to for some reason, their refusal does not cause any surprise. They are not compelled to perform the errand or task, and usually the older person will eventually do it himself, as in this story.

The hunter must, therefore, confront his mother-in-law directly, violating the general pattern of avoidance between them. He returns the insult to his male achievement by chopping off the old lady's head.

His wife, meanwhile, has missed the insult and its consequence because she has been off gathering in another place. G!kon//'amdima first learns of the trouble when she sees that her mother's blood has flowed out and dried. The blood brings the knowledge of death just like the uterine fluid of the elephant girl which flows to her parents' camp. Then follows a motif which is widespread in Africa, that of the smoky fire utilised to conceal tears (Alan Dundes, personal communication, Aug. 1974). In some versions, G!kon//'amdima's husband, lulled by this ruse, goes on playing his musical hunting bow or lies back in masculine satisfaction, thinking lazily about taking his wife to bed. In one version there is a definite suggestion that G!kon//'amdima is bored silly with her husband's bow-playing – he has played it so much for so long. 'Wa-wa-wa-wo!' It sometimes goes on all night. 'Does this bow still deserve to live?' she asks herself, in one version. Out comes the big knife and, once it is heated red-hot, G!kon//'amdima uses it to avenge her mother. Striking in these

episodes of G!kon//'amdima's story, just as when she appears as the
elephant girl, is the theme of revenge and counter-revenge. Some
storytellers use the words /xao, 'to pay', and !hun/xao, literally, 'to
kill-pay', to describe the acts of vengeance among the in-laws. It has
been very hard to find out whether vengeance forays ever actually
took place to any great extent, or whether the Ju/'hoansi merely like
to think of themselves as having a glorious fighting past. In any case,
the folktales concentrate a great deal upon friction between allied
groups as expressed in terms of attack and counter-attack.

Insult between in-laws leads to retaliative murder, which is then
in turn avenged. For this last act of vengeance, G!kon//'amdima must
flee from affinal pursuers who wish to avenge their brother's death.
To elude them she tosses various obstacles over her shoulder,[13]
chiefly different kinds of thorns, and finally escapes by invoking the
aid of a raincloud. The cloud is almost like a familiar. In one version
it hides her in its darkness and then drops hail on her pursuers for
her:

> And the hail broke the strings of Kha//'an's and !Xoma's
> loincloths, so they just stood there naked. And the bows and
> arrows they had, with which they had been stalking her, just fell
> apart, beaten by the hail and the rain.
>
> So the brothers and the rain went back to their village
> together. And there the rain danced with them and danced with
> them and danced with them and made their things fall apart
> and ruined everything they had.

In a version collected by Lorna Marshall (10 Feb. 1953), 'the boys had
no more arrows. The poison was wet.' The cold familiars of the
heroine have turned aside the hot, male aggression.

The younger brothers pursue G!kon//'amdima with bows and
arrows, 'stalking' her as if she were an animal. It is a toss-up whether
they have come to marry her or to kill her. Again the metaphorical
equivalence of sex and hunting is reinforced. Her reaction to their
aggression is to launch an attack on their maleness and on their
hunting power. She enjoins the raincloud to break their bows and
arrows and the strings of their loincloths so that they stand finally, in

one version, *thasi n/a'ang*, 'wearing only their penises'. As two Kauri men said to me, 'A man has to have a loincloth if he wants to dance real medicine; a loincloth also makes a person run faster if he's chasing an animal.'

G!kon//'amdima's child is her helper in the flight episode. The little girl is a guinea fowl, a bird which gives good, audible warning of human approach, whether in bush or barnyard. Thanks to the guinea fowl, the thorns, and the rain, G!kon//'amdima eludes her pursuers.

The final episode is again that of the magical gemsbok horn. This horn, called a =*u*, is given to G!kon//'amdima by her grandmother. !Unn/obe put in an aside with this detail as she told her version of the story: 'Even long ago the Ju/'hoansi had this thing, a gemsbok horn to blow upon just like the one Old /Ukxa uses today. When you blow on it, it goes '*odi, odi, chodi*' – that is how it sounds.' The magical horn was specifically stated to be gemsbok.

One is reminded immediately of the tiny medicine bows and quivers, made of gemsbok horn, which outsiders have for so long called 'Bushman love bows' but which were really magical objects used in vengeance contexts by great *n/omkxaosi*. The detail is interesting, too, in the light of the beliefs about the power of supernatural gemsboks discussed in Section Two. The verb used to describe the action of the gemsbok horn is *xoian*. This word contains the meanings 'to curse' and 'to grind into powder'. It appears that this climax is the final downfall of the heroine's brothers-in-law.

But in one version the final adventure of G!kon//'amdima does not end with the mere vanquishing of yet another husband. After being hounded and harassed by a series of male adversaries, tricked, bereaved, killed, sought against her will in marriage, and pursued like wild game, the virtuous heroine has her final triumph by actually turning into a meat animal. /Asa N!a'an's version ended, 'Then G!kon//'amdima changed herself into something else, and became a steenbok. Her heart became a steenbok, the steenbok that the Ju/'hoansi shoot and take home to cook and eat. The first steenbok was once a person's heart, G!kon//'amdima's heart.'

The metaphor has come full circle. A woman pursued as meat

becomes meat by her own will, and since that time people have had game.

Here is the culminating facet of women's symbolic power. They are not only the providers of plant food and of sexual 'meat', but in their actions upon men and in their acts of will they cause game to exist and to be brought down. Men's sexuality, in contrast, has been likened in this story to plant food.

In the next series of stories, men's roles as providers of meat are explored. These stories deal with tricks played by Kaoxa, a male, upon women. The close balancing of trickery in these tales – in fact the equal pendulum-swings between preponderance of male power and preponderance of female power – provide further insight into Ju/'hoan attitudes on this crucial issue.

IV

Men and Women

I have heard the old people talk, and they say that this man
Kaoxa had two wives. They were all living together somewhere,
they and their children. And the man began all the trouble.

He went hunting one day: he went off hunting and was
searching for animals but couldn't find any. (Just as I heard the
story, I'm telling it to you.) And since he didn't see any animals,
he went home and they all went to sleep. In the morning he got
up and went hunting again. He hunted and hunted but didn't
see an animal. He knew that everyone in the camp was dying of
hunger. He said to himself, 'O, what am I going to do? What am
I going to take home for my wives to eat?'

Then he saw a tall tree. He climbed and climbed until he sat
in the top of it. Then he jumped out. When he hit the ground his
anus came out. It popped right out of his arse. So he cut it off
and sliced it up like meat. He sliced it into strips and put it in his
bag. Then he took grass and stopped up his empty arse. He
stopped himself up and went home with that meat. When the
sun was low he came to his camp.

The children cried 'Ho, ho, father has killed an animal, father
has killed an animal!'

Kaoxa kept his front turned toward the others.

'Don't go behind my back, you scamps,' he said to the

children. But they danced around until they were behind his
back anyway. They saw the grass sticking out of his arse and
couldn't imagine what it was. So they just went on praising him
for coming home with meat.

Kaoxa spread out the meat to dry. He took out one strip and
gave it to his older wife to roast. When it was done, she took it
out of the fire and knocked the ashes off it. Then she started to
pound it to make it soft. But it was so hard that it bounced out of
her hands and landed in Kaoxa's lap.

Then it disappeared. It had already gone back into Kaoxa's
arse. They looked for it and looked for it. Kaoxa kept a straight
face and just sat there. They looked and looked but couldn't find it.

'What on earth can have happened to it?' asked the wives.
'There's no dog here, so what can have taken it?' So they roasted
another piece.

This time the older wife said to the younger, 'You roast it and
knock the ashes off; let's see what will happen this time.' So the
younger wife roasted it. While she was pounding it the same
thing happened.

The wives said, 'This has got to stop. Tomorrow we're going
to have a look at this meat by daylight. This kind of thing is
something we've never seen before.' They hung the rest of the
meat in a tree, and everybody went to sleep.

In the morning when they got up the meat was all gone.

It had all gone back into Kaoxa's arse. The wives were very
surprised. They left the camp together asking each other, 'What
is this fellow up to? He's trying to torment us. Let's go and look
for bush food and think of a way to fool him.'

So they went off and soon they found a *tamah* melon. When
they saw it, they sat down and cut it open and took out the
seeds. Then they went home.

'What shall we do?' they said to each other. 'Let's cut off our
labia and hang them up to dry. Then we can pound them up
with the *tamah* seeds and set them aside for his food. When he
gets home he'll have something to eat, all right. He fooled us,
didn't he?'

So they did just what they said they would. They ate plain
melon with the children. Then they filled a bowl with the bad
stuff and set it aside for their husband.

When Kaoxa came home they took the bowl and gave it to
him. He started to eat it, and then said, '*Ai*. Who gave you two
such a nice piece of hide to pound up with the *tamah* seeds?'

'Um, where was it, um ... in an abandoned camp. We found
the skin of a baby giraffe. Someone had scraped it and rolled it
up and hung it inside a hut. It had rotted, and hunger got the
better of us, so we took it.'

'O!' said Kaoxa. 'It tastes so good and salty!'

Then they were all finished eating, and they went to sleep.
Kaoxa slept badly. He tossed and turned. He tried to sleep, but
the smell of what he had eaten kept bubbling up from his
insides into his nostrils. Finally he got really angry, and said,
'Oh, what on earth have those women given me to eat? What
can possibly be smelling so foul? I'll fix them ... they'll be sorry!'

In the morning they all got up and Kaoxa said, 'I'm going to
go off in this direction. Now you two gather carefully in this
other direction.'

Then he went off walking away from the camp. He walked
and walked, and as he walked he was thinking very hard. 'What
am I going to do to those two women?' He walked some more
and then he saw a nice *n=ai* tree.

Now today the balls of edible gum from this tree are red and
sweet. That's because on that day Kaoxa took his own testicles
and hung them up in the *n=ai* tree.

Then he went back to his wives, and said, 'I've found some very
nice gum. Tomorrow I'll take you both there so you can eat some.'

'Hooray for our husband!' shouted the wives. 'Where did you
find it?'

Over there,' he said. 'And I'm not fooling you, even though
you deceived me yesterday – no, I don't do that sort of thing. I
haven't a thought of that kind in my head.'

They all slept and when they got up in the morning they set
off. When they got to the *n=ai* tree the wives said, 'Yes, indeed,

it's nice gum! Ooo! Let's look for long sticks to poke it down with. Where will we find a long stick?'

But Kaoxa said, 'Oh, no, if you poke these balls of gum, all the gum will spill out. Why don't you climb the tree and get right up to them and bite them? That way you won't lose any of the gum.'

So the wives went up the tree. One went to one part of the tree and the other went somewhere else. They bit into the balls of gum – and the terrible things broke right into their mouths!

Kaoxa ran off, and his wives began to scream. They came down out of the tree crying, 'What are we going to do? What kind of man is this who has made us eat his bad things?' They complained and cried for a while, and then they left the tree. They thought of what they could do to get back at their husband.

'Let's make a baby giraffe,' they said to each other. 'And tomorrow he can go to kill it.'

So they spent the day doing that. They made the tracks of a big giraffe and the tracks of a baby giraffe. They made the tracks together, so that it looked like the baby giraffe was suckling. Then they dug a pit and defecated until it was full. They fashioned a baby giraffe from their defecations, and then said to each other, 'It's time to go home.'

When their husband came back to camp they said to him, 'We found a baby giraffe in the bush. Where were you hunting that you missed the giraffe? A cow giraffe has given birth, and we saw her. We saw the baby giraffe lying on the ground after it was born. Tomorrow we'll go back there so you can kill it.'

Kaoxa said, 'My wives, my wonderful wives.' He was very happy. In the morning they got their things together and went after the baby giraffe. Kaoxa took his spear with him. 'I'll stab it with my spear,' he said.

But the wives disagreed. 'If you spear it all the blood will run out. We don't want the blood to spill; we want to eat every bit of that baby giraffe. Why do you want to spear it? Just jump and grab it. Then we'll help you kill it.' So Kaoxa jumped. *!'am*! he

landed in the middle of the pile of shit. The wives ran off. Kaoxa
lay there and shouted. He wiped himself off, muttering, 'Death
take their crotches! Are these women crazy?'

Finally he was free of the stuff and walked away. As he
walked he thought and thought. 'What am I going to do to those
wives of mine?' Then he saw some bush food that people call
='angg=oa [Bauhinea macrantha]. Seeing them, he decided to
make a big patch of ='angg=oa bushes. He did that. But they
weren't just bushes: they looked like ='angg=oa but they were
really people. When he had stood the ='angg=oa people in a
clump like he wanted them, Kaoxa went home. He said to his
wives, 'There's a patch of ='angg=oa over there. Tomorrow we'll
go and peel some and roast them to eat. We'll shell them and
pound them and bring them home to eat.'

'All right,' said the two wives. They slept, and in the morning
they packed their things and went to the ='angg=oa patch.

Kaoxa was the first to get there because the women were
walking slowly. He whispered to the ='angg=oa, 'I'm bringing
you some people who have really done me wrong. Now you
just sit there and wait for them. I'm going on ahead.'

When Kaoxa had got right into the main clump of ='angg=oa
he called out to his wives, 'Come on and walk faster. Catch up
with me so we can eat some ='angg=oa.'

As the wives came into the clump of bushes, the ='angg=oa
people began to beat them with sticks. They beat them and beat
them and cracked their heads open. The wives cried and cried
for help, but Kaoxa was gone: he had run away.

'Hey,' the wives yelled. 'What sort of husband is this who has
married us and then treats us this way? Why should such a big
important person treat people like this? Why doesn't he take
good care of us? Instead he's tormenting us.' The two wives
went home. They stayed there until their husband came.

'By the way, we didn't see any ='angg=oa,' they said to him.
'All we saw was a bunch of people. We went into the midst of
them and they nearly beat us to death.'

'You must have got lost,' said Kaoxa. 'You went the wrong

way. There's another camp over there and you stumbled right
into it.'

'But we were following your footsteps and that's how we
nearly got killed!'

But Kaoxa said, 'Impossible. I didn't see anybody at all on the
trail that I took.'

The wives lived in discontent for some time. Kaoxa was
satisfied and fed them well, but they were discontented just the
same.

One day one of the wives said, 'I think I'll go and visit my
family.'

Kaoxa refused, and said, 'No, you're not; we're staying here.
Why should we go and visit them – they never visit us.'

So they stayed. But the wife got restless. 'How can I get
away?' she wondered.

One day when Kaoxa and his son went hunting, she simply
ran off alone. The other wife sat in the camp alone and waited
for her husband to return.

The wife who had left did not return. The other wife stayed at
the camp alone, waiting for her husband. He was off hunting
but he did not bring home anything for her to eat. Hunger
began to work upon her, and she grew very thin. Soon she had
no fat on her buttocks – they were nothing but skin.

One day Kaoxa killed a fat eland far from his camp and came
home at last to bring the news.

'Hai? Where's my other wife?' he asked.

'Oh, she's left,' answered the wife who had stayed.

'And you?' asked Kaoxa 'why do you look so terrible?'

'Hunger, obviously,' she replied.

'Well, if you're going to look like this I'm leaving,' said
Kaoxa. 'You're probably just starving yourself so you'll have an
excuse to leave me and run after other men. I'm leaving, and
you'll just have to sit here. I'm not interested in a woman who's
so thin. You're awfully thin and ugly and you don't interest me
at all.'

With that, Kaoxa took his son and began packing up their

belongings. The wife just sat there. Kaoxa packed all his things into a string carrying bag. As they were leaving, his son put out his hand and drew his mother to her feet.

'Please, mother, follow us, I beg you,' he said.

So she walked secretly behind them when they left. After they had walked a long while, father and son sat down to rest. The son sneaked to where his mother was and found her a comfortable place to sit. Kaoxa rested and ate something and then they travelled further.

After a while the son asked his father, 'Are we almost there?'

'Don't worry – the meat is there. We'll come to it,' answered Kaoxa.

When they came to the dead eland, Kaoxa and his son began cutting it up right away. Kaoxa skinned it and broke its body open. Then he took out its intestines. He dipped out the chyme with his cupped hands and dumped it on the ground. He was still dipping out the chyme when his son said to him, 'Father, let mé take the chyme and throw it away for you. I want to watch the dung beetles eat it.'

[Aside:] The son wanted the chyme to smooth on the ground for his mother, so she would have a nice place to sit.

So the father gave it to him and the child sat his mother upon it. Then he came back.

'Father!' he said. 'Won't you give me that bit of fat so I can watch the dung beetles eat it?'

Kaoxa cut out the piece of fat for him and he went and gave it to his mother to eat.

The son went back and forth between his father and his mother. He spent the whole day taking bits of food to his mother one by one. He and his father would eat a little and then he would take something like the bladder and go to his mother.

'I'm going to play with the dung beetles and eat my meat over there,' the son would say. Then he would go and give whatever it was to his mother.

At last the sun hung low in the sky. Kaoxa said, 'Since it's so late already, I think we'll just go to sleep and wait until morning to fetch water.'

'All right,' said his son. He went and told his mother. Then they all went to sleep. The wife slept in one place and her husband and son slept together not far away. In the night the son went to check on his mother several times. In the morning Kaoxa went off to fetch water, leaving his son in their new camp. When he was gone, the son told his mother to come and sit with him in the camp. Today she was fat, and very beautiful. She sat with her son in the camp as if she were a lovely python girl.

When a little time had passed, Kaoxa returned and saw her. '*Hai*! Is this my son who's sitting with such a beautiful woman? Who can it be?' He asked his son, 'Has your mother returned?'

'Yes, mother has come,' he answered.

'What has she been eating that makes her look so good?'

'I don't know: she looked like this when she got here,' he said. Kaoxa dropped his water containers and ran to his wife.

He climbed on top of her and right away he began screwing her very hard.

Her son cried, 'Hey! Didn't you nearly kill my mother with hunger, and then abandon her so that I had to feed her myself? Who do you think made her beautiful again? If you think you're going to screw her now, I'll fix you!'

Kaoxa was still lying on top of his wife and refused to get off.

'Father, give me your axe so I can sharpen it and eat the eland bones,' said his son. 'Hand me the whetstone too.' All the while Kaoxa lay on top of his wife and continued to screw her. Suddenly ... (snap!) The boy had chopped his father in two with the axe! He did it to get him off his mother.

[Aside:] He no longer wanted his mother to be his mother; he wanted to marry her.

Then he lifted up his father's body. He took the top half and threw it one way, and threw the bottom half the other way.

'When did *you* suddenly grow up?' asked his mother, as she sat up.

'Will you make a fire so we can warm ourselves, mother?' he asked.

'Certainly, my son.'

'I'm not your son any more.'

'Well, what am I going to call you now? How about my little brother?' But he refused that name too.

'My nephew?' But he refused again.

'What am I going to call this child?' she wondered out loud. 'My husband?' (snap!) That was all he wanted. He jumped up and ran to the fire. He was looking for =u=usi, these little black insects that smell bad and crawl around near the fire. When he saw some he lay down in their midst. He wanted them to bite his penis so it would swell up and he would be able to do what he wanted. Well, the =u=usi bit him nearly to death. His penis swelled up until it was enormous. It was so big he couldn't take his mother with it.

He had spoiled his own chances! The things that went on long ago ... This is what the old people tell, and this is what I have heard.

Told by !Unn/obe N!a'an, Kauri, Botswana, 1972

DISCUSSION: THE BALANCE OF SEXUAL POWER

Stories about G!ara or Kaoxa, such as these involving him and his wives in a struggle for power, do not deal with the remote, sky-dwelling creator god of Ju/'hoan religious conception but with a very earth-bound trickster. Some of his many bumbling exploits have been presented in the foregoing text.

How are we to account for the fact that the same group of names (Hice, Hoe, G!ara, G//aoan, and so on) is applied to two apparently different beings, one all too human, the other a god?

One possibility and perhaps the best, is to see creator and trickster as two facets of a single important character.

Other suggestions, though, have been advanced by a number of writers. Schapera presents an array of conceptions from the religious systems of all the Khoisan peoples and shows the mutual influences and borrowings which took place among them. He is careful to make the point that these interrelated systems are markedly different from the Bantu religious systems which surround them today.[14]

Using Schapera's compilation and the reports of the many other researchers who have worked on the religious beliefs of the several Khoisan groups, Lorna Marshall (1962:233) has presented a possible explanation for the dual Ju/'hoan conception. She surmises that the sky god concept came in as a result of Bergdama and Khoi influence. The name Hoe was probably adopted by the Ju/'hoansi from the Bergdama, whose central religious concept, Schapera (1930:398) tells us, was an elaborately described creator god who controlled the weather and gathered about him in his sky home the souls of the dead. Further, the name Hice apparently found its way to the Ju/'hoansi from the Narons and =Kao//'ae (Auen), who were much influenced by the Khoi concept of *Heitsi Eibib*, 'a sort of ancestral hero ... who is worshipped at his graves where he is prayed to for success in hunting, etc.'

Though the picture is as yet very confusing, especially when the beliefs and mythology of the Cape and Basutoland Bushmen peoples are brought into it, it appears that the dual conception shared with the Ju/'hoansi by a number of central and northern Bushman groups may represent beliefs from two different historical strata. What these strata may be in any precise terms is, of course, extremely difficult to say. Another possible explanation is that both concepts were anciently held by Bushman peoples at some time, but came to share a name or set of names.

For now, let us merely note that the trickster incarnation seems to belong to an entirely separate realm of belief from that of the Ju/'hoan creator. The virtually complete absence in the folktales of details associated with the sky god, the lesser god, the spirits of the dead, and other supernatural beings discussed by Ju/'hoansi in the same cosmological vein gives support to the making of this distinction. A similar separation held for the Greek epic figures who were also supposed to have been gods. As Havelock (1963:171) writes, 'the Homeric saga is itself largely indifferent to the gods as objects of cult ... cult subsists only at the margins of the story, not at its centre'. For both Ju/'hoan and Greek oral tradition, then, it seems as if the earthly exploits of the gods were placed in a separate realm from their roles in religion as creators and divinities.

Turning to the characteristics shown by Kaoxa (or G!ara, G//aoan, and others) in the tales, we note that his adventures can be described as a series of tricks on other characters. He tricks women, some of whom are his wives, he tricks his brothers-in-law (who appear in many forms) and he tricks a number of different animals. Kaoxa's tricks sometimes have serious and sometimes merely funny outcomes. In the case of the tricks played on his wives (and returned by them), the outcomes are usually funny, ending in mutual discomfiture and impasse. In the cases of tricks he plays on animals and his strange brothers-in-law, the consequences are sometimes of obvious concern to the life of mankind. But both sorts of trick serve serious ends by creating social meanings.

Real 'Creation' tales as such, unlike the adventures of this buffoon figure, involve a sentient creator (see Boas 1915:329). Though the Ju/'hoansi do not have tales about the benefactions of the sky god Kaoxa, they do say in conversation that he created this or that. Some accounts of his creations seem to contradict the folktale accounts of accidental discoveries made by Kaoxa the trickster. The contradictions provide additional support for viewing the two figures as belonging to separate areas of belief.

In the Ju/'hoan trickster tales with beneficial outcomes for mankind, Kaoxa is usually involved with an antagonist who possesses magical or superhuman powers. The benefaction comes about through his desire to possess these powers, or their fruits, for himself. In the tales of his tricks on women, however, there is a balance between his powers and theirs. In fact, the major theme of these stories appears to be 'tit for tat'. Back and forth the trickeries fly, sex for sex, excrement for excrement. There is a dynamic quality about these exchanges, a muscular balance, a 'working relationship' in the most active of senses. We learn much about the relative potencies attributed to men and women in Ju/'hoan society by observing this objectified balance.

It is very much the world of adult relationships with which the series deals. This is not merely childish muck-slinging. The humour of each trick and counter-trick lies in giving the social dynamic an objective form in terms of gobbets and piles of filth. We as outsiders are not the only ones who learn about Ju/'hoan social attitudes in this way: as Elizabeth Marshall Thomas noted in one of her transcriptions of the series (14.2.53), 'There has been much hilarity from the adults listening to this story but the children have been listening to it openmouthed and without a smile.' Real learning is going on in this recreational context.

Part of the children's education is seeing separate spheres of interest defined for the sexes. The men are hunters, the women, gatherers. But transgression of the boundary between these realms does not bring supernatural sanctions in the world of the tales. Instead it is detailed graphically what happens in the human world if men step too far into the women's sphere and vice versa. The tales are 'didactic', but only by indirection; they outline the consequences of social action rather than preach.

There is a specific equation made in the tales between women's sphere and women's sexuality, and between men's sphere and men's sexuality. Incursions into these spheres by the opposite sex most often take the form, in these tales, of sexual befoulment. Men can hunt, and one weapon they can use against women is deception about the fruits of the hunt. They can bring home anything and call it meat. Similarly, women can put amazing ingredients into plant foods they have gathered and secretly prepared.

However, an absolute distinction of women and plants versus men and meat is not made in these stories, and Ju/'hoan practice is not that strict either. In the various versions Kaoxa uses animal instruments like springbok, antbear ribs, duikers' chests, baby wildebeests, and his own extruded and biltonged (dried, cured) anus to fool his wives or befoul them sexually; but just as often he employs vegetable materials like balls of red tree gum, =*'angg=oa* bushes and their pods, or *kito'an* fruits to do his dirty work. The wives, similarly, use not only vegetable products such as *tamah* melon seeds, *kito'an* fruits, and =*'angg=oa* but also the feet, skin, or blood of a baby giraffe or eland to do theirs.

In general, the women trick their husband into eating their sexual parts or falling into a pit of sexual secretions or excrement. He tricks them into biting into his testicles or anus or makes love to them in the guise of dead meat. In a version collected by Melvin Konner (personal communication, Feb. 1971), he is reconstituted after one such episode from his own penis, which the wives have discarded thinking it is only the penis of an antbear. In some versions both Kaoxa and his wives get into each other's stomachs by pretending to be plant food, then laugh or giggle there, making life unbearable. One informant explicitly said that Kaoxa wanted to make love to the women so he tricked his way inside them by turning into ripe *kito'an*, which looks like a red cucumber. When the wives are eaten in turn, they sometimes pop right out through Kaoxa's stomach wall and he has to be sewn up again by obliging flies. 'This is the same thing you did to us!' the wives crow.

A trick is thus a retaliation for another trick. In the text just presented, told by a woman storyteller, 'The man began all the trouble', and the wives' tricks are their reaction to it. For a while, in the field, I thought that Kaoxa was always the initiator of the tricks. He was, when the storytellers were women. But one day I heard the story from an old man.

'/Xoan N!a'an's been telling you all wrong,' he said. 'She hasn't told you that it was the women who began it, in the beginning.'

He then proceeded to tell the story himself, starting out, 'The women lived and thought, What shall we do to this man?' One day they played around as if they were urinating, but really they were getting together a pile of sexual secretions. Then they dug a big hole ...'

For men, doubtless, it seems as if women begin all the trouble. The admirable balance of this trick series allows both men and women to express vexation at each other by starting it where they please.

There might seem some overbalancing in the direction of male importance in that Kaoxa is personified, while his wives are not even named. The folktale wives, as women, however, do have social ammunition which is uniquely their own. In a motif which recurs in some versions (and also in other Ju/'hoan stories), they taunt their husband by comparing him to the males in their own family. He wants to spear the 'baby giraffe', but they say that if their uncles or fathers or older brothers were there, they would leap right upon it and kill it so no blood would be lost. His competitive spirit lands him right in the hole, where they want him.

In another story the women get back at Kaoxa by overdoing their roles as women. The trickster chides his wives for not building a house, and when they do build it, just in time for the rains, they build it so well that he cannot find the door.

He sloshes about outside while they sit in comfort and laugh at him. He blows and blows his magic gemsbok horn, but shelter does not appear for him.

One message of the trick series, then, as well as of the adventures of G!kon//'amdima, is that women are in a strong position in Ju/'hoan society. That they 'like meat', for instance, is not just taken as a whim, to be gratified or not as males choose, but as a biological and social fact with which men must creditably reckon. If they do not, they risk the censure, not only of women but of other males, in particular of males in their wives' families of birth. The need to have a good working relationship with in-laws is a powerful social force on the behaviour of husbands towards their wives.

Finally, in the last episode of the trick series, it is clear that Kaoxa even risks the murderous fury of his own son by withholding meat – but taking sex – from the boy's mother. Ultimately he is unseated and nearly replaced by this son as his wife's sexual partner, just because he has failed to heed the elementary social stipulation that 'women like meat'.

Chapter Seven

Technology and Metaphor

Oh, foolish man. Why do you marry that
which is meat and call it a wife?

G/ui Bushman

Life's greatest danger consists in the fact ... that
man's food consists entirely of souls.

Iglulik Inuit

... all relationships between things, material goods, precious
objects and values, are in fact relationships between men,
relationships which men express and dissemble at the same
time... this, all anthropologists must understand and
recognize as the aim of all their theoretical labors.[1]

French anthropologist

Ju/'hoan stories show us that a metaphorical equation of women
with meat animals and men with their hunters can provide a plentiful
landscape for social comment. As I suggested in the Introduction, this
simple transposition in the folklore provides a wealth of provocative
figures and situations for the exploration of social relatedness.
Women demand meat as their social right, and they get it – otherwise

187

they leave their husbands, marry elsewhere, or make love to other men.

At the same time women 'are meat' to men, to be pursued with bows and arrows and 'eaten' with relish if the men are successful. Last, women triumph over the cannibal and incestuous mistakes of men by choosing to transform themselves into the meat that they both 'like' and 'are like'. They maintain their social position by insisting on being their own, quite adequate, powerful selves.

Referring to transpositions like this in other cultures, Maurice Godelier (1977) speaks of the 'phantasmic nature' of social relations as known through their representations. It is in fact not rare but generally true, he says, that the real conditions of life in society gradually become 'ethereal' as they appear in expressive forms. 'Fetishised' representations of society in art have a strangely inside-out or upside-down character, with relations between people appearing to be relations between things, and vice-versa.

What are we to make of the apparent universality of these transpositions? Does it indicate that this kind of metaphorical operation has been selected for through time, because of its usefulness within the mental technology of human societies? Trying to answer these questions will raise the following problems:

1. whether folklore 'reflects' society or 'refracts' it,
2. what 'work' may be done for society in the 'special reality' of art forms,
3. what relation is borne by the ordinary reality of ethnography to the special reality of art, and
4. what adaptive value can be suggested for expressive forms in general?

FOLKLORE: REFLECTION OR REFRACTION OF CULTURE?

It is clear that folklore does not mirror cultural reality in any simple way. Texts do 'speak about the world,' says Ricoeur (1976:37), but not descriptively. Instead, an oral performer uses cultural materials as any artist uses the elements of his art. Both build upon the interest which members of the culture have in these elements from previous experience of them. 'If the narrative tradition does mirror culture,' writes Harold Scheub (1977:345), 'it does so only in intricate, aesthetically perceived forms, which ultimately have the same effect on an audience as art and music do.'

The relation of dramatised, imaginary events to practical reality and their role in facilitating social and economic survival is therefore far from easily perceived. Instead of 'reflecting' nature or even social ideals in any literal way, folklore comments on both with great obliqueness, often seeming bizarre and incomprehensible in its fracturing of the normal order of reality. Dramatic confrontation between characters may be replaced by interactions among objects.

Characters may act in ways which appear to contradict their actions at other times. Yet somehow, from this kaleidoscope of contradictory views of the human condition, vital information and rules for conduct are extracted by audiences.

Joseph Russo and Eric Havelock, both interested in this didactic capacity of narrative, have suggested useful explanations for the puzzling contradictions to be found in the Greek epics. Russo (1978:49) sees the momentary creation of atypical situations which resolve into a renewed world order as the best way to reinforce 'the social, political, and cosmic normalities'. Havelock (1978b) writes that special language use such as that in epic reflects a paradoxical awareness of social and anti-social attitudes in man, both of which must be taken account of. He also emphasises that pragmatic attitudes must of necessity vary according to various situations. If the same character appears to act differently sometimes, what is being stressed is the situational appropriateness of his action rather than the character as an unvarying type.

Victor Turner (1967) and the literary critic Morse Peckham (1965) have more recently advanced a somewhat different but equally attractive view. They see aesthetic movements as 'liminal' in that they suspend the ordinary cultural rules of logic and equivalence in favour of a freer kind of contemplation. Art reveals, in this view, the fragments from which the supposedly coherent world is built and dares to recombine them in new ways which may be significant.

David Lewis-Williams (1981), writing on the rock art of Bushman peoples, goes further with this view to stress that art is 'dialogic' in character. It discourses upon valued ideas by putting them into dramatic confrontation with each other, and what it teaches comes out of this confrontation. In other words, it is not didactic in any simple sense but is so indirectly, rather as a debate might be.

A provocative essay by the anthropologist Jean Briggs (1982) takes a related perspective on the educational effect of dramatic games played by the Inuit with their children. Briggs offers convincing evidence that adherence to desired values is cemented by dramatised conflict over them which is experienced vividly in the games. She quotes Birket-Smith's Iglulik shaman ('man's food consists entirely of souls') as I have done at the beginning of this chapter, to indicate that aggression is problematic for the Inuit.

'Ostensibly, they enjoy it when the object of the aggression is an animal and fear it when the object is human ... but in a hunting society it is not easy to keep animals and men comfortably compartmentalized' (Briggs 1982:115). The problem of aggression is 'solved' by being explored, looked at from all sides; a dangerous blend of its elements is memorably experienced and resolved in vicarious form, in this case through a dramatic game.

Briggs's view is a useful one for students of other hunting-gathering societies: the Bushman 'problem' with women and meat is clearly similar. The 'foolish man' of G/ui Bushman folklore and his counterpart in Ju/'hoan stories, G!kon//'amdima's husband, know very well the differences between animals and people. But it is so important to distinguish between the correct aggressive attitudes towards the two – one for killing, one for sex – that the lesson is reinforced through the imaginary sense of dangerous confusion that can be harmlessly roused in the folktales.

This approach suggests, in fact, a comprehensive understanding of the 'positive' uses of 'negative' or 'upside-down' representations. The Ju/'hoan trickster, for example, like similar figures in the folklore of other hunter-gatherers, is a bumbling, almost anti-human character through whose exploits the realm of proscribed behaviour is dramatically explored.

And yet world order is established somehow, in spite of and even because of all his mistakes. Children and adults learn right behaviour partly by observing the consequences and participating in the danger of wrong behaviour. This is not just a modern educational truism: complex, dramatic playing through of the 'wrong way' as an aid to internalisation of the 'right way' seems to be an ancient device of cultural reinforcement that we are only now coming to understand.

Moreover, transpositions in meaning, such as food and souls for the Iglulik, meat and women for the Ju/'hoansi, create at one stroke the possibility for fruitful exploration into social and economic issues. The ways in which women's strengths may be probed are manifold if women are not limited to appearing in human form. The ways a man's plans may backfire on him are unexpectedly numerous if his food has the capacity to turn itself at whim into souls.

For Ju/'hoansi, women may be represented or suggested in tales by the moon, honey, breast milk, pythonesses, certain kinds of skin bag, gentle rain, and uterine fluids which appear to have minds of their own. Men and the inhabitants of their domain, which includes hot medicine smoke, weapons and arrow poison, ungentle rain, and the sun, interact with female figures and objects in dramatic situations. There is some concentration by Ju/'hoan women and girls on the telling of women's tales, and there is also some by men and boys on the tales that are mostly about men. But both are familiar with all the tales, especially those, the most numerous group, which deal with men and women in dramatic confrontation. No matter which sex appears to have the upper hand at any given moment, the stories are 'making sense' to both men and women. This making of sense in stories has everything to do with contexts that are outside of stories. Semantics internal to a story have a two-way relationship with external cultural circumstances. Meaning that is also meaningful in art draws its significance from actuality. But the nature of the comment upon reality made in a representation may be paradoxical in the extreme. Reality may be turned on its head in order to be seen better. This process may in turn affect how reality is later viewed. It is a dialectical process, in other words, this making of sense. For the Ju/'hoansi, power issues and gender issues are at the core of social reality, but the elements of the balance negotiated by society are semantic terms. And the balance must be negotiated and renegotiated, just as sense must be made and remade each time an old story is told anew. The semantic relationships for framing social issues originate in the 'freer' world of stories, where men and women may sling muck and unspeakable insults at each other. An old story told for generations may provide a framework for 'new' bad words to be bandied about, or it may allow for a slight balance-shift in sexual power, due perhaps to historical circumstances, to be explored.

Stories' comments are not just passive representations: they generate sense for circumstances beyond the stories themselves. They deal in actualities, the prime realities of social experience, but they do so dialectically: they constantly 'make new sense' by reflecting upon social reality as currently understood. The sexual balance of power so prominent in Ju/'hoan tales is just one of the social issues explored in storytelling. Many other areas of social and economic life – in fact all aspects of adaptation – are also affected by the creative processes of the expressive forms.

THE 'SPECIAL REALITY' OF ORAL FORMS

The hidden teaching capacities, and the sense-making functions, of folklore and dramatic games suggest we examine in a general way the 'work' such forms may perform in society.

I advance the possibility that certain social tasks may be accomplished exclusively in the special world of expressive forms. It seems, to begin with, that this world is a realm of play whose rules not only allow but demand a heightened manipulation of reality for social ends. It has the capacity to involve individuals at a deeper level than their mere participation in a shared cognitive system. There is a kind of cultural rumination endlessly going on there, a milling process that brings the unseen into harmony with the seen, the old with the new; all aspects of the ongoing life of society are its grist. Both Bateson (1972) and Godelier (1977) have remarked upon this important unifying 'work' done by artistic forms in bringing together visible and invisible structures of cultural life. Expressive forms may perhaps accomplish things for society, in other words, that can be done in no other way. In the region of 'special realities' lies a huge reservoir of adaptive potential for our species, since images of reality, being phantasmagoric, are virtually limitless, and can encompass immense change.

Such a view should allow us to understand the place in culture of what seems on the surface to be supererogatory artistic behaviour, which is actually integral to the life of traditional societies. Individuals and social groups act through expressive forms to articulate meanings that must be shared in order to perpetuate society as an entity of shared understandings. The forms work by containing, exploring, commenting on, turning inside out, and in a myriad ways reinforcing the cognised models (to use Rappaport's apt term) which keep cultural systems continuing in their environments.

Put broadly, they embody what Reichel-Dolmatoff (1971:xv) calls 'the meaning of the environment, the native's *intelligence du milieu*': it is clear how very social this concept of '*intelligence*' must be, and of what vital importance therefore are the expressive mechanisms which fix and convey it.

The 'special reality' of art forms, then, makes a specific communicative contribution to culture. In this perspective, folklore, rock paintings, dramatic games, dance, and other expressive forms should be regarded as integral parts of the communication systems required to make certain adaptations successful. In the case of the Ju/'hoansi, despite recent changes, the wresting of a livelihood from a harsh, semi-arid environment for a very long time with handmade tools, depending as absolutely as it has upon social co-operation of a very particular sort, has been intimately connected with the dramatic verbal and visual arts which both 'make sense' and provide a framework for survival information.

ETHNOGRAPHY AND 'SPECIAL REALITY'

The realm of art, as we have seen, juggles with the elements of ordinary reality for special purposes. What then can ordinary reality, here the ethnography of the Ju/'hoansi, tell us about the meaning of the elements which are used in folktales? For one thing, it can tell us what associations the items and relationships which appear in folklore have in other contexts. All such connections are potential contributors to an item's metaphorical meaning. Both everyday discourse and the world of oral expression provide us with linguistic proof that certain associations are indeed made; if we further understand an item's uses in non-verbal contexts we have an added depth of association to draw upon. The symbolism of the tales, explored in previous sections, expands our knowledge of Ju/'hoan cognitive symbolism in general. The concepts of the trance dance give us insight into concepts used to generate agreements and consensus in daily contexts.

Oral tradition, then, gives us up-to-date information about contemporary symbolism: we can hear the connections being made by storytellers themselves, the carriers of tradition, and can see them being corroborated by audiences. Existing ethnography can be utilised to further strengthen the case for certain associations, and can provide a depth of reference, for the non-native, to simulate the native's past cultural experience. Gathered correctly, then, the data of belief, as revealed through expressive forms, are as real as any other kind of data, and they can be handled as precise tools.

At the basis of this approach to the cultural truth contained in artistic forms is a respect for the integrity of cultural metaphors as they are presented. Like Lewis-Williams (1982:431) in his analysis of Bushman rock painting, we can take 'metaphors preserved in Bushman ethnography' as data in themselves needing no further abstraction by us. Rather than reduce them to a bare system of equivalences, it is fruitful to take these sometimes contradictory cultural metaphors where and as we find them, as constitutive elements not only of expressive life but of attitudes toward life in general. Life's necessary information, its understandings and techniques, together form its mental technology, a realm absolutely dependent on metaphor for meaning and communication. Metaphors for everyday contexts are honed upon their use in special contexts – and the reverse is also true. Thus if we refer them clearly to ethnography, oral texts can clarify vital cultural concerns.

Throughout this book we have been looking at some of the fundamental problem points of Ju/'hoan Bushman life as revealed by an ethnographic analysis of their ritual and folklore. We have seen that the following crucial areas – sickness, initiation, hunting, childbirth, weather, and danger from carnivores – are related to each other by five key metaphors of transformation. Each of these metaphors, in turn, is connected with the symbolic power of animals. Animals function as operators to mediate within pairs of opposite states of being toward desirable outcomes of coolness, maturity, well-being, safety and transcendence. The Ju/'hoansi's use of metaphoric animal power to influence environment gives us clues about how they regard their environment and their relationship to it. Certain areas of life for the Ju/'hoansi – like the pursuit of animal protein in a sparse, semi-arid environment – are chancy, and men resort to supernatural power to supplement knowledge and skill.

Folklore and other symbolic expressions provide social scientists with abundant primary data, both about environmental adaptation and about attitudes toward the social and supernatural worlds on which agreement and action are based.

Further, we have seen from the foregoing discussion of the Ju/'hoansi's male and female creation stories and of the give-and-take of power between men and women, that one basic symbolic scheme which readily emerges for this folklore is founded in a polarity between men and women, the two main social categories. References to women's puberty rites in the tales symbolise the establishment of one vision of world order, men's, another. However, the two creations are analogous in structure. Ju/'hoan people, telling the stories, use the same sand diagram to describe both creations.

The equal-but-different male and female symbolic roles extend to many events and items which interact in the tales. Women are connected with gathered foods, the moon, cold, water, protection from heat, menstruation, breast milk, *san* power, herbivorous animals, and a number of other 'female' attributes. Men are associated with hunted foods, heat, fire, the sun, trance, curing, arrows and arrow-poison, carnivores, and medicine smoke. In no story, however, does one of these sets of attributes appear to the exclusion of the others; always they are in dynamic interaction with each other. In women's stories we always hear what the men are hunting, for example; in men's stories the women's activities are rarely far removed from the scene of action. In stories involving ritual, where for example men are preparing to initiate boys, women are always sitting by their fires pounding ochre for the ceremony.

Mediation between the opposite sexual spheres centres around a comprehensive metaphor linking eating and intercourse. Men hunt and 'eat' women as carnivores prey on herbivores. Fat as a liquid solid, the 'cool' result of the union of hot and cold, is used as an alternative mediator. The consumption of fat is metaphoric of the sexual mediation between semen (hot) and menstrual blood (cold).

Mediation solves cognitive problems generated by the necessarily bounded nature of cultural categories. From the mediation between opposing spheres comes drama, the possibility of forward movement into desired resolutions. Thus symbolic mediation is an essential ingredient of imaginary narrative, providing both impetus and realistic action in the events and changes of plot. Its capacity to make believable drama among characters and objects is a vital part of its mnemonic function. It has been adaptive both because it reinforces social categorisation by temporarily rearranging it and because it makes important attitudes dramatically memorable.

Symbolic mediation ideas developed in the freer world of expressive forms like trance dancing and stories do service in other contexts. Metaphors which appear in folklore are in common use in everyday life. Dahm N!a'an, a Ju/'hoan man, described a good hunter as fearful of eating or sleeping with his wife lest his poison get cold because she smelled of milk and *san*. Coming home after a successful hunt, however, such a hunter would greet his wife with special fervour. He would 'praise the meat', Dahm N!a'an said, lying next to his wife with his face between her breasts. He would see her buttocks and her legs and would be happy 'because the meat had fat and was fat'. Eating, and sleeping with, are equated symbolically in this statement. Milk and *san* are also equated. Both pairs of words represent contact with female power which would cause the arrow poison to get cold. The hunter would fail in the hunt. When he comes home successful, however, he can immerse himself joyfully in the things which tie animals and women together. It is hard to tell, even in this piece of everyday discourse, which meat – animal or woman – is being discussed. The metaphors tying women to the enchanted, hunted prey are so intricate as utterly to defy untangling.

For another instance of this intricacy, consider the identification of women dancers with cow elands in the Eland Bull Dance of men-arche. The menstruating girl is secluded in a hut. The other women dance around the hut for her.

Nicholas England (1968:596) has written this evocative account of the women's movements:

Eland dancing is heavier and more deliberate than any other. It can perhaps be best described as a moderately slow, flat-footed run in which the body weight is allowed to settle firmly on each alternate foot as it is planted on the ground; indeed, at the moment of impact, all of the dancer's flesh sags toward the ground, graphically illustrating the direction of the weight. And her body ornaments follow the motion downwards, adding a small but clear clicking sound effect to the movement. The feet land flat and firm on each step, producing a thud in the sand. And all of this occurs at the moment of the sharp sound – 'clink' describes it best in words – from the adze-blades, for the dance step follows the beat of the /'aisi [adzes] exactly. The entire effect conjures a picture of the grandly muscular, fleshy eland, trotting along unhurriedly in the veld. In fact, informants say that the clinking of the /'aisi is used purposely to imitate the sound that the eland makes under such circumstances.

There seems to be an association of animal fat, women's reproductive ripeness, and the sound of clinking metal used to initiate the characteristic clicking sound made by elands' leg bones when they walk. In fact, sleek-skinned, fertile G!kon//'amdima's clinking bangles are one of her most constant attributes.

In one version of the story the heroine (here named !Au!aua instead of G!kon//'amdima) is apprehended by her pursuers because of the sound of her ornaments.

> After a while, they heard someone coming down to the water. Kha//'an said to his younger brother, 'Here she comes.' But !Xoma contradicted him, saying, '*Yau*. When !Au!aua comes down you'll know her by the sound of her approach. Do you think !Au!aua is so poor that we will not hear the clinking of her bracelets and her anklets? There will be no doubt about it when she comes.'
> So they waited until they heard '*n/enu, n/enu, n/enu, n/enu*'; she came down with her bangles clinking...

In another story Kaoxa's wife, this time appearing as a *=hamsa* bird, dances gracefully, making the clinking sound '*!a=ain, !a=ain, !a=ain*'. In a description by the curer Kxao Giraffe of the Eland Bull Dance, the same idiophone appeared: 'Other times an eland will come to where the people are singing. It comes toward them and arrives at where they are. When people sing the Eland Song – '

Biesele: 'When a young girl first menstruates?'

Kxao Giraffe: 'Yes, friend, *!a-ain !a=ain !a=ain*, that's how the eland arrives.'

In the background of complex metaphors like these lie specific ethnographic realities, here those of technological advance. Dahm N!a'an's statement about the hunter and his wife sums up attitudes about women and hunting which are directly linked to the technology of the poisoned arrow. In the menstrual dance, with its equation of women and muscular, fleshy eland antelopes, the technologically innovative metal adze-blades and their stereotyped clinking sound, *!a=ain*, have become constant and important ritual elements.

Patricia Vinnicombe (1972:198) has suggested an evolutionary framework for Bushman rock paintings which can be extended to help us better understand the complex metaphors of Bushman folk-tales.

The framework she suggests is the stone-age environment as confronted by a revolutionary new technology, the bow and arrow, and by the ritual which went along with its use. I would further note that it is the poisoned arrow that has profoundly affected the hunters' socio-economic arrangements and art up to today. For once an effective arrow poison has been developed, hunters no longer need to wound animals mortally with their arrows but only to pierce their skins. Thus much of their hunting skill centres around the tracking of the poisoned animals during the hours or days they take to die.

P.V. Tobias (1965:77) has related this feature of Bushman technology to their development of an acute reliance on veld-craft. This system of knowledge and belief, as we have seen, is reflected prominently in ritual and folklore. Much is made, symbolically, of the personal and social discipline accompanying the poison technology. Avoidance of sex and women prior to hunting is prescribed in the idiom of 'hot' poison and its 'cold' antitheses.

Further, not only women, but also the male hunters themselves, are symbolically identified with game animals at certain times. When a Ju/'hoan man has put a poisoned arrow into an animal, his actions until the animal dies are said to be reflected in its actions. Thus he must move carefully, observing a number of ritual cautions, while waiting for the poison to do its work.

There is a peculiarly intimate identification between hunter and prey, then, at these times. It is traceable to the period in hunting with poison during which a man can actively do no more but must rely on the orderly working out of forces which he has set in motion but which are stronger and greater than he is. The hunter's reliance on probability and on providence (conceived to have supplied men with arrow poison) is thus symbolically underscored. During this period the hunter's actions are no longer overtly practical but become a kind of metaphorical system of action depending on symbolic identification with the prey. The hunter's manner must be circumspect and his demeanour grave: he must project only humility about his accomplishment in getting an arrow into the animal, or his prey, it is believed, will shrug off the poison's effects and bound away.

Clearly, social technology as well as material technology has metaphorical underpinnings. Ju/'hoan hunting ritual with its dynamic expositions reinforces social relationships which are adaptive in connection with the new technology. Reasoned, ritually disciplined, highly social hunting involving a lifetime of learning and of sharing information, with shared arrows denoting shared protein needs, underscores the necessary social relationships within small groups of hunters whose members have absolute reciprocal dependence upon one another.

In present-day folktales and ritual, references to the poison technology are accompanied by some to a newer one, the technology of metal. Metal implements such as the adze of the menstrual dance are more prominent in ritual and in modern tale repertoires than in the ones of a hundred years ago because metal has become prominent and powerful in daily life for the majority of the Bushmen.

Like the gemsbok dancing which was replaced in a rapidly spreading wave by the new giraffe tradition, bone or stone implements have been superseded by metal ones in the tales. The metal tools ring with a new sound – they function in tales and ritual as concentrations of the idea of great durability and sharpness. Adzes, knives, axes, metal spearpoints, awls, branding irons – all play crucial roles. The introduction of metal, which has only displaced stone for some implements during the lifetimes of middle-aged men now living,[2] has had an effect on expressive forms comparable to that of the revolutionary technology of the poisoned arrow. I have been able in this book to give only a few examples of the metaphorical treatment of technology in Ju/'hoan oral tradition. However, Ju/'hoan folklore, ritual, and expressive life in general are absolutely 'shot through' with such allusions and cross-references. Why this should be the case – in other words, what the adaptive significance of this kind of metaphoric expression may be – is our last topic for discussion.

THE ADAPTIVE VALUE OF EXPRESSIVE FORMS

Expressive forms both codify and condense meaning.

Condensation is accomplished partly by redundancy of reference, partly by the widely allusive interconnections among the items and attributes chosen to bear significance in an expressive system. Condensation produces economy: if experience gained in one context can be used, through metaphorical connections, in other contexts, a kind of mental efficiency is promoted. Such condensation is adaptive because it allows a smaller amount of experience to have a larger experiential impact. Metaphor, in other words, has a multiplier effect on experience.

For this reason, it seems probable that human sapience has been based since its beginnings on such metaphorical processes. Sapience as we know it has required that a repertoire of dominant image and image relationships be selected for each culture or group, out of the welter of sensory experience available. These images and relationships have been closely tied to the structures of description, inference, and persuasion used socially to make decisions and generate consensus. Storytellers clearly play an active role in all this, both in holding old meanings current by keeping juggled items 'in the air' of culture and allowing new ones to enter the game when appropriate.

As items used metaphorically gather meaning through time, they may perform in different media and contexts, solving cognitive problems of relatedness and dysfunction. Processes of metaphorical mediation resolving oppositions in the world view (such as our five folk concepts) are also used as fundamental metaphors for social processes. As such, they play a vital role in forging and maintaining community.

Underlying metaphors necessarily shape decision-making. With longtime foragers such as the Ju/'hoansi, animal imagery permeates thought about relatedness, subsistence, and co-operation. Taken together, such metaphorical expressions and their use not only describe but dynamically link man, society, and environment.

As we have seen, for oral peoples it is specifically their non-written expressive forms which contain and convey many of their instrumental, active metaphors. Folklore and other genres are thus integral parts of oral communication systems, and they perform real work in the storage and transfer of knowledge.

Looking at Ju/'hoan folklore as part of the communication system which makes an entire adaptation possible, we begin to see the storytellers' work as both symbolic in nature and thoroughly practical in effect. Because it generates social agreement, it is actually a form of action on game, on aggregations of people, on reciprocity in human relations, on cycles in activity and residence. It also acts to resolve tensions generated by the living styles of the hunting and gathering adaptation.

Ultimately, the historical success of this adaptation in all its variants is itself a piece of data for which we must account. Among human societies, hunter-gatherers have been 'tenured' much longer than any others: we must confront the fact that their apparently 'irrational' thought systems, with working metaphors couched in various artistic genres and performing real communicative functions, indeed embody some of the essentials of their adaptation. We know little, as yet, about the time-depth of ancient relevancies. Symbol systems are full of the past in ways very complexly related to the present. We know that ideologies lag behind new economic arrangements, but we have not found a way to measure or evaluate this lag in the symbolic forms. But like scientific ideas, symbolic ideas that 'work' often enough and well enough to be useful, that give coherence to contemporary belief and continuity to tradition, will be called upon again and again for different tasks. They will be stretched for service to the reasonable limits of their applicability. When /Asa N!a'an told her story about G!kon//'amdima's heart turning into a steenbok, I asked her how it happened that a human heart could become an animal. Her answer made use of a folk concept in a way I had not heard before, but which made perfect sense in the light of its other uses. It made clear something that all the metaphors had pointed to, that womanly power and manly power and the power of shamans, of n/omkxaosi, are really one power, a power in turn coterminous with the identical powers of creation and healing. /Asa N!a'an said, 'Her heart left G!kon//'amdima's upper back through her n//ao spot and became a steenbok, and that was the first meat.'

Notes

PREFACE

1. I have chosen to use the so-called !Kung people's name for themselves, Ju/'hoan (pl. Ju/'hoansi), which means 'ordinary people' along with the widely-used 'Bushman' appellation for the click-speaking hunter-gatherers of Southern Africa. 'San', favoured by some scholars, is pejorative in the Nama (Hottentot) language. The Bushmen, though they have names for their different linguistic subdivisions, have no collective term for themselves.

INTRODUCTION: 'WOMEN LIKE MEAT'

1. The /Xam, now extinct, were a linguistic subdivision of the Bushmen living in the western part of what is now South Africa. They spoke a 'Southern Bushman' language which had five clicks.
2. The Ju/'hoansi or !Kung are a linguistic subdivision of the Bushmen living in north-western Botswana, northern Namibia, and southern Angola. The largest group of living Bushmen, their language belongs to the 'Northern Bushman' group of languages and has four clicks.
3. *Buchu* is the /Xam word for an aromatic herbal powder believed to have magical properties, particularly in healing and in inducing trance. A similar substance is called *san* by the Ju/'hoansi.

PART I
CHAPTER ONE: THE JU/'HOANSI AND THEIR FOLKLORE

1. In tracing the connection of Bantu-speakers' folklore and Khoikoi

(Hottentot) folklore with that of the Bushmen, I draw heavily on a remarkable series of personal communications sent to me since 1973 by Mrs Sigrid Schmidt of Hildesheim, West Germany. Mrs Schmidt has the most extensive knowledge of the subject among the students of Khoisan folklore today.

2. W.J.G. Loots's Doctoral Thesis (1961) – The Hare and the Tortoise – is the sole example known to me.

3. 'Khoisan' is a term coined by Leonard Schultz-Jena in 1928 to include both the pastoral Khoikoi (pejoratively called 'Hottentot' by the Dutch settlers) and the hunting-gathering San (Bushmen), who in some ways were similar to the Khoikoi in both physical characteristics and culture.

4. See 'Linguistic Perspective' and 'Bushman Origins and Migrations', in L. Marshall (1976:24-29).

5. Sigrid Schmidt, (1970:48) citing A. Coetzee, S.C. Hattingh, W.J.G. Loots and P.D. Swart, 1967. Tiperegister van die Afrikaanse Volksverhaal. *Tydskrif vir Volkskunde en Volkstaal* 23, 3-4.

6. The chance that the heroine tales might prove to be an important 'cycle' in Ju/'hoan folktales was first brought to my attention by Melvin Konner.

PART II
CHAPTER ONE: TRADITION AND CREATIVITY IN JU/'HOAN
RELIGION AND FOLKLORE

1. *Oryx gazella*, a large antelope.

2. A teaching videotape, *That is how it was: Beh N!a'an Talks About the Beginnings of Giraffe Medicine,* was made at this time by Thomas Dowson and myself.

3. The !Xoo people of Bere, ninety miles south-east of Ghanzi and some two hundred miles from Tjum!kui, speak an unrelated 'Southern Bushman' language but were dancing and singing giraffe songs when I visited them in 1972.

4. Richard B. Lee, 'The Haba-utwe Oration', personal communication, 1973.

CHAPTER TWO: UNDERSTANDING JU/'HOAN TALES

1. *'Msi*, food in general as well as plant food in particular, is the unmarked category. This linguistic point is of interest when we consider that a larger proportion of Ju/'hoan subsistence is provided by gathering than by hunting.
2. For a lengthy treatment of this topic, see McCall (1970).
3. Available from Documentary Educational Resources, 101 Morse Street, Watertown, Mass. USA.
4. National Geographic television film, aired 17 May, 1974.
5. Lorna Marshall, personal communication (Namibia), and my own observations (Botswana).

CHAPTER THREE: SELECTED TALES AND ANALYSIS

1. Lorna Marshall (1957:235) has spelled them =*gani* and //*ghui*.
2. Bleek and Lloyd (1968:339). *N!ow* or *n!ao* is not confined to the Ju/'hoansi: similar beliefs have been reported for the G/ui and even for the extinct /Xam of the Cape; see D. Bleek 1932. Customs and beliefs of the /Xam Bushmen: Part IV, Omens, wind-making, clouds. *Bantu Studies* VI, 336. Sigrid Schmidt is working on a related concept among the Nama.
3. *Zizyphus mucronata* Willd., 'buffalo thorn'.
4. One storyteller commented, 'It was that she was pregnant, of course. She hid herself to have her children.'
5. Richard B. Lee, 'How Jackal Spoiled the World' (unpublished), and field notes, 4 April, 1969.
6. Compare the Earth Diver motif (A-T A 812) found as far away as Siberia and North America, in which the creator sends down animals to try to bring up earth out of the water. After a number of animals have failed, one succeeds, and the earth is established.
7. This chapter has been much concerned with themes of initiation appearing in Ju/'hoan folklore. Girls' menarchal rites and their possible relationship to one of the heroine's songs were discussed. Connections between the 'Ceremony of the First Kill' and the tale of 'The Branding of the Animals' were suggested. The two

initiation complexes appear to balance and many of the parallels
seem plausible, but there is another consideration to deal with.
When the word 'initiation' is used by anthropologists in connection with Ju/'hoan religion, it is to a third ceremony, not yet
mentioned, that they refer.

That ceremony is called *tcoqma*. It is a ritual of secret learning
and ordeal.Rather little is known about *tcoqma* by anthropologists. What information does exist about this month-long seclusion
for young boys comes for the most part from interviews. Few
outsiders have ever seen the ceremony performed.

Because I do not believe that the symbolism of *tcoqma* enters to a
great extent into Ju/'hoan folklore, I will not summarise here what
little is known of it. The Ju/'hoansi at Kauri and Dobe in Botswana
and in the Nyae Nyae area of Namibia still speak of it with great
enthusiasm, and with respect for its secrecy; men in their forties still
bear its scarifications between their eyebrows. But it appears to be
receding in importance, perhaps even dying out.

'We don't do it any more,' men say, or '*Tcoqma* has gone back
to its home in the south.'

Whether *tcoqma* as a tradition at one time 'came through' the
Ju/'hoan area, as people say, and is now 'leaving' it, or whether
(as is highly possible) it is so secret that Ju/'hoan men do not want
to speak of it, is hard to say. That a new dance tradition may take
a place by storm for a while is evident in the women's drum dance
now coming into northern Botswana from the Mbukushu of the
Okavango swamps and Barakwengo of the Caprivi Strip. Some
researchers, for instance Nicholas England and Lorna Marshall,
feel that *tcoqma* may reflect Bantu influence. It has been suggested
that hunting traditionally fulfilled the need for a completely
separate province for males in Bushman society, so that harsh
ordeals were not necessary for initiation into manhood (Allan
Forbes, personal communication, 1974). Bushman trance-curers,
too, are predominantly male, and their power much acknowledged. The prominence of these other male spheres supports the
idea that *tcoqma* may reflect Bantu influence.

However, it is not just the Botswana Ju/'hoansi of today who have danced it in the recent past. In the 1950s the relatively isolated Nyae Nyae Ju/'hoansi were separating their adolescent boys from the community every few years to dance with them at the *tcoqma* camp in the bush, to subject them to the great cold of the winter nights, to hunger, thirst, and exhaustion. During the dancing the initiates were told about the habits of the meat animals, and that they should respect the animals as one respects kin (John Marshall, personal communication, 1974).

The most extensive discussion of *tcoqma* I am aware of in the literature appears in Nicholas England's thesis (1968, 1992). He has compiled the available written sources on *tcoqma* and related rituals in other Bushman groups in an attempt to shed light on its practice among the Nyae Nyae Ju/'hoansi. From interviews with informants he concludes that *tcoqma* came to the Ju/'hoansi through contact with a different Bushman group to the south. This group, in turn, may have been influenced by Bantu tradition. The arrival of *tcoqma* in Nyae Nyae occurred during the lifetime of the parents of the grandparental generation of the 1970s. This account fits well with what the neighbouring Botswana Ju/'hoansi told me about *tcoqma*'s recent entry from the south.

8. The soft call of this bird, like its name, begins with a nasal click which is different from any of the other clicks. Apparently the sound is an imitation of the call of this bird. I am using //'*om* to symbolise it.

9. The two groups of stories have both real connections and real distinctions between them. The main distinction is that they are usually told separately. Of the thirty or so performances I heard in Botswana which included a heroine, only two (and two more collected by Elizabeth Marshall Thomas and Lorna Marshall, 7.1.53 and 10.2.53) connected this episode at the spring with the *n=ah* tree to the complex series of adventures which comprise the heroine cycle. Another distinction is that in the stories of the jackal's treachery to her older sister, the heroine is always a python. Sometimes this python is referred to as 'another G!kon//'amdima.'

10. From a version collected by Lorna Marshall among the G/ui, July 2, 1955.

11. As we proceed with the discussion of the stories, instances of this equation will be noted as we come to them. For a condensed treatment of this topic, the reader is referred to McCall 1970. See also the film *The Hunters*, by John Marshall; and Lorna Marshall 1959.

12. There is a faint echo here of the 'humorous' mistake made by the jackal's grandmother when the jackal has died from the arrow poison. In both cases an old lady wrongly puts something which belongs in the food category – the $n=ah$ seeds or the *dchuun* bulbs – into a sexual context; menstruation or the genitals of her son-in-law. As in the jackal story, where cannibalism follows close on this confusion, this second mistake too has serious consequences.

13. The Obstacle Flight motif (D 672) is spread throughout the world and has been carefully traced by a number of folklorists (see, for example, Aarne 1936). This motif is usually associated with flight from supernatural beings, such as ogres (313, 327), the devil (314) or a magician (325) (Aarne and Thompson 1928). In only one tale-type is it associated with flight from humans, and that is in type 502 where a prince flees from his cruel stepmother. Another difference is that the thorns flung by G!kon//'amdima do not transform themselves into magical objects – they are obstacles already. The author Bessie Head wrote from eastern Botswana (personal communication, 1973), 'Bakalanga people told me here they strew thorns on the way when fleeing the Matabele and at one time that must have been a common means of defense against an enemy.' (Of course the Bakalanga historical accounts may have folkloric incorporations.) But the raincloud, and in one version the 'bowls of rain' the heroine packs up to take with her, are clearly magical objects.

14. I. Schapera (1930), Appendix: 'Comparative Note on Bushman and Hottentot Religion,' pp. 395-399.

CHAPTER FOUR: TECHNOLOGY AND METAPHOR

1. Thomas 1959; Birket-Smith 1959:166; Godelier 1975 respectively.

2. John Yellen, personal communication, autumn 1973.

Bibliography

Aarne, Antti. 1936. *Die Magische Flucht*. Folklore Fellows Communications 92, Helsinki.

Aarne, Antti and Thompson, Stith. 1928. *The Types of the Folktale*. Folklore Fellows Communications 74. Helsinki.

Abrahamson, Hans. 1951. The origin of death: Studies in African mythology. *Studia Ethnographica Uppsalensia* 3, 28-33.

Bascom, W.R. 1973. Folklore, verbal art, and culture. *Journal of American Folklore* 86, 374-81.

Bateson, Gregory. 1972. *Steps to an Ecology of Mind*. New York: Ballantine.

Biesele, Megan. 1971. Hunting in semi-arid areas: The Kalahari Bushmen today. *Botswana Notes and Records*. Special Edition No. 1, Proceedings of Botswana Society Conference on Sustained Production from Semi-Arid Areas, Gaborone.

—— 1974a. A note on the beliefs of modern Bushmen concerning the Tsodilo Hills. *Newsletter of the South West Africa Scientific Society* 15(3).

—— 1974b. A contemporary Bushman's comments on the Brandberg paintings. *Newsletter of the South West Africa Scientific Society* 15(7) and 15(8).

—— 1975a. Folklore and Ritual of !Kung Hunter-Gatherers. Doctoral Thesis, Department of Anthropology, Harvard University, Cambridge, Mass.

—— 1975b. Song texts by the Master of Tricks: Kalahari San thumb piano music. *Botswana Notes and Records* 7.

—— 1976a. Aspects of !Kung Folklore. In R.B. Lee and I. DeVore (eds), *Kalahari Hunter-Gatherers*. Cambridge, Mass: Harvard University Press.

—— 1976b. Environmental Planning and Botswana's Basarwa (Bushman) Citizens: A Progress Report. Prepared for IDEP/UNEP Conference on Environmental Planning and 'Poorly Integrated' Minorities in Africa. Mauritius, April.

—— 1978a. Religion and Folklore. In P.V. Tobias (ed.) *The Bushmen*. Cape Town: Human and Rousseau.

—— 1978b. Sapience and Scarce Resources: Communication Systems of the !Kung and Other Foragers. Paper presented at the International Conference on Hunter-Gatherers, Paris. Published in *Social Science Information* 17(6).

—— 1982. Review of Sigrid Schmidt, *Marcher aus Namibia*, Eugen Diederichs Verlag, Dusseldorf. In *Research in African Literatures*, 13(4).

—— 1983a. Interpretation in rock art and folklore: Communication systems in evolutionary perspective. *South African Archaeological Bulletin* Goodwin Series 4.

—— 1983b. Review of Jan Knappert, *Namibia: Land and Peoples, Myths and Fables*, Leiden, Brill. *Research in African Literatures*, 14(3).

—— 1983c. Interpretation in rock art and folklore: Communication systems in evolutionary perspective. *South African Archaeological Bulletin* Goodwin Series 4, June, 54-60.

—— 1986a. How hunter-gatherers' stories 'make sense': Semantics and adaptation. In Biesele and Tyler1986.

—— 1986b. How Hunter-Gatherer's Pictures 'Make Sense': South African Rock Art and Bushman Folklore. Prepared for conference The Longest Record: The Human Career in Africa, Berkeley, California, April.

—— 1986c. 'Anyone with sense would know': Tradition and Creativity in !Kung Narrative and Song. In R. Vossen and K. Keuthmann (eds), *Contemporary Studies in Khoisan*. Hamburg: Helmut Buske Verlag.

—— (ed.). *The Past and Future of !Kung Ethnography: Critical Reflections and Symbolic Perspectives*. Hamburg: Helmut Buske Verlag.

—— 1988. The Peabody Museum and 'the Culture of Imagery' Review of *From Site to Sight: Anthropology, Photography and The Power of Imagery*. Curtis Hinsley and Melissa Banta, exhibit catalogue. In *Exposure* (magazine).

—— 1990a. Educational Policy Affecting Ju/'hoansi in Independent Namibia: Minority Needs in Nation-Building Context. 6th International Conference on Hunting and Gathering Societies, Fairbanks, Alaska, May.

—— 1990b. *Shaken Roots: Bushmen of Namibia Today*. With photographs by Paul Weinberg. Johannesburg: Environmental Development Agency.

—— 1990c. Review of M. Guenther, 1989. *African Studies* 49, August.

Biesele, M., Guenther, M., Hitchcock, R., Lee, R.B. and Macgregor, J. 1989. Hunters, Clients, and Squatters: The Contemporary Socioeconomic Status of Botswana Basarwa. *African Study Monographs* 9(2).

Biesele, M. and Howell, N. 1981. 'The Old People Give You Life': Aging Among !Kung Hunter-Gatherers. In P. Amoss and S. Harrell (eds), *Other Ways of Growing Old*. Stanford University Press.

Biesele, M. and Tyler, Stephen A. (eds), 1986. Toward an oral hermeneutics. *Cultural Anthropology* (Special Issue) May.

Birket-Smith, Kai. 1959. *The Eskimos*. London: Methuen.

Bleek, D.F. 1936. Customs and beliefs of the /Xam Bushmen: Part VIII, More about sorcerers and charms. *Bantu Studies* 10,131.

Bleek, W.H.I. 1864. *Reynard the Fox in South Africa: Hottentot Fables and Tales*. London: Trubner.

Bleek, W.H.I. and Lloyd, L.C. 1923. *The Mantis and his Friends*. Cape Town: Maskew Miller.

—— 1911. *Specimens of Bushmen Folklore*. London: George Allen. Facsimile reprint, Cape Town: Struik, 1968.

Blurton Jones, N.G. and Konner, M.J. 1976. !Kung Knowledge of Animal Behavior or: The Proper Study of Mankind is Animals. In R.B. Lee and I. DeVore (eds), 1976.

Boas, Franz. 1915. Mythology and Folktales of the North American Indians. In F. Boas *et al.* (eds), *Anthropology in North America*. New York: Stechert.

Briggs, Jean. 1982. Living Dangerously: The Contradictory Foundations of Value in Canadian Inuit Society. In Eleanor Leacock and Richard B. Lee (eds), *Politics and History in Band Societies*. Cambridge: Cambridge University Press.

Bruner, Jerome. 1968. *Toward a Theory of Instruction*. New York: W.W. Norton.

Chadwick, H.M. and N.K. 1946. *The Growth of Literature*. New York: Macmillan.

Clark, J. Desmond. 1970. *The Prehistory of Africa*. New York: Praeger.

Dickens, Patrick. 1991. Ju/'hoan orthography in practice. *South African Journal of African Languages* 11(1), 99–104.

Dorson, Richard (ed.). 1972. *African Folklore*. Bloomington: Indiana University Press.

Ebert, James I. 1976. Hunting in Botswana's Past and its Role in a Developing Botswana. University of New Mexico Development Report to the Botswana Government No. 13.

England, Nicholas. 1968. Music among the Zu'/'wa-si of South West Africa and Botswana. Doctoral Thesis, Department of Music, Harvard University.

—— 1992. *Music among the Ju/'hoansi and Related Peoples of Namibia, Botswana and Angola*. New York: Garland Publishing.

Fourie, L. 1928. The Bushmen of South West Africa. In L. Fourie, H. Vedder, and T. Hahn (eds), *The Native Tribes of South West Africa.*, Cape Town: Cape Times.

Godelier, Maurice. 1975. Modes of Production, Kinship, and Demographic Structures. In M. Bloch (ed.), *Marxist Analyses and Social Anthropology*. London: Malaby.

—— 1977. *Perspectives in Marxist Anthropology*. Cambridge: Cambridge University Press.

Goody, Jack. 1977. *The Domestication of the Savage Mind*. Cambridge: Cambridge University Press.

Goody, Jack and Watt, I.P. 1963. The Consequences of Literacy. *Comparative Studies in History and Society* 5, 304-45.

Guenther, Mathias G. 1989. *Bushman Folktales: Oral Traditions of the*

Nharo of Botswana and the /Xam of the Cape. Stuttgart: Franz Steiner Verlag.

Havelock, Eric. A. 1963. *Preface to Plato*. Cambridge, Mass.: Harvard University Press.

—— 1978a. The Alphabetization of Homer. In Eric A. Havelock and Jackson P. Hershbell (eds), *Communication Arts in the Ancient World*. New York: Hastings House Publishers.

—— 1978b. *The Greek Concept of Justice*. Cambridge, Mass.: Harvard University Press.

Heinz, H.-J. 1966. Social Organization of the !Ko Bushmen. Master's Dissertation, University of the Witwatersrand.

Hitchcock, Robert K. 1982. Prehistoric Hunter-Gatherer Adaptations. In R. Renee Hitchcock and Mary R. Smith (eds), *Settlement in Botswana*. Johannesburg: Heinemann.

Hoernlé, A.W. 1918. Certain rites of transition and the conception of *!nau* among the Hottentots. *Harvard African Studies* 2.

Hymes, Dell. 1981. *'In Vain I Tried To Tell You': Essays in Native American Ethnopoetics*. Philadelphia: University of Pennsylvania Press.

Innis, Harold. 1951. *The Bias of Communication*. Toronto: University of Toronto Press.

Katz, Richard. 1976. Education for Transcendence: !Kia-Healing with the Kalahari !Kung. In R.B. Lee and I. DeVore (eds), 1976.

Leach, E.R. 1970. *Claude Lévi-Strauss*. New York: Viking.

Lee, Richard B. 1968. The Sociology of !Kung Bushman Trance Performances. In R. Prince (ed.), *Trance and Possession States*. Montreal: R.M. Bucke Memorial Society.

—— 1969. !Kung Bushman Subsistence: An Input-Output Analysis. In A.P. Vayda (ed.), *Environment and Cultural Behavior*. New York: Natural History Press.

—— 1973. The Evolution of Technical Civilizations. In C. Sagan (ed.), *Communication with Extra-Terrestrial Intelligence*. Cambridge, Mass: M.I.T. Press.

—— 1976. Introduction. In Lee and Devore (eds), 1976.

—— 1984. *The Dobe !Kung*. New York: Holt, Rinehart and Winston.

Lee, Richard B. and DeVore, I. (eds), 1976. *Kalahari Hunter-Gatherers*. Cambridge, Mass: Harvard University Press.

Lewis-Williams, J. David. 1981. *Believing and Seeing: Symbolic Meaning in San Rock Paintings*. London: Academic Press.

—— 1982. The economic and social context of southern San rock art. *Current Anthropology* 23(4).

Lewis-Williams, J. David and Biesele, Megan. 1978. Eland hunting rituals among northern and southern San groups: Striking similarities. *Africa* 48(2).

Lord, Albert. 1978. *The Singer of Tales*. New York: Atheneum.

Loots, W.J.G. 1961. Die Herkoms, Ontwikkelung en Verspreding van die Reisiesverhale, Deels I, II. Doctoral Thesis, University of the Witwatersrand.

Luria, A.B. 1976. *Cognitive Development: Its Cultural and Social Foundations*. Cambridge, Mass.: Harvard University Press.

Maingard, L.F. Notes on health and disease among the Bushmen of the southern Kalahari. *Bantu Studies* 11(3), 285-94.

Marshall, John. *The Hunters* (film). Documentary Educational Resources, 5 Bridge St. Watertown, Mass.

—— 1974. *Bushmen of the Kalahari* (television film). National Geographic.

Marshall, Lorna. 1957. N!ow. *Africa* 27.

—— 1959. Marriage among !Kung Bushmen. *Africa* 29.

—— 1960. !Kung Bushman bands. *Africa* 30.

—— 1961. Sharing, talking, and giving: Relief of social tensions among !Kung Bushmen. *Africa* 31(3).

—— 1962. !Kung Bushman religious beliefs. *Africa* 32.

—— 1969. The medicine dance of the !Kung Bushman. *Africa* 39.

—— 1976. *The !Kung of Nyae Nyae*. Cambridge, Mass: Harvard University Press.

McCall, Daniel G. 1970. *Wolf Courts Girl: The Equivalence of Hunting and Mating in Bushman Thought*. Africa Series No.7. Athens, Ohio: Ohio University Center for International Studies.

McLuhan, Marshall. 1962. *The Gutenberg Galaxy: The Making of Typographic Man*. Toronto.

Metzger, Fritz and Ettighoffer, P.C. 1951. *Und Seither Lacht e Hyäne*. Windhoek: John Meinert.

Ong, Walter. 1967. *The Presence of the Word*. New York: Simon and Schuster.

—— 1982. *Orality and Literacy*. London: Methuen.

Orpen, J.M. 1874. A Glimpse into the Mythology of the Maluti Bushman. *Cape Monthly Magazine* 9.

Ortega y Gasset, Jose. 1972. *Meditations on Hunting*. New York: Scribner's.

Parry, Milman. 1971. *The Making of Homeric Verse: Collected Papers*. Adam Parry (ed.). Oxford: Oxford University Press.

Peckham, Morse. 1965. *Man's Rage for Chaos: Biology, Behavior, and the Arts*. Philadelphia: Chilton Books.

Pfeiffer, John. 1982. *The Creative Explosion: An Inquiry into the Origins of Art and Religion*. New York: Harper and Row.

Radin, Paul (ed.). 1952. *African Folktales and Sculpture*. Bollingen Series 32. New York: Pantheon Books.

—— 1972. *The Trickster*. New York: Schocken.

Reichel-Dolmatoff, G. 1971. *Amazonian Cosmos: The Sexual and Religious Symbolism of the Tukano Indians*. Chicago: University of Chicago Press.

Ricoeur, Paul. 1976. *Interpretation Theory: Discourse and the Surplus of Meaning*. Fort Worth, Texas: TCU Press.

Ridington, Robin. 1978. Hunting and Gathering World View in Relation to Adaptive Strategy. Paper presented at the First International Conference on Hunting-Gathering Societies, Paris.

Russo, Joseph. 1978. How, and What, Does Homer Communicate? The Medium and Message of Homeric Verse. In Eric A. Havelock and Jackson P. Hershbell (eds), *Communication Arts in the Ancient World*. New York: Hastings House Publishers.

Schapera, I. 1930. *The Khoisan Peoples of South Africa*. London: Routledge and Kegan Paul.

Scheub, Harold. 1971. Translation of African Oral Narrative- Performances to the Written Word. *Yearbook of Comparative and General Literature* 20, pp. 28-36.

—— 1977. Body and image in oral narrative performances. *New Literary History* 8(3).

Schmidt, Sigrid. 1970. Europäische volkserzählungen bei den Nama und Bergdama. *Fabula* 2(1/2).

Schoeman, P.J. 1957. *Hunters of the Desert Land*. Cape Town: Howard Timmins.

Shepard, Paul. 1972. Introduction. In José Ortega y Gasset, 1972.

—— 1973. *The Tender Carnivore and the Sacred Game*. New York: Scribner's.

Silberbauer, George. 1963. *Bushman Survey Report*. Gaborones: Bechuanaland Government.

—— 1965. *Report to the Government of Bechuanaland on the Bushman Survey*. Gaborones: Bechuanaland Government.

—— 1978. Political Process in G/wi Bands. Paper presented at the First International Conference on Hunting and Gathering Societies, Paris.

Snyman, J.W. 1970. *An Introduction to the !Xũ Language*. Cape Town: A.A. Balkema.

Tedlock, Dennis. 1977. Toward an oral poetics. *New Literary History* 8(3).

Testart, Alain. 1978. Milieu naturel, mythologie et organisation sociale. *Social Science Information* 15, 415-26.

Theobald, Robert. 1972. *Habit and Habitat*. Englewood Cliffs, N.J.: Prentice-Hall.

Thomas, Elizabeth Marshall. 1959. *The Harmless People*. New York: Knopf.

Thomas, E.W. 1950. *Bushman Stories*. Cape Town: Oxford University Press.

Thompson, Stith. 1932-1934. *Motif-Index of Folk Literature*. Indiana University Studies, Vols. xix to xxiii. Bloomington, Indiana.

—— 1951. *The Folktale*. New York: Dryden Press.

Thompson, Stith and Roberts, W.E. 1960. *Types of Indic Oral tales.* Folklore Fellows Communications No. 18. Helsinki.

Tobias, P.V. 1965. Bushman Hunter-Gatherers: A Study in Human Ecology. In D.H.S. Davids (ed.), *Ecology in Southern Africa.* The Hague: W. Junk.

Tonkinson, Robert. 1978. *The Mardudjara Aborigines: Living the Dream in Australia's Desert.* New York: Holt, Rinehart and Winston.

Turner, V.W. 1967. *The Forest of Symbols.* Ithaca, N.Y.: Cornell University Press.

Vedder, H. The Nama. In L. Fourie, H. Vedder, and T. Hahn (eds), *The Native Tribes of South West Africa.* Cape Town: Cape Times.

Vinnicombe, Patricia. 1972. Myth, motive and selection in Southern African rock art. *Africa* July.

Westphal, E.O.J. 1963. The linguistic prehistory of Southern Africa: Bush, Kwadi, Hottentot, and Bantu linguistic relationships. *Africa* 33(3).

Wiessner, Pauline. 1982. Risk, Reciprocity and Social Influence in !Kung San Economics. In E. Leacock and R. Lee (eds), *Politics and History in Band Societies.* Cambridge: Cambridge University Press.

Winterhalder, Bruce, and Smith, Eric A. (eds). 1981. *Optimal Foraging Strategies.* Chicago: Chicago University Press.

Yengoyan, Aram. 1979. Economy, society, and myth in Aboriginal Australia. *Annual Review of Anthropology* 8, 393-415.

SELECTED BIBLIOGRAPHY: KHOISAN FOLKLORE REFERENCE SOURCES

DISCUSSED IN THIS WORK

Bleek, Dorothea. 1928. *The Naron: A Bushman Tribe of the Central Kalahari.* Cambridge University Press for the University of Cape Town, Publications of the School of African Life and Languages.

Bleek, Dorothea *et al.* 1923. *The Mantis and his Friends: Bushman Folklore.* Cape Town: Maskew Miller.

Bleek, W.H.I. and Lloyd, Lucy. 1911. *Specimens of Bushman Folklore.* London: George Allen.

Guerreiro, Manuel Viegas. 1968. *Bochimanes !Khu de Angola.* Lisbon: Instituto de Investigaçao Cientifica de Angola.

Marshall, Lorna. 1962. !Kung Bushman religious beliefs. *Africa* 32(3).

Metzger, Fritz and Ettighoffer, P.C. 1951. *Und Seither Lacht die Hyäne.* Windhoek: John Meinert.

Orpen, J.M. 1874. A glimpse into the mythology of the Maluti Bushmen. *Cape Monthly Magazine* July.

Silberbauer, George. 1965. *Report to the Government of Bechuanaland on the Bushman Survey.* Gabarones: Bechuanaland Government.

Thomas, Elizabeth Marshall. 1959. *The Harmless People.* New York: Knopf.

ADDITIONAL

Bleek, Dorothea. Special speech of animals and the moon used by the /Xam Bushmen. *Bantu Studies* 10, 163-99 (from prose narratives with texts and translations).

Dorman, S.S. 1925. *Pygmies and Bushmen of the Kalahari.* London. (Several San narratives paraphrased in English, mostly apparently Bantu borrowings. San linguistic group undesignated.)

Hewitt, Roger. 1976. An Examination of the Bleek and Lloyd Collection of /Xam Bushman Narratives, with Special Reference to the Trickster, /Kaggen. Doctoral Thesis, School of Oriental and African Studies, University of London.

Leeuwenburg, J. 1970. A Bushman-legend from the George District. *South African Archaeological Bulletin* 25, 145-6.

Potgieter, F.F. 1955. *The Disappearing Bushmen of Lake Chrissie.* Pretoria: Van Schaik. (Batwa, two tales in English, one with text, one obviously of Swazi origin.)

Schoeman, P. 1957. *Hunters of the Desert Land*. Cape Town: Howard Timmins.

Seubring, G. 1934. Three Bushmen and Hottentot tales. *Journal of American Folklore* XLVII.

Thomas, E.W. 1950. *Bushman Stories*. Cape Town: Oxford University Press. (Twenty-nine stories told by a man whose mother was a Hei-//om, father a !Kung, in Nama Khoi language. Appear to be for the most part Nama stories.)

Von Weilligh, G.B. 1921. *Boesman Stories*. Cape Town. (Four volumes, two of which are devoted to 'myths and legends,' and 'animal fables,' 25 narratives in each category. Collected during the 1880s from /Xam informants within 100 miles of Katkop, where the Bleeks collected. Contains several versions of Bleek tales. However, the tales are in Afrikaans and have been translated to conform to Afrikaaner aesthetic canons.)

Index